Outcome Based Education

A PRACTICAL GUIDE FOR HIGHER EDUCATION TEACHERS

From Theory to Practice - Achieving Academic Quality, Accreditation and Ranking

DEEPESH DIVAAKARAN

ISBN 979-8-89277-792-6

Dedication

To My Beloved Wife Archana,

You are my pillar of strength, my source of inspiration, and my unwavering support. Your love, understanding, and encouragement have fuelled my journey in the education industry. Thank you for standing by my side through every challenge and triumph. This dedication is a testament to the love and bond we share.

To My Wonderful Children Daivik and Esha,

You are the driving force behind my pursuit of excellence. Your curiosity, enthusiasm, and zest for learning ignite my passion for transforming education. I dedicate this book to you, with the hope that it will inspire you to embrace the power of education and pursue your dreams with unwavering determination.

To My Parents,

Your unwavering belief in my potential and your constant encouragement have shaped the person I am today. You have instilled in me the values of hard work, perseverance, and lifelong learning. This dedication is a tribute to your unwavering support and love.

To my Mentor Dr. Ramesh Unnikrishnan, Milan Ganatra and Dr. Manoj George,

Your guidance, wisdom, and mentorship have played a pivotal role in my professional growth. Your invaluable insights and belief in my abilities have been instrumental in shaping my career. I am forever grateful for your guidance and support.

To My Family,

Your unwavering support, love, and belief in me have been the bedrock of my success. Your encouragement and understanding have propelled me forward in my journey. This dedication is a token of my gratitude for your presence in my life.

To my Best Friends Kanchan Patil and Vincy Baby,

Your friendship has been a source of joy, laughter, and unwavering support. Your presence in my life has made the journey even more meaningful and fulfilling. I dedicate this book to you as a symbol of our cherished bond.

To my Colleagues and Well-Wishers,

Your collaboration, insights, and shared passion for education have been invaluable in my professional journey. Your unwavering support and encouragement have inspired me to push boundaries and strive for excellence. This dedication is a tribute to our collective efforts in transforming education.

This book is a testament to the love, support, and inspiration I have received from each one of you. Your presence in my life has enriched my journey and made it more rewarding. I am deeply grateful for your unwavering belief in me.

With heartfelt gratitude,

Deepesh Divaakaran

Contents

Preface

Welcome to the world of Outcome-Based Education (OBE) and its transformative potential in shaping the future of education. This book is a comprehensive guide that explores the principles, strategies, and implementation of OBE in educational institutions. It is designed to assist educators, administrators, and curriculum developers in understanding and effectively adopting the principles of OBE to enhance student learning and success.

Education is evolving rapidly, and it is crucial for educational institutions to adapt to the changing needs and demands of the 21st-century learners. Outcome-Based Education offers a student-cantered approach that focuses on clearly defining the desired learning outcomes and aligning instructional practices to achieve those outcomes. This shift from a traditional teaching-cantered approach to a learner-cantered approach is fundamental to preparing students for the complexities and challenges of the modern world.

In this book, I will delve into the four pillars of OBE that form the foundation for its successful implementation: Clarity of focus, Designing down, High expectations, and Expanded opportunities. These pillars serve as guiding principles for curriculum design, instructional strategies, and assessment practices, ensuring that education is purposeful, meaningful, and impactful.

Throughout the chapters, I will explore each pillar in detail, providing theoretical frameworks, practical examples, and case studies to illustrate their application in real-life educational settings. I will discuss the importance of setting clear learning outcomes, breaking down the curriculum into manageable units, establishing high standards of performance, and providing diverse learning opportunities for all students.

Additionally, this book will address various aspects of implementing OBE, such as assessment and evaluation, faculty development, and stakeholder engagement. I will provide guidance on designing effective assessments that align with learning outcomes, strategies for professional development to support faculty in embracing the OBE approach, and methods for involving stakeholders in the educational process.

It is my hope that this book will serve as a valuable resource and guide for educators and educational leaders who are committed to enhancing student learning and preparing them for success in an ever-changing world. By embracing the principles and strategies of OBE, we can create educational environments that empower students, foster their critical thinking and problem-solving skills, and equip them with the competencies needed to thrive in their personal and professional lives.

I extend my sincere gratitude to all the educators, researchers, and practitioners who have contributed to the field of Outcome-Based Education, paving the way for a more student-centered and outcome-driven approach to learning. It is your dedication and insights that have shaped this book and its content.

I invite you to embark on this journey with me as we explore the power of Outcome-Based Education and its potential to revolutionize education for the better. Let us work together to create educational experiences that inspire, empower, and prepare our students for a future full of possibilities.

Happy reading and transformative learning!

Sincerely,

Deepesh Divaakaran

About Author

Throughout my career in the education industry, I have been driven by a deep passion for transforming the landscape of education in India. With over 15 years of experience as a serial Edu-Tech Entrepreneur and expertise in Quality Assurance, Accreditation, and Ranking, I have had the privilege of working with esteemed institutions like the JAIN GROUP, NMIMS, SRI SAIRAM, IHRD, and numerous private and government universities.

In 2018, I founded three innovative products that have revolutionized education: proCampuz, Edmojo, and QuickFee. proCampuz quickly gained recognition as an academic resource platform, providing students and faculty members with easy access to a vast array of educational resources. Edmojo, an outcome-based learning management system, empowered students to achieve their goals and objectives. QuickFee streamlined fee management processes, simplifying payments for educational institutions.

Recognizing the impact of my work, Leo1, a highly esteemed company incubated by Google and recognized by Forbes, acquired my academic resource platform in 2021, rebranding it as Leo1 Campus. This acquisition marked a significant milestone in my journey, as I became an integral part of Leo1's leadership team, playing a key role in securing substantial funding for the company.

Driven by an unyielding desire to push the boundaries of innovation, I founded Four32 AI Labs in 2023. This cutting-edge platform harnesses the power of Artificial Intelligence (AI) and Machine Learning (ML) to revolutionize accreditation and ranking in the education industry. With my visionary leadership, I envision a future where AI and ML redefine educational experiences and outcomes, paving the way for a more advanced and personalized education system.

I have dedicated myself to simplifying the education experience for both students and faculty members, continuously striving for excellence. My unwavering dedication and relentless pursuit of innovative solutions contribute to the growth and development of education in India, making a positive impact on the lives of the Gen Z population.

As an author, my mission is to provide educators, administrators, and curriculum developers with practical guidance and effective strategies to successfully embrace and implement Outcome-Based Education (OBE). In this book, I aim to bridge the gap between theory and practice, offering a comprehensive resource that supports educators in designing purposeful and meaningful learning experiences for their students.

With my extensive experience in curriculum design, instructional practices, and assessment strategies, I bring valuable insights to the table. Having conducted various workshops, training sessions, and consultations with diverse educational institutions, I understand the challenges and opportunities that come with implementing OBE principles.

My unwavering belief in the transformative power of education fuels my passion for OBE and Education Industry as a whole. I am convinced that by equipping students with the necessary knowledge, skills, and competencies, we can empower them to thrive academically, professionally, and personally. Through this book, I aspire to contribute to the ongoing dialogue on educational reform and inspire positive change in the field of education.

Within these pages, I draw upon my experiences, expertise, and research to provide practical strategies and insights that educators can readily apply in their classrooms and institutions. I present a step-by-step approach to implementing OBE, addressing key considerations such as curriculum design, assessment practices, and instructional strategies. Real-life examples and case studies further illustrate the successful implementation of OBE in various educational contexts.

I invite you to embark on this transformative journey with me as we explore the principles and practices of OBE. Together, we can create meaningful learning experiences that prepare our students for a future of success and fulfilment.

Let the journey begin.

Introduction

As someone who has worked with over 150 universities and colleges in India, I have gained extensive experience in implementing Outcome Based Education (OBE) and helping institutions achieve their goals. Through my work, I have helped more than 15,000 faculty members to understand the principles of OBE and to design effective learning outcomes, assessment rubrics, and teaching strategies that align with those principles. I have also been instrumental in implementing quality assurance in the field of education, helping institutions to achieve the highest grades in NAAC, maximum scores in NBA and higher rankings in NIRF.

Experience with OBE:

Through my work with universities and colleges across India, I have seen first-hand the power of Outcome Based Education to improve teaching and learning outcomes. I have worked with institutions to develop learning outcomes that are aligned with the needs of their students and the demands of their respective fields. I have also helped faculty members to design effective assessment rubrics that measure student learning in a fair and accurate way. By doing so, I have helped institutions to achieve better student outcomes and to prepare their graduates for success in their careers.

Insights into Quality Assurance:

As part of my work, I have been instrumental in implementing quality assurance in the field of education. By working with institutions to develop and implement effective quality assurance mechanisms, I have helped them to achieve the highest grades in NAAC and maximum scores in NBA, Top ranking in NIRF. I understand the importance of ensuring that programs are meeting their goals and that students are achieving the desired learning outcomes. Through my work, I have developed strategies for ensuring that institutions are meeting their quality assurance goals and that they are continuously improving the quality of their programs.

Role of Technology:

As a serial entrepreneur who has founded a company that developed an LMS based on OBE, I have a deep understanding of the role of technology in Outcome Based Education. I believe that technology can be a powerful tool for facilitating learning and assessment in an OBE framework. By using technology, institutions can collect and analyse data on student learning outcomes in real-time, which can help them to improve teaching and learning outcomes. I have seen the power of technology first-hand and believe that it will continue to play an increasingly important role in the future of education.

New Education Policy 2020:

As a passionate follower of the new education policy, I believe that Outcome Based Education is an important aspect of the policy's goals. The policy aims to provide students with a holistic education that prepares them for success in the 21st century and in the era of Industry 4.0. Outcome Based Education can help institutions to achieve this goal by focusing on the development of skills and competencies that are essential for success in the modern world. I believe that teachers who embrace Outcome Based Education will be well-positioned to align with the policy's goals and to prepare their students for success in the years to come.

By sharing my personal experience with Outcome Based Education, I hope to provide readers with practical insights and guidance on how to implement OBE in real-world situations. I believe that by doing so, we can help institutions to improve the quality of their programs and to prepare their graduates for success in their chosen fields.

Why I wrote this Book?

As someone who has worked in the field of education for many years, I have seen first-hand the importance of providing students with a high-quality education that prepares them for success in their chosen careers. However, I have also seen how challenging it can be for educators to achieve this goal. Many traditional approaches to education are focused on delivering content and assessing students based on their ability to memorize and regurgitate information. This approach often does not equip students with the skills and competencies that they need to succeed in the modern world.

Outcome Based Education offers a solution to this problem by focusing on the development of skills and competencies that are essential for success in the 21st century. However, I also understand that implementing Outcome Based Education can be a challenge for many educators, particularly those who are new to the approach.

This book is my attempt to make the process of implementing Outcome Based Education simpler and more accessible for higher education teachers. By sharing my personal experience, providing practical guidance, real-world examples, and tools and resources for teachers, I hope to help educators unlock the full potential of Outcome Based Education in their courses and programs. I believe that by doing so, we can help institutions to improve the quality of their programs and to prepare their graduates for success in their chosen fields. Ultimately, my goal is to help educators transform teaching and learning in higher education and to provide students with the knowledge, skills, and competencies that they need to succeed in the modern world.

Purpose and Goal of this Book

The purpose of this book is to provide higher education teachers with a practical guide to implementing Outcome Based Education (OBE) in their courses and programs. By reading this book, teachers will gain a better understanding of what OBE is, why it is important in higher education, and how to design effective learning outcomes, assessment rubrics, and teaching strategies that align with OBE principles.

Goals of this Book

- Provide an overview of Outcome Based Education and its key principles.
- Explain the importance of OBE in higher education.
- Offer practical guidance on how to design effective learning outcomes and assessment rubrics that align with OBE principles.
- Provide guidance on how to implement OBE in the classroom, including how to align course content with learning outcomes, how to assess student learning using rubrics, and how to provide feedback to students.
- Offer practical tools and resources for teachers, such as templates for writing learning outcomes and assessment rubrics.
- Provide guidance on how to evaluate the effectiveness of OBE in higher education, including how to collect and analyse data on student learning outcomes and how to use that data to improve teaching and learning.
- Help teachers to understand how to map Program Outcomes (POs) and Program Education Objectives (PEOs) to individual courses within the program and how to assess whether the POs and PEOs have been met.
- Encourage teachers to incorporate technology into their OBE approach to teaching and learning.
- Offer a comprehensive guide that helps higher education teachers to successfully implement Outcome Based Education in their courses and programs.
- By achieving these goals, this book aims to help higher education teachers make the transition to Outcome Based Education and to improve the quality of teaching and learning in their courses and programs.

Overview of topics covered

Introduction to Outcome Based Education (OBE): Provide an overview of OBE and its key principles, including the importance of focusing on learning outcomes and aligning teaching, learning, and assessment to those outcomes.

Designing Effective Learning Outcomes: Discuss the process of designing effective learning outcomes, including how to use Bloom's taxonomy and other frameworks to develop outcomes that are measurable, clear, and aligned with program goals.

Creating Assessment Rubrics: Offer guidance on how to design effective assessment rubrics that align with OBE principles and measure student learning in a fair and accurate way.

Aligning Course Content with Learning Outcomes: Explain how to align course content with learning outcomes, including how to select appropriate teaching strategies and assessment methods that support the achievement of those outcomes.

Assessing Student Learning: Provide guidance on how to assess student learning using rubrics and other assessment methods, including how to provide effective feedback to students.

Evaluating the Effectiveness of OBE: Discuss how to evaluate the effectiveness of OBE in higher education, including how to collect and analyse data on student learning outcomes and how to use that data to improve teaching and learning.

Mapping Program Outcomes (POs) and Program Education Objectives (PEOs) to Individual Courses: Explain how to Define PO and PEO effectively. Explain how to map POs and PEOs to individual courses within the program and how to assess whether the POs and PEOs have been met.

Quality Assurance: Offer guidance on how to ensure quality assurance in the implementation of OBE, including how to meet the accreditation requirements of agencies like NBA, NAAC, NIRF, ABET, AMBA, EQUIS, and AACSB.

Implementation Strategies: Provide practical strategies for implementing OBE in higher education, including how to engage faculty, students, and other stakeholders in the process, and how to overcome common challenges and obstacles.

Chapter 1

Defining Outcome Based Education

Outcome Based Education (OBE) is an approach to teaching and learning that places a strong emphasis on defining and measuring student learning outcomes. With OBE, educators start by defining what students should know and be able to do by the end of a course or program, and then design learning activities, assessments, and teaching strategies that are aligned with those outcomes. This approach shifts the focus from teaching content to teaching skills and competencies, and from assessing what students know to assessing what they can do with that knowledge.

OBE is based on the idea that student learning outcomes should be the primary driver of curriculum design, instruction, and assessment. This means that educators need to be intentional about what they want students to learn and be able to do, and then design instruction and assessments that align with those learning outcomes. By doing so, OBE ensures that students are well-prepared for success in their careers and that they have the skills and competencies that they need to be effective in the modern world.

OBE has become increasingly popular in higher education, particularly in response to the changing needs of employers and the demands of a rapidly evolving global economy. By focusing on learning outcomes, OBE helps to ensure that students are equipped with the knowledge, skills, and competencies that they need to succeed in the workforce and in their personal lives.

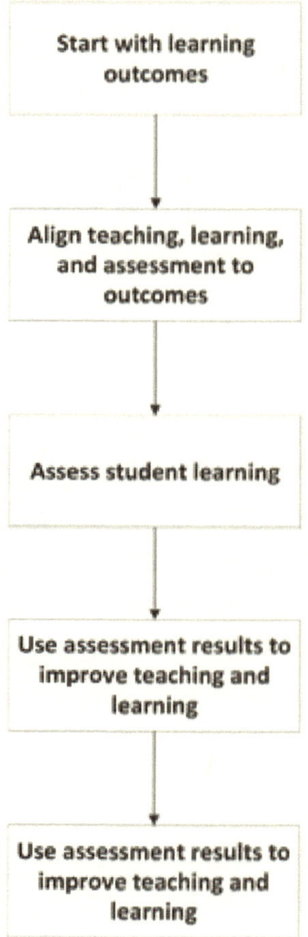

Figure 1: Empowering students through Outcome Based Education: Shifting the focus from knowledge to skills and measuring what truly matters.

Start with learning outcomes: The first step in Outcome Based Education is to define clear, measurable learning outcomes for students. These outcomes should describe what students should know and be able to do by the end of a course or program.

Align teaching, learning, and assessment to outcomes: Once the learning outcomes have been defined, educators should design teaching strategies, learning activities, and assessments that are aligned with those outcomes. This ensures that students are learning the skills and competencies that are needed to achieve the outcomes.

Assess student learning: Throughout the course or program, students should be assessed on their progress toward the defined learning outcomes. This can be done using a variety of assessment methods, such as tests, projects, essays, or presentations.

Use assessment results to improve teaching and learning: The results of the assessments can be used to improve teaching and learning by identifying areas where students are struggling or where the teaching strategies may not be effective. Educators can then adjust their teaching strategies or assessments to better align with the learning outcomes.

Evaluate program effectiveness: Finally, educators should evaluate the effectiveness of the program by looking at how well students are meeting the defined learning outcomes. This evaluation can be used to make improvements to the program, such as modifying the learning outcomes, adjusting teaching strategies, or changing assessments.

1.1 Traditional Education System

The history of Indian education can be traced back to ancient times, when traditional systems of learning, such as the Gurukul system, were prevalent. In these systems, students lived with a guru or teacher and learned through a process of observation, imitation, and practice.

During the colonial period, the British established a system of education in India that was designed to produce a class of people who could serve as clerks and administrators in the colonial administration. This system was largely focused on producing a small number of elites who were trained in English and western-style education.

After India gained independence in 1947, the government began to focus on expanding access to education and developing a system that was more relevant to the needs of the country. This led to the establishment of a national system of education that was based on the principles of democracy, equality, and social justice.

Over the years, the Indian education system has undergone significant changes and reforms. In the 1960s and 1970s, there was a focus on expanding access to education and promoting equity and social justice. In the 1980s and 1990s, there was a shift towards privatization and greater autonomy for educational institutions. More recently, the government has introduced reforms aimed at improving the quality of education and promoting innovation and entrepreneurship.

Today, the Indian education system is a complex and diverse system that includes a wide range of institutions, from traditional Gurukul-style schools to modern universities and technical institutes. Despite the challenges and limitations, education continues to be seen as a key factor in promoting social and economic development in India.

India has a large and diverse education system, with a wide range of schools, colleges, and universities. According to the Ministry of Education, Government of India, there are over 1.5 million schools in India, including government, private, and aided schools. These schools are categorized into primary, upper primary, secondary, and higher secondary schools, and provide education to students from ages 6 to 18 years.

In addition to schools, India has over 47,000 colleges and universities that provide higher education to students. These include universities, deemed universities, colleges, and institutes that offer undergraduate, postgraduate, and doctoral programs in a wide range of disciplines.

The higher education sector in India is regulated by various bodies, including the University Grants Commission (UGC), All India Council for Technical Education (AICTE), National Council for Teacher Education (NCTE), and the Bar Council of India, among others.

Overall, the education system in India is a complex and diverse system that provides education to millions of students across the country. However, there are still significant challenges and disparities in access and quality of education, particularly in rural and underprivileged areas. The Indian government has introduced several reforms in recent years, including the National Education Policy 2020, to address these challenges and improve the quality and accessibility of education in India.

The traditional education system in India has had a significant impact on the current state of the Indian education system and has contributed to several challenges that still exist today. Here are a few of the challenges that are related to the traditional education system in India:

Rote learning: One of the main challenges of the traditional education system in India is its emphasis on rote learning and memorization of information, which does not necessarily develop critical thinking or problem-solving skills.

Lack of student engagement: The traditional education system in India can be teacher-centered, with little emphasis on active student engagement and participation in the learning process. This can lead to disinterest and disengagement among students.

Limited access: Historically, the traditional education system in India was only accessible to a privileged few, and this has contributed to disparities in education access and outcomes that still exist today.

Inflexibility: The traditional education system in India can be inflexible, with a fixed curriculum and little room for innovation or adaptation to changing needs or circumstances.

Limited vocational education: The traditional education system in India has historically focused on academic education, with limited emphasis on vocational education and training, which can be a barrier to employment opportunities for some students.

Traditional Education

An Inflexible Education System

Traditional Education	Curriculam	Teaching	Standard Assessment	Academic Performance
In a traditional education system, classrooms are typically structured with desks arranged in rows facing the front where the teacher stands.	In the traditional education system, the curriculum is typically defined based on predefined standards and its rigid.	In the traditional education system, teachers play a crucial role in delivering the curriculum based on the standards defined in the syllabus.	Standard assessments are often provided to all students regardless of their individual capabilities, and these assessments can be rigid in their design and format.	Academic performance is often measured based on a rigid assessment system. This leads to a disparity between students' actual capabilities derived from these assessments.

Figure 2: Challenges in the Traditional Education System: Rote learning, lack of student engagement, limited access, inflexibility, and limited vocational education.

Addressing these challenges requires a fundamental shift in the approach to education, with greater emphasis on student-cantered and outcomes-based education that fosters critical thinking, problem-solving, and lifelong learning. The Indian government has introduced several reforms in recent years to address these challenges, including the National Education Policy 2020, which aims to promote a more holistic and flexible approach to education that emphasizes the development of 21st-century skills.

Outcome Based Education (OBE) can be an effective approach to address some of the challenges of the traditional education system in India. Here are a few ways in which OBE can help to transition the Indian education system:

Focus on learning outcomes: OBE places a strong emphasis on clearly defining learning outcomes and aligning teaching and assessment methods to these outcomes. This can help to shift the focus away from rote learning and memorization, and towards the development of critical thinking, problem-solving, and other 21st-century skills.

Student-centered approach: OBE is a student-centered approach that encourages active participation and engagement in the learning process.

This can help to promote greater student engagement and motivation and can help to address the issue of disinterest and disengagement among students.

Flexibility: OBE is a flexible approach that allows for innovation and adaptation to changing needs and circumstances. This can help to address the issue of inflexibility in the traditional education system in India and can help to promote a more dynamic and responsive education system.

Alignment with industry needs: OBE places a strong emphasis on the development of skills and competencies that are relevant to industry needs and employment opportunities. This can help to address the issue of limited vocational education in the traditional education system in India and can help to prepare students for the workforce.

Overall, OBE can help to transition the Indian education system by promoting a more student-centered, outcomes-based, and flexible approach to education that is aligned with the needs of the 21st-century world. By emphasizing the development of critical thinking, problem-solving, and other key skills, OBE can help to prepare students for success in a rapidly changing and complex global environment.

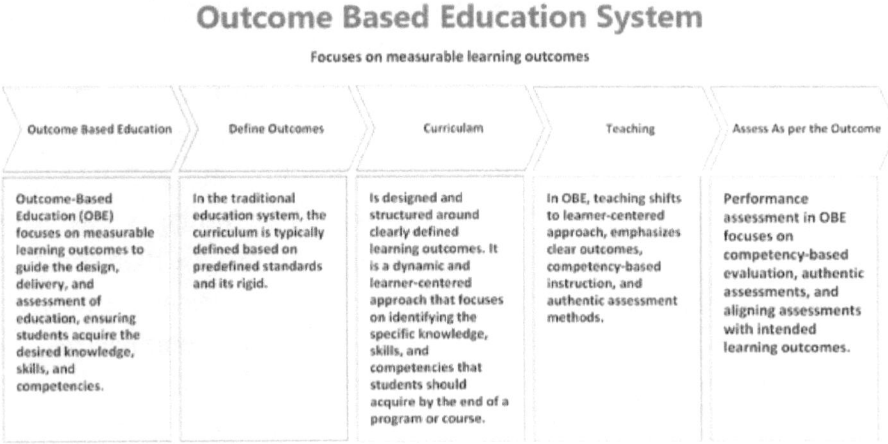

Figure 3: Transitioning Indian Education: Embracing Outcome-Based Education for a student-centered, flexible, and industry-aligned approach."

The figure illustrates the transition of the Indian education system towards Outcome-Based Education (OBE). It depicts the key features and benefits of OBE, including the focus on learning outcomes, student-centered approach, flexibility, and alignment with industry needs. These elements are interconnected, showcasing how OBE can address the challenges of the traditional education system in India. The figure highlights the importance of embracing OBE to foster critical thinking, problem-solving, and lifelong learning, ultimately preparing students for success in the 21st-century world.

Outcome Based Education (OBE) is an effective approach to teaching and learning for several reasons:

1. **Clarity of learning outcomes:** OBE emphasizes the development of clear and measurable learning outcomes that are aligned with the needs of students, society, and the economy. This clarity of learning outcomes helps to focus teaching and learning on what is important and relevant and helps to ensure that students are learning the skills and competencies that are necessary for success.

2. **Student-centered approach:** OBE is a student-cantered approach that focuses on the needs and interests of individual students. This approach encourages active participation and engagement in the learning process, and helps to promote greater motivation, ownership, and responsibility for learning.

3. **Focus on skills and competencies:** OBE places a strong emphasis on the development of skills and competencies, such as critical thinking, problem-solving, communication, and collaboration, that are essential for success in the 21st-century world. This focus on skills and competencies helps to ensure that students are prepared for the challenges and opportunities of the future.

4. **Integration of assessment and teaching:** OBE emphasizes the integration of assessment and teaching, with assessment being used to inform teaching and learning throughout the process. This helps to ensure that students are continually receiving feedback and support and helps to promote a culture of continuous improvement in teaching and learning.

Overall, OBE is an effective approach to teaching and learning because it emphasizes clarity of learning outcomes, a student-cantered approach, the development of skills and competencies, the integration of assessment and teaching, and flexibility. These characteristics help to ensure that students are prepared for success in the 21st-century world, and that teaching and learning remain relevant and responsive to the needs of society.

1.2   Four pillars of Outcome based Education (OBE)

Outcome-Based Education (OBE) is an educational approach that focuses on clearly defining the desired outcomes of learning and designing instructional activities to achieve those outcomes. It aims to shift the focus from teaching to learning by emphasizing the importance of student achievement and competency. OBE is based on four pillars that provide a framework for implementing OBE effectively in educational institutions. These four pillars are Clarity of focus, Designing down, High expectations, and Expanded opportunities. In this discussion, we will explore each of these pillars in detail, providing real-life examples to illustrate their significance.

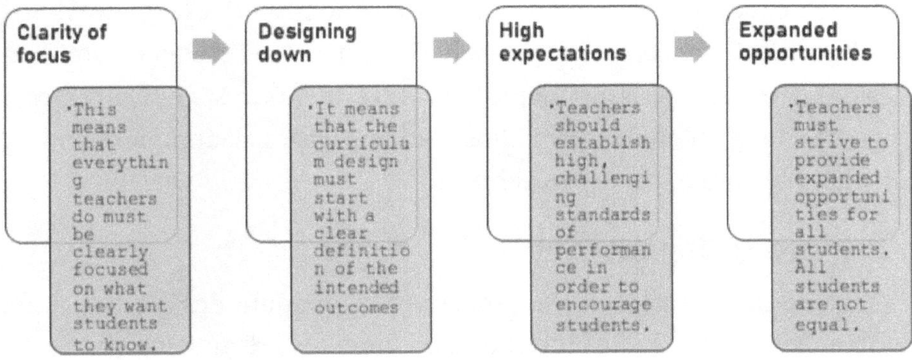

Figure 4: Building the Foundation: Exploring the Four Pillars of Outcome-Based Education (OBE)

The figure represents the four pillars of Outcome-Based Education (OBE): Clarity of focus, Designing down, High expectations, and Expanded opportunities. These pillars form the foundation of OBE, guiding educators in implementing this educational approach effectively. Each pillar is represented by a distinct shape, highlighting its unique contribution to OBE. The figure demonstrates the interconnectedness of these pillars, emphasizing their collective role in promoting student achievement and competency. Through real-life examples, we will delve into each pillar, showcasing how they shape the learning experience and drive positive outcomes in OBE.

1.2.1 Clarity of focus

Clarity of focus means that everything teachers do must be clearly focused on what they want students to know. It involves setting clear and specific learning outcomes or objectives that guide instructional planning and assessment. By having a clear focus, teachers can align their teaching strategies and activities with the intended learning outcomes, ensuring that students acquire the necessary knowledge, skills, and competencies.

Example: In a mathematics class, the clarity of focus can be demonstrated by setting specific learning outcomes, such as solving complex equations, understanding geometric principles, and applying mathematical concepts in real-world scenarios. Teachers can then design their lessons, assignments, and assessments to specifically target these learning outcomes, providing students with a clear understanding of what they are expected to achieve.

1.2.2 Designing down

Designing down refers to the process of curriculum design that starts with a clear definition of the intended outcomes. It involves breaking down the desired learning outcomes into smaller, manageable units and aligning them with specific courses or instructional modules. This approach ensures that each component of the curriculum is purposefully designed to contribute to the overall achievement of the learning outcomes.

Example: In a nursing program, designing down would involve identifying the desired learning outcomes related to patient care, clinical skills, and ethical practices. These outcomes can then be further broken down into specific competencies and integrated into individual courses, such as anatomy and physiology, pharmacology, and patient assessment. Each course would be designed to address the specific learning outcomes within its domain, creating a coherent and interconnected curriculum.

1.2.3 High expectations

High expectations imply that teachers establish challenging standards of performance to encourage students to strive for excellence. By setting high expectations, teachers inspire students to go beyond their comfort zones, take risks, and reach their full potential. High expectations foster a culture of continuous improvement and motivate students to excel in their learning journey.

Example: In an English literature class, high expectations can be demonstrated by challenging students to critically analyse complex literary works, engage in meaningful discussions, and produce well-researched essays. By setting high standards of performance, teachers push students to develop strong analytical and communication skills, encouraging them to think critically and express their ideas effectively.

1.2.4 Expanded opportunities

Expanded opportunities mean that teachers strive to provide diverse and inclusive learning opportunities for all students. It recognizes that students have different learning styles, abilities, and backgrounds, and it is essential to create an inclusive and supportive learning environment that caters to their individual needs. By providing expanded opportunities, teachers promote equity and ensure that every student has access to quality education.

Example: In a visual arts class, expanded opportunities can be offered by providing a range of artistic mediums, techniques, and projects that cater to different interests and abilities. Teachers can create a supportive and inclusive classroom environment where students feel comfortable expressing their creativity and exploring their unique artistic talents. This approach allows students with varying levels of artistic ability to participate and thrive in the learning process.

The four pillars of Clarity of focus, designing down, High expectations, and Expanded opportunities form the foundation of Outcome-Based Education (OBE). Implementing these pillars in an educational institution creates a student-centered learning environment that fosters clarity, alignment, excellence, and inclusivity. By understanding and embracing these pillars, academic members can effectively design and deliver instruction that empowers students to achieve their learning outcomes and succeed in their academic and professional pursuits.

1.3 Key Principle and Components of Outcome based Education (OBE)

In Outcome Based Education (OBE), key principles refer to the fundamental ideas, values, and beliefs that guide the design, implementation, and evaluation of teaching and learning practices. These principles reflect the fundamental goals and objectives of OBE and are intended to provide a framework for the development of student-centered, outcomes-based approaches to education.

1.3.1 Some of the key principles of Outcome based Education (OBE)

Clarity of learning outcomes: This principle emphasizes the importance of developing clear and measurable learning outcomes that are aligned with the needs of students, society, and the economy. Clarity of learning outcomes helps to ensure that teaching and learning are focused on what is important and relevant and helps to ensure that students are learning the skills and competencies that are necessary for success.

Student-centered approach: This principle emphasizes the importance of focusing on the needs and interests of individual students. A student-centered approach encourages active participation and engagement in the learning process, and helps to promote greater motivation, ownership, and responsibility for learning.

Focus on skills and competencies: This principle emphasizes the importance of developing skills and competencies, such as critical thinking, problem-solving, communication, and collaboration, that are essential for success in the 21st-century world. This focus helps to ensure that students are prepared for the challenges and opportunities of the future.

Integration of assessment and teaching: This principle emphasizes the importance of integrating assessment and teaching, with assessment being used to inform teaching and learning throughout the process. This helps to ensure that students are continually receiving feedback and support and helps to promote a culture of continuous improvement in teaching and learning.

Continuous improvement: This principle emphasizes the importance of ongoing evaluation and refinement of teaching and learning practices to ensure that they remain relevant and responsive to the needs of students, society, and the economy. Continuous improvement involves collecting and analysing data on student learning outcomes and teaching and learning practices and using this data to inform changes and improvements to the curriculum, teaching and learning strategies, and assessment practices.

Overall, the key principles of OBE provide a framework for the development of student-cantered, outcomes-based approaches to education that are focused on developing the skills and competencies that are necessary for success in the 21st-century world. We will see more on this in later chapters.

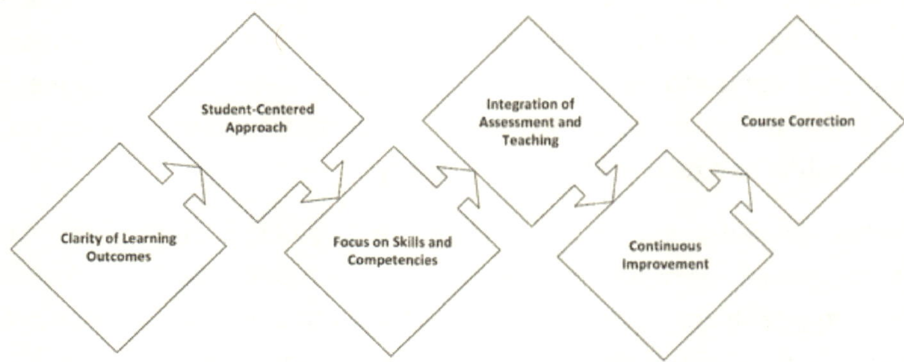

Figure 5: Guiding Principles of Outcome-Based Education (OBE): Fostering Clarity, Student-Centeredness, and Continuous Improvement

The diagram illustrates the key principles of Outcome-Based Education (OBE). Clarity of learning outcomes ensures that teaching focuses on relevant skills and competencies aligned with students' needs. A student-centered approach promotes active engagement and motivation. The focus on skills and competencies prepares students for the future. Integration of assessment and teaching ensures continuous feedback and support. Continuous improvement involves evaluating and refining practices based on data analysis. Course correction allows for adjustments to enhance the teaching and learning process. Together, these principles create an effective OBE framework.

Each principle is depicted as a pillar, symbolizing its significance and influence on the educational process. The figure showcases the interconnected nature of these principles, emphasizing their collective role in promoting meaningful and relevant education. Through the exploration of these principles in later chapters, we will gain a deeper understanding of how they shape OBE practices and enhance student learning outcomes.

1.3.2 Components of Outcome Based Education (OBE)

Outcome Based Education (OBE) is an approach to education that emphasizes the development of clear and measurable learning outcomes, a focus on skills and competencies, a student-centred approach, and the integration of assessment and teaching. Here are the main components of OBE, explained in detail:

Learning Outcomes

Learning outcomes are the foundation of OBE. They are clear and measurable statements that describe what students will know, understand, and be able to do upon completion of a course or program. Learning outcomes should be aligned with the needs of students, society, and the economy, and should be developed collaboratively by faculty, students, employers, and other stakeholders. The process of developing learning outcomes should involve identifying the knowledge, skills, and competencies that students need to succeed in their chosen field or career, and ensuring that these outcomes are specific, measurable, achievable, relevant, and time-bound (SMART).

Curriculum Design

Curriculum design is the process of aligning teaching and learning activities with learning outcomes. The curriculum should be designed to enable students to achieve the learning outcomes and should be organized into coherent and sequenced learning experiences. The curriculum should be flexible, with opportunities for students to choose from a range of learning experiences and should be grounded in research-based teaching and learning practices.

Teaching and Learning Strategies

Teaching and learning strategies should be designed to enable students to achieve the learning outcomes. They should be student-centered, with a focus on active participation, collaboration, and problem-solving. Teaching and learning strategies should be aligned with the needs and interests of individual students and should be based on research-based teaching and learning practices.

Assessment and Evaluation

Assessment and evaluation are an integral part of OBE. Assessment should be aligned with the learning outcomes and should be designed to measure student achievement of the intended learning outcomes. Assessment should be varied and authentic, and should involve a range of assessment methods, such as essays, projects, presentations, and exams. Assessment should be used to inform teaching and learning and should provide students with feedback on their progress towards achieving the learning outcomes.

Continuous Improvement

Continuous improvement is a key component of OBE. It involves ongoing evaluation and refinement of teaching and learning practices to ensure that they remain relevant and responsive to the needs of students, society, and the economy. Continuous improvement involves collecting and analysing data on student learning outcomes and teaching and learning practices and using this data to inform changes and improvements to the curriculum, teaching and learning strategies, and assessment practices.

Overall, the main components of OBE are learning outcomes, curriculum design, teaching and learning strategies, assessment and evaluation, and continuous improvement. These components work together to provide a student-centered, outcomes-based approach to education that prepares students for success in the 21st-century world.

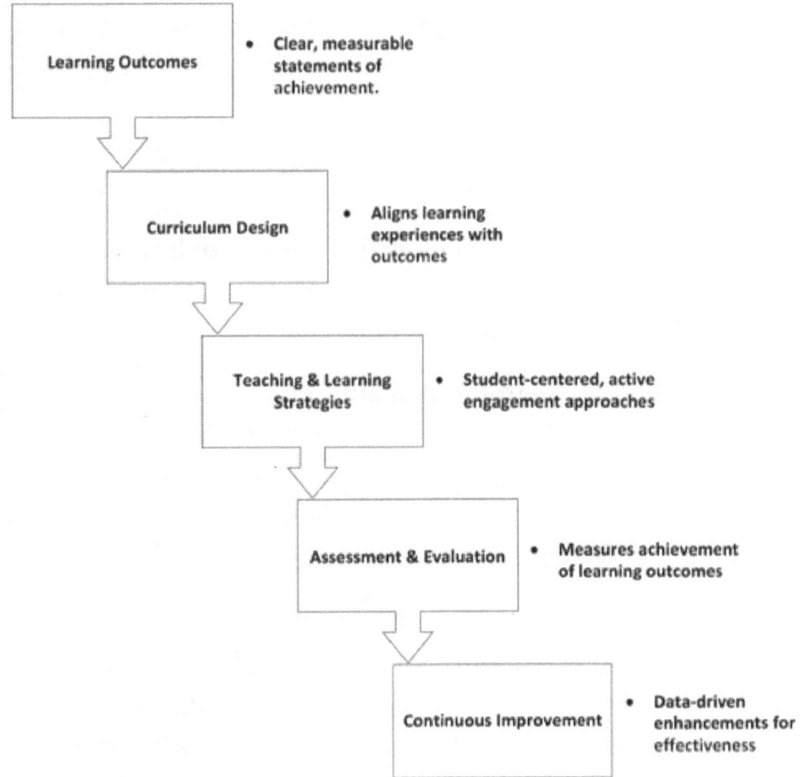

Figure 6: Components of Outcome-Based Education (OBE): Building Blocks for Student-Centered Learning

The figure illustrates the key components of Outcome-Based Education (OBE): Learning Outcomes, Curriculum Design, Teaching and Learning Strategies, Assessment and Evaluation, and Continuous Improvement. Each component is represented as a building block, highlighting its essential role in constructing a student-centered educational experience. The interconnection among these components signifies their integration and mutual influence on promoting effective teaching and learning. Learning outcomes serve as the OBE foundation, guiding curriculum design, which in turn informs the selection of appropriate teaching and learning strategies. Assessment and evaluation are woven throughout the process, providing feedback to students, and informing continuous improvement efforts. Together, these components shape the OBE framework, fostering a holistic and outcomes-driven approach to education.

1.4   Implementing Outcome Based Education in your Institutions

Implementing Outcome Based Education (OBE) can be a powerful way for colleges to make their programs more effective. Here are some steps that colleges can take to implement OBE:

Develop clear and measurable learning outcomes: The first step in implementing OBE is to develop clear and measurable learning outcomes that are aligned with the needs of students, society, and the economy. Learning outcomes should be specific, measurable, achievable, relevant, and time-bound (SMART), and should be developed collaboratively by faculty, students, employers, and other stakeholders.

Align curriculum and teaching strategies with learning outcomes: Once the learning outcomes have been developed, the next step is to align the curriculum and teaching strategies with the learning outcomes. This involves designing the curriculum to enable students to achieve the learning outcomes, and developing teaching strategies that are aligned with the needs and interests of individual students.

Implement varied and authentic assessment: Assessment is a critical component of OBE and should be varied and authentic. Assessment should be designed to measure student achievement of the intended learning outcomes, and should involve a range of assessment methods, such as essays, projects, presentations, and exams.

Collect and analyse data: Data collection and analysis is an essential component of OBE. Colleges should collect and analyse data on student learning outcomes and teaching and learning practices and use this data to inform changes and improvements to the curriculum, teaching and learning strategies, and assessment practices.

Provide professional development: Implementing OBE may require professional development for faculty and staff. Colleges should provide opportunities for faculty and staff to learn about OBE, and to develop the skills and competencies necessary for successful implementation.

Overall, implementing OBE requires a commitment to student-centered, outcomes-based approaches to education, and a willingness to continuously evaluate and improve teaching and learning practices. By implementing OBE, colleges can help to ensure that their programs are effective, relevant, and responsive to the needs of students, society, and the economy.

1.5   Continuous improvement

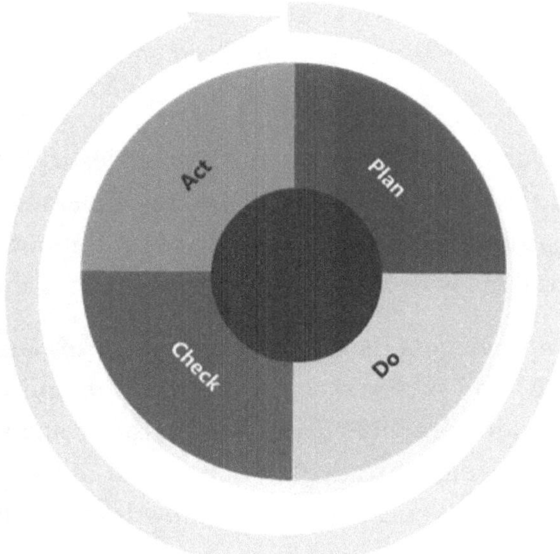

Figure 7: Continuous Improvement in Outcome-Based Education (OBE): The PDCA Cycle

The figure represents the continuous improvement process in Outcome-Based Education (OBE) using the Plan-Do-Check-Act (PDCA) cycle.

This cycle serves as a systematic approach to evaluating and refining teaching and learning practices.

Plan: In this stage, educators plan and define the desired learning outcomes, curriculum design, and teaching strategies based on student needs and the goals of the educational institution.

Do: In this stage, educators implement the planned teaching and learning activities, ensuring that they are aligned with the identified learning outcomes.

Check: This stage involves assessing student learning outcomes and collecting data through various methods such as assessments, student feedback, and program evaluations. The data is then analysed to determine the effectiveness of the teaching and learning practices.

Act: Based on the data analysis, educators act by making necessary adjustments and improvements to teaching and learning strategies, curriculum design, or assessment methods. This step ensures continuous refinement and enhancement of educational practices.

The PDCA cycle creates a feedback loop, allowing educators to continuously evaluate and improve their practices to better meet the needs of students, society, and the economy. By implementing this cycle, educational institutions can foster a culture of continuous improvement and provide students with an enhanced learning experience.

Continuous improvement is a key component of Outcome Based Education (OBE) and involves ongoing evaluation and refinement of teaching and learning practices to ensure that they remain relevant and responsive to the needs of students, society, and the economy. Here's how continuous improvement helps, and how it can be measured and implemented:

Benefits of Continuous Improvement: Continuous improvement helps to ensure that teaching and learning practices are always improving, leading to better outcomes for students and a better alignment with the needs of society and the economy. It helps to identify areas for improvement and provides a process for addressing them. Additionally, it encourages a culture of ongoing learning and growth among faculty and students.

Measurement of Continuous Improvement: Continuous improvement can be measured using a range of methods, including assessment data, student feedback, faculty feedback, and program evaluation. Assessment data can provide information about student learning outcomes, while student and faculty feedback can provide insights into the effectiveness of teaching and learning practices. Program evaluation can provide an overall assessment of the effectiveness of the program.

Implementation of Continuous Improvement: Implementing continuous improvement involves a commitment to ongoing evaluation and refinement of teaching and learning practices. It involves collecting and analysing data on student learning outcomes and teaching and learning practices and using this data to inform changes and improvements to the curriculum, teaching and learning strategies, and assessment practices. It also involves creating a culture of continuous learning and growth among faculty and students.

Overall, continuous improvement is a critical component of OBE, and helps to ensure that teaching and learning practices remain relevant and effective. By measuring and implementing continuous improvement, colleges can ensure that their programs are aligned with the needs of students, society, and the economy, and provide students with the skills and competencies necessary for success in the 21st-century world.

Chapter 2

Understanding Campus Success System Framework (CSSF)

Designing clear and measurable learning outcomes is a critical component of Outcome Based Education (OBE). Learning outcomes are statements that describe what students are expected to know and be able to do by the end of a course, program, or educational experience. Here are some key steps in designing learning outcomes:

Identify the intended learning: The first step in designing learning outcomes is to identify the intended learning. This involves identifying the knowledge, skills, and competencies that students are expected to acquire because of the educational experience.

Use action verbs: Learning outcomes should use clear and specific action verbs that describe what students will be able to do because of the educational experience. Examples of action verbs include "analyse," "evaluate," "synthesize," "create," "demonstrate," and "apply."

Make outcomes measurable: Learning outcomes should be measurable, which means that they should describe the level of mastery that students are expected to achieve. This can be done using rubrics, assessment criteria, or other tools that allow for the objective evaluation of student performance.

Ensure alignment: Learning outcomes should be aligned with the curriculum, teaching strategies, and assessment practices. This helps to ensure that teaching and learning are focused on achieving the intended learning outcomes and helps to promote greater clarity and coherence in the educational experience.

Involve stakeholders: Designing learning outcomes should be a collaborative process that involves input from faculty, students, employers, and other stakeholders. This helps to ensure that the learning outcomes are relevant and responsive to the needs of all stakeholders.

Figure 8: Aligning Core Values, Direction, Outcomes, and Systems for Effective Outcome-Based Education

This diagram illustrates the interconnected components of Outcome Based Education (OBE), emphasizing the importance of aligning core values, direction, outcomes, and systems to achieve successful educational outcomes.

At the start, we have the concept of core values, which represent the fundamental beliefs and principles that guide the behaviour and actions of individuals or the entire campus community.

The next component is the direction, which represents the chosen path or course of action that the campus will undertake to support and uphold its core values. The direction provides a clear vision and purpose for the educational institution.

As we move forward, we come to the outcomes, which are the defined and measurable statements that represent the desired knowledge, skills, and competencies that students should attain. These outcomes are aligned with the chosen direction and serve as a guide for curriculum design, instruction, and assessment.

Finally, we have the systems, which are the operational processes and structures that support the implementation and achievement of the desired outcomes. These systems ensure that the direction is followed, the core values are upheld, and the outcomes are effectively pursued and measured.

The quote "People should work on the system, and the system should work for Campus" emphasizes the collaborative effort required from individuals within the educational institution to contribute to the success of OBE. It highlights the importance of aligning efforts and utilizing effective systems to drive positive outcomes.

Overall, this diagram conveys the importance of integrating core values, direction, outcomes, and systems in the context of OBE, demonstrating how they work together to create a purposeful and effective educational experience for students.

Designing clear and measurable learning outcomes is a critical component of OBE. By designing learning outcomes that are aligned with the needs of students, society, and the economy, colleges can help to ensure that their programs are effective, relevant, and responsive to the needs of all stakeholders.

2.1 Practical Approach of Designing Effective Outcomes for CSSF

Here's a practical approach to designing learning outcomes, along with a hierarchy of different levels of learning outcomes:

Start with the program goals: The first step in designing learning outcomes is to start with the program goals. These are the overarching statements that describe what the program is intended to achieve. For example, a program goal might be "to develop graduates who are proficient in critical thinking."

Identify the program outcomes: Once you have identified the program goals, the next step is to identify the program outcomes. These are the specific statements that describe what students will be able to do because of the program. For example, a program outcome might be "students will be able to analyse complex problems and develop effective solutions."

Develop course-level outcomes: Once you have identified the program outcomes, the next step is to develop course-level outcomes. These are the specific statements that describe what students will be able to do because of each course. For example, a course outcome might be "students will be able to identify the key components of a complex problem and develop a detailed analysis."

Use Bloom's Taxonomy: When developing course-level outcomes, it can be helpful to use Bloom's Taxonomy, which is a framework for classifying learning objectives based on cognitive complexity. Bloom's Taxonomy consists of six levels, from lowest to highest: Remembering, Understanding, Applying, Analysing, Evaluating, and Creating.

Use action verbs: When writing learning outcomes, it's important to use clear and specific action verbs that describe what students will be able to do. Using action verbs also helps to ensure that the outcomes are measurable. Examples of action verbs at different levels of Bloom's Taxonomy include:

Remembering: List, Define, Identify

Understanding: Summarize, Explain, Interpret

Applying: Solve, Demonstrate, Apply

Analysing: Analyse, Compare, Evaluate

Evaluating: Assess, Evaluate, Judge

Creating: Design, Create, Invent

* More about this in later section of this chapter

Ensure alignment: Finally, it's important to ensure that the course-level outcomes are aligned with the program outcomes and the program goals. This helps to ensure that teaching and learning are focused on achieving the intended learning outcomes and helps to promote greater clarity and coherence in the educational experience.

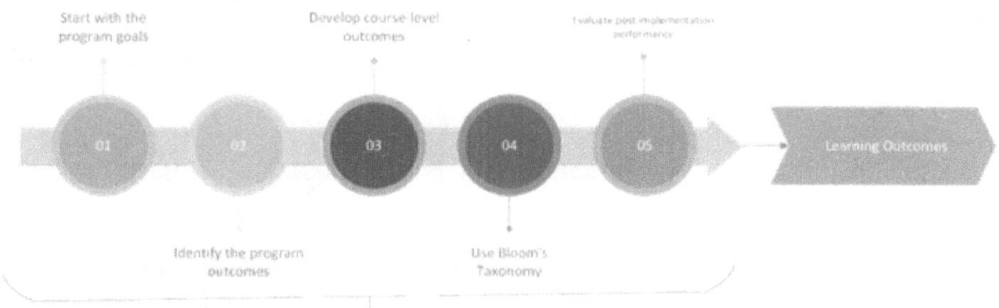

Figure 9: Designing Learning Outcomes: A Step-by-Step Approach

This horizontal diagram illustrates the step-by-step approach to designing learning outcomes, starting from program goals, and progressing to course-level outcomes. The process involves careful consideration of program objectives, alignment with Bloom's Taxonomy, and the use of action verbs.

On the left side of the diagram, we have the program goals, which represent the overarching statements that describe what the program aims to achieve. These goals provide the foundation for the development of specific learning outcomes.

Moving towards the right, we have the program outcomes, which are the specific statements that describe what students will be able to do because of the program. These outcomes are derived from and aligned with the program goals, reflecting the desired knowledge, skills, and competencies of graduates.

Next, we have the course-level outcomes, which are specific statements that describe what students will be able to do because of each course within the program. These outcomes are developed based on the program outcomes and provide a more detailed focus on the knowledge and skills to be acquired within individual courses.

The diagram also highlights the importance of using Bloom's Taxonomy, a framework that classifies learning objectives based on cognitive complexity. By considering the different levels of Bloom's Taxonomy, educators can ensure that course-level outcomes reflect a range of cognitive abilities, from remembering and understanding to applying, analysing, evaluating, and creating.

Additionally, the use of action verbs is emphasized to articulate the expected student abilities clearly and specifically. Action verbs help to ensure that the outcomes are measurable and observable, allowing for effective assessment and evaluation of student achievement.

Finally, the diagram emphasizes the importance of alignment, ensuring that course-level outcomes are aligned with both the program outcomes and the program goals. This alignment helps to ensure a cohesive and purposeful educational experience, where teaching and learning activities are directly linked to the intended learning outcomes.

Overall, this horizontal diagram provides a visual representation of the step-by-step approach to designing learning outcomes, highlighting the significance of program goals, program outcomes, course-level outcomes, Bloom's Taxonomy, action verbs, and alignment in the process.

Overall, designing learning outcomes is a critical component of OBE. By developing clear and measurable learning outcomes at the program and course levels, colleges can help to ensure that their programs are effective, relevant, and responsive to the needs of all stakeholders.

2.2   Campus Success System Framework (CSSF)

Campus Success system Framework (CSSF) is a framework designed by me to ensure campuses effectively designs the Learning Objectives. Learning objectives are laid out at various level and should be reflection of Campus Success System Framework (CSSF). The overall Campus Success System Framework (CSSF) is based on Core Value of the Institute. In any campus when I focus on designing effective Learning objectives we start with the basis. We first look at what are the underlying values of the campus? Are they defined? Are they well published in the campus or not?

2.2.1   5 Keys steps to identify your Campus core Values

Identifying the core values of a campus is an important step in developing a strategic plan for an educational institution. Core values are the principles and beliefs that guide the actions and decisions of the institution. Here are 5 key steps in identifying the core values of a campus:

Step 1: Conduct a review of the institutional mission and vision.

The institutional mission and vision often provide a good starting point for identifying the core values of a campus. These documents typically articulate the institution's overall goals and aspirations and can help to identify the values that are most important to the institution.

Step 2: Engage stakeholders.

Engaging stakeholders can help to ensure that the core values are relevant, meaningful, and aligned with the needs and aspirations of all stakeholders. This can include faculty, staff, students, alumni, employers, and other members of the community. Stakeholders can be engaged through surveys, focus groups, and other forms of feedback.

Step 3: Analyse existing policies and practices

Analysing existing policies and practices can help to identify the values that are already embedded in the institution's culture. For example, if the institution has a strong commitment to sustainability, this may be reflected in its policies on energy use, waste reduction, and transportation.

Step 4: Identify the values that are most important.

Based on the institutional mission and vision, stakeholder feedback, and analysis of existing policies and practices, the core values of the campus can be identified. These values should reflect the institution's culture and identity and should guide decision-making and actions at all levels of the institution.

Step 5: Communicate the core values.

Once the core values have been identified, it's important to communicate them to the campus community. This can be done through the development of a mission and vision statement, the establishment of a code of conduct, and the integration of the core values into institutional policies and practices.

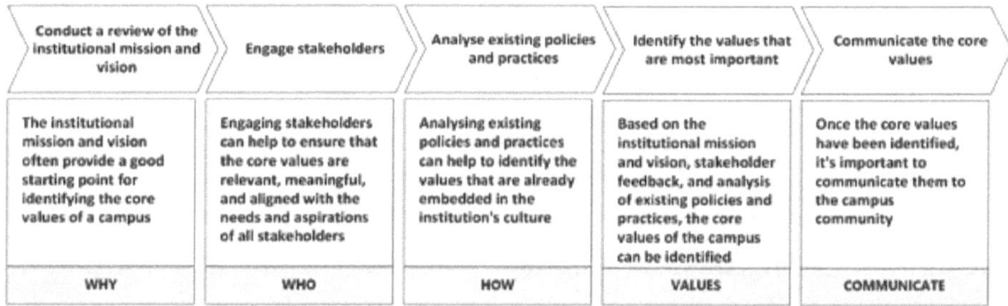

Figure 10: 5 Steps to Identify Your Campus Core Values

This diagram illustrates the five key steps involved in identifying the core values of a campus. These steps provide a systematic approach to ensure that the core values are meaningful, relevant, and aligned with the needs and aspirations of the institution and its stakeholders.

Overall, identifying the core values of a campus is a critical component of developing a strategic plan for an educational institution. By engaging stakeholders, analysing existing policies and practices, and identifying the values that are most important, colleges can develop a clear and compelling set of core values that guides their actions and inspires their community.

2.3   Why Campus Core Values are Important

Good values are the foundation of any successful organization, including educational institutions. A campus that upholds good values is more likely to achieve its vision and mission, as these values guide decision-making and actions at all levels of the institution. Here are some ways that good values can lead to the creation of a good vision and mission for an institution:

Alignment: Good values ensure that the actions and decisions of the institution are aligned with its vision and mission. For example, an institution that values academic excellence is more likely to have a mission focused on providing students with a rigorous and challenging education.

Culture: Good values create a positive and supportive culture within the institution, which can attract and retain talented faculty and staff, as well as motivated and engaged students. This positive culture can contribute to the achievement of the institution's vision and mission.

Accountability: Good values create a sense of accountability within the institution, as faculty, staff, and students are held to high standards of conduct and performance. This accountability can help to ensure that the institution remains focused on its vision and mission, and that resources are allocated effectively to achieve its goals.

Innovation: Good values can foster a culture of innovation within the institution, as faculty and staff are encouraged to think creatively and explore new approaches to teaching, research, and service. This can help the institution to achieve its vision and mission by staying at the forefront of its field and adapting to changing needs and trends.

Overall, good values are essential for creating a positive and effective educational institution. By upholding these values, institutions can ensure that their actions and decisions are aligned with their vision and mission, that they create a positive culture, that they remain accountable to their stakeholders, and that they foster a culture of innovation and continuous improvement.

2.3.1   Good Core Values Leads Excellent System that define Excellence

1. **Creation of Proper Direction** – The path campus will undertake to support Core values of campus.
2. **Creation of Effective Outcomes** – The defined measurable statements to support the desired direction.
3. **Creation of Good Systems** – The defined operational process that support the desired Outcomes.

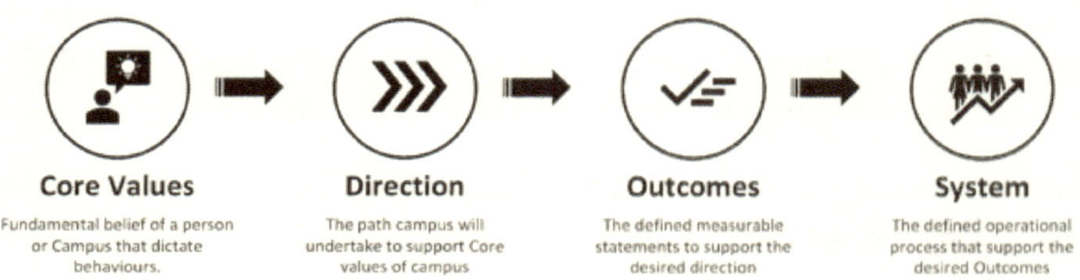

Figure 11: Aligning Core Values, Direction, Outcomes, and Systems for Effective Outcome-Based Education

2.3.2   People should work on system, and system should work for Campus

The individuals working within the campus community and the systems and processes in place should be focused on achieving the goals and objectives of the institution. Here are some key points to consider:

People working on the system: This refers to the individuals within the campus community who are responsible for developing, implementing, and maintaining the various systems and processes that are needed to run the institution. These individuals may include administrators, faculty, staff, and students. It is their responsibility to ensure that the systems and processes are designed and implemented in a way that supports the goals and objectives of the institution.

The system working for the campus: This refers to the idea that the systems and processes in place should be designed and implemented in a way that supports the goals and objectives of the institution. This includes ensuring that the systems are efficient, effective, and responsive to the needs of the campus community. When the system is working for the campus, it helps to support the success of the institution as a whole.

By working together to develop and implement effective systems and processes, individuals within the campus community can help to ensure that the institution is able to achieve its goals and objectives. This requires a commitment to collaboration, innovation, and continuous improvement, as well as a willingness to challenge and refine the systems and processes as needed to ensure that they are meeting the needs of the institution.

As we have seen that **Great Directions are possible when it is measurable** and hence it is imperative that we define our statements which clearly explains what our direction should be.

Great directions are an essential component of any successful institution, including educational institutions. However, in order to achieve these great directions, they must be measurable. Here are some reasons why measurability is important for great directions:

Clarity: Measurable directions provide clarity about what needs to be achieved and how success will be measured. This helps to ensure that everyone in the campus community is working towards the same goals and objectives.

Focus: Measurable directions help to focus the institution's resources and efforts on the most important priorities. By measuring progress towards specific goals, the institution can identify areas where additional resources or attention may be needed.

Accountability: Measurable directions create a sense of accountability within the institution, as faculty, staff, and students are held to specific standards of performance. This helps to ensure that the institution remains focused on its goals and objectives, and that resources are allocated effectively to achieve its goals.

Continuous Improvement: Measurable directions facilitate continuous improvement by providing a framework for assessing progress and identifying areas where additional effort or resources may be needed. By measuring progress towards specific goals, the institution can identify areas where it is excelling and areas where it needs to improve.

Overall, measurable directions are essential for achieving great directions within an educational institution. By providing clarity, focus, accountability, and a framework for continuous improvement, measurable directions help to ensure that the institution is able to achieve its goals and objectives and provide a high-quality education to its students.

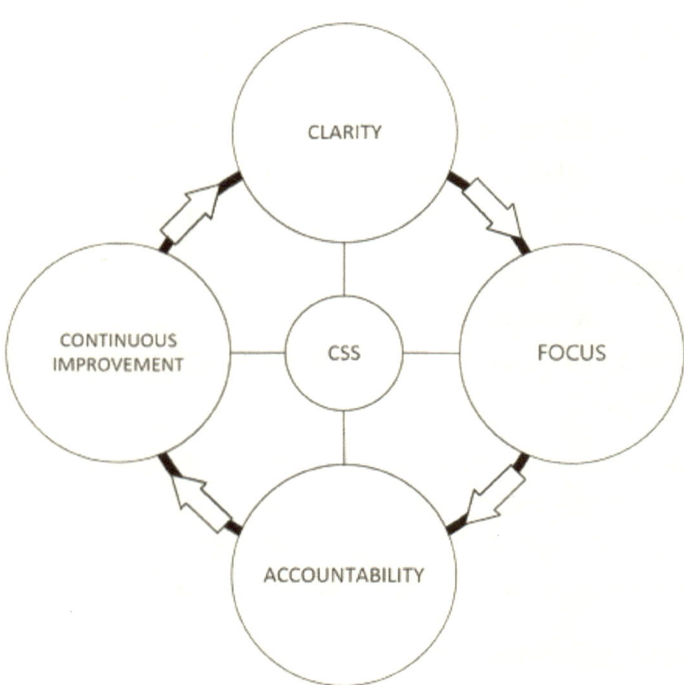

Figure 12: Measurability: The Key to Achieving Great Directions

This diagram emphasizes the importance of measurability in achieving great directions within educational institutions. It highlights how measurability provides clarity, focus, accountability, and a framework for continuous improvement. By measuring progress towards specific goals and objectives, institutions can ensure that they are working towards the same priorities, allocating resources effectively, and holding themselves accountable for performance. Measurability ultimately helps institutions achieve their goals and provide a high-quality education to students.

Chapter 3

Campus Success Statements Framework (CSSF)

Campus Success System Framework (CSSF) is a framework of policies, practices, and strategies that are designed by me to help educational institutions achieve their goals and objectives. This system is typically focused on improving student outcomes, enhancing the quality of teaching and learning, and promoting the overall success of the campus community. Here are some key components of a Campus Success System Framework (CSSF):

Mission and vision: A clear and compelling mission and vision are essential for a Campus Success System. These statements should articulate the institution's goals and aspirations and provide a framework for decision-making and action.

Leadership: Strong leadership is essential for a Campus Success System Framework (CSSF). This includes leaders at all levels of the institution, including administrators, faculty, and staff. Effective leaders are able to inspire and motivate their teams, and provide direction and guidance as needed.

Continuous improvement: A Campus Success System Framework (CSSF) should be focused on continuous improvement, with a focus on enhancing student outcomes and improving the quality of teaching and learning. This requires a commitment to data-driven decision-making, and a willingness to challenge and refine existing practices as needed.

Engagement: Engagement of stakeholders is essential for a Campus Success System Framework (CSSF). This includes faculty, staff, students, alumni, employers, and other members of the community. Engagement can take many forms, including surveys, focus groups, and other forms of feedback.

Resources: Adequate resources are essential for a Campus Success System Framework (CSSF). This includes funding, personnel, and infrastructure. Institutions must ensure that resources are allocated effectively to achieve their goals and objectives.

Overall, a Campus Success System Framework (CSSF) is a comprehensive framework for achieving the goals and objectives of an educational institution. By focusing on student outcomes, enhancing the quality of teaching and learning, and promoting the overall success of the campus community, this system can help institutions to provide a high-quality education and prepare students for success in their chosen fields.

3.1 Layers of Campus Success System Framework (CSSF)

The **Campus Success System Framework (CSSF)** is a holistic approach to improving outcomes in higher education institutions. It is based on the idea that success in higher education is not just about individual courses or programs, but rather about creating a cohesive and coordinated system that supports student learning and success from beginning to end. The **Campus Success System Framework (CSSF)** is composed of four layers: **Syllabus Success, Graduate Success, Alumni Success, and Campus Success**. Each layer builds upon the previous layer to create a comprehensive and integrated system for achieving success in higher education.

The first layer of the Campus Success System Framework (CSSF), Syllabus Success, focuses on the development and implementation of effective curricula and instructional materials that support student learning and success. This includes creating clear learning outcomes, assessments that align with those outcomes, and teaching strategies that are engaging and effective.

The second layer, Graduate Success, focuses on the successful completion of a program of study by students, and the acquisition of the knowledge, skills, and competencies needed to succeed in their chosen field. This layer includes tracking the success of graduates in finding employment or enrolling in graduate programs and using this data to continually improve programs.

The third layer, Alumni Success, focuses on the long-term success of graduates in their chosen careers or endeavours. This includes providing career development services to alumni and establishing a network of alumni mentors to help alumni advance in their careers.

The fourth and final layer, Campus Success, focuses on the overall success of the institution in achieving its mission and goals, as reflected in measures such as enrolment, retention, graduation rates, and reputation. When the previous layers are successful, it leads to overall success for the campus.

By implementing the Campus Success System Framework (CSSF), institutions can create a coordinated and comprehensive approach to improving outcomes in higher education. This approach helps to ensure that students are well-prepared for their chosen fields, alumni are successful in their careers, and the institution is successful in achieving its mission and goals.

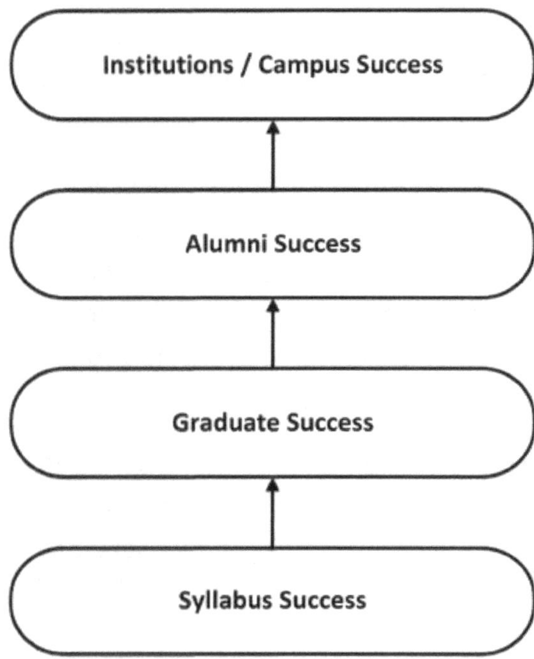

Figure 13: Building Success in Higher Education: The Campus Success System Framework (CSSF)

This diagram illustrates the Campus Success System Framework (CSSF) as a holistic approach to improving outcomes in higher education institutions. It showcases the four layers of the system: Syllabus Success, Graduate Success, Alumni Success, and Campus Success. Each layer builds upon the previous one, creating a comprehensive and integrated system that supports student learning and success throughout their educational journey.

The diagram visually represents how each layer contributes to a cohesive and coordinated system, promoting student success, alumni achievements, and institutional excellence. By implementing the Campus Success System Framework (CSSF), higher education institutions can create an environment that fosters continuous improvement and maximizes positive outcomes for all stakeholders involved.

Let us elaborate on the four layers of Campus Success System Framework (CSSF) that you have identified and provide examples of how each layer can lead to success at the subsequent layer.

Syllabus Success: The first layer of the Campus Success System Framework (CSSF) is Syllabus Success. This refers to the development and implementation of effective curricula and instructional materials that support student learning and success. When a syllabus is successful, it should include clear learning outcomes, assessments that align with those outcomes, and teaching strategies that are engaging and effective. For example, a university might redesign a course syllabus to include more interactive learning activities or incorporate technology to enhance student engagement.

Graduate Success: The second layer of the Campus Success System Framework (CSSF) is Graduate Success. This refers to the successful completion of a program of study by students, and the acquisition of the knowledge, skills, and competencies needed to succeed in their chosen field. When graduates are successful, they are well-prepared to enter the workforce or pursue advanced studies. For example, a university might track the success of its graduates in finding employment or enrolling in graduate programs and use this data to continually improve its programs.

Alumni Success: The third layer of the Campus Success System Framework (CSSF) is Alumni Success. This refers to the long-term success of graduates in their chosen careers or endeavours. When alumni are successful, they serve as ambassadors for the institution, and help to attract new students and support the institution's mission. For example, a university might establish a network of alumni mentors or offer career development services to help alumni advance in their careers.

Campus Success: The final layer of the Campus Success System Framework (CSSF) is Campus Success. This refers to the overall success of the institution in achieving its mission and goals, as reflected in measures such as enrolment, retention, graduation rates, and reputation.

When a campus is successful, it can attract and retain talented faculty and staff, provide high-quality educational experiences to students, and contribute to the advancement of knowledge and society. For example, a university might invest in infrastructure or research initiatives to enhance its reputation and attract new students and faculty.

To illustrate the impact of these four layers of the Campus Success System Framework (CSSF), let's consider a hypothetical case study. A university redesigns the syllabus for one of its core courses, incorporating more interactive learning activities and aligning assessments more closely with learning outcomes. As a result, student engagement and retention in the course improve, and more students successfully complete the program. These graduates are well-prepared for their chosen fields and can find employment or enrol in graduate programs at high rates. Over time, these graduates become successful alumni, serving as mentors and ambassadors for the institution. This success translates to overall success for the campus, with increased enrolment, improved reputation, and expanded research opportunities.

Numerical proofs of the impact of the Campus Success System Framework (CSSF) can be seen in measures such as retention rates, graduation rates, alumni employment and graduate school enrolment rates, and rankings in national and international surveys of higher education institutions. For example, a university that implements the Campus Success System Framework (CSSF) might see improvements in retention rates from year to year or see a higher percentage of graduates entering high-demand fields. These measures can be used to track progress and make data-driven decisions about the institution's strategic priorities.

3.2 Case Studies

3.2.1 Syllabus Success initiative at The University of Texas at Austin

- A study of the Syllabus Success initiative found that courses that underwent syllabus revisions had higher student engagement and success rates than courses that did not undergo revisions. Specifically, the study found that course success rates (defined as the percentage of students who earned a grade of C – or better) increased by an average of 4.4 percentage points for courses that underwent syllabus revisions.

- Another study of the Syllabus Success initiative found that courses that underwent syllabus revisions received higher overall course evaluations from students than courses that did not undergo revisions. Specifically, the study found that courses that underwent revisions had an average overall course evaluation score that was 0.21 points higher (on a 5-point scale) than courses that did not undergo revisions.

- UT Austin also tracks retention rates for its students, and data from the university shows that retention rates have been steadily increasing over the past few years. For example, the retention rate for first-time, full-time freshmen at UT Austin was 93.6% for the Fall 2020 semester, up from 92.2% in Fall 2016.

These data suggest that the Syllabus Success initiative has had a positive impact on student engagement, success, and retention rates at UT Austin. By revising course syllabi to include clear learning outcomes and assessments that align with those outcomes, UT Austin has been able to improve the quality of instruction and support student learning and success.

Please note: The information provided here is for general informational purposes only. We make no representations or warranties of any kind, express or implied, about the completeness, accuracy, reliability, suitability, or availability of the information. Any reliance you place on such information is strictly at your own risk.

3.2.2 Graduate Success Initiative at the University of California, Los Angeles (UCLA)

According to data from UCLA, 86% of recent graduates were employed or pursuing advanced degrees within six months of graduation. This figure is based on a survey of the Class of 2020 conducted by UCLA's Career Centre.

Data from UCLA's Centre for Education Statistics shows that the six-year graduation rate for first-time, full-time undergraduate students who entered UCLA in Fall 2014 was 91.7%. This is higher than the national average six-year graduation rate for public four-year institutions, which was 62% for students who entered in Fall 2014, according to data from the National Centre for Education Statistics.

UCLA also tracks student outcomes through its annual "First Destination Survey," which surveys recent graduates about their employment and educational activities after graduation. According to the most recent survey, 96% of respondents from the Class of 2019 were employed or pursuing further education within six months of graduation.

These data suggest that the Graduate Success initiative at UCLA has been successful in preparing graduates for successful careers and further education. By providing career development services and support to students as they transition from college to the workforce, UCLA has been able to help its graduates achieve high levels of success after graduation.

Please note: The information provided here is for general informational purposes only. We make no representations or warranties of any kind, express or implied, about the completeness, accuracy, reliability, suitability, or availability of the information. Any reliance you place on such information is strictly at your own risk.

3.2.3 Alumni Success initiative at the University of Michigan

- According to data from the University of Michigan, 95% of its graduates are employed, pursuing further education, or engaged in other meaningful activities within six months of graduation. This figure is based on a survey of the Class of 2020 conducted by the university's Career Centre.

- Data from the University of Michigan's "Post-Graduation Activity Report" shows that the most common industries for recent graduates to enter are consulting, finance, technology, healthcare, and education. In addition, a significant percentage of graduates enter fields related to public service and the arts.
- The University of Michigan also tracks outcomes for its alumni over time. According to data from the university's Alumni Association, 96% of alumni reported being satisfied with their experience at the university, and 86% said they would choose to attend the university again if given the opportunity.
- This was only possible because the University successfully implemented and kept measuring effective learning outcomes and the result was evident in the Success of Graduates.

These data suggest that the Alumni Success initiative at the University of Michigan has been successful in helping graduates to achieve meaningful careers and contribute to society in a variety of fields. By providing career development and networking opportunities to alumni, the university has been able to help its graduates succeed long after they leave campus.

Please note: The information provided here is for general informational purposes only. We make no representations or warranties of any kind, express or implied, about the completeness, accuracy, reliability, suitability, or availability of the information. Any reliance you place on such information is strictly at your own risk.

3.2.3 Campus Success System at the University of Central Florida

- The University of Central Florida (UCF) has seen significant improvements in retention rates in recent years. For example, the university's retention rate for first time-in-college students increased from 82.5% in Fall 2010 to 89.7% in Fall 2019.
- Graduation rates have also improved at UCF. According to data from the National Centre for Education Statistics, the six-year

graduation rate for first-time, full-time undergraduate students who entered UCF in Fall 2014 was 71.7%. This is higher than the national average six-year graduation rate for public four-year institutions, which was 62% for students who entered in Fall 2014, according to data from the National Centre for Education Statistics.

- UCF has also seen improvements in alumni employment and graduate school enrolment rates. According to data from the university's Career Services Office, 88% of UCF graduates who responded to a survey were employed or pursuing further education within six months of graduation in 2019.

- In addition, UCF has achieved high rankings in national and international surveys of higher education institutions. For example, UCF was ranked #16 among public universities in the United States by U.S. News & World Report in its 2022 rankings and was ranked #21 in the world among universities under 50 years old by Times Higher Education in its 2021 rankings.

These data suggest that the Campus Success System has had a significant impact on measures such as retention rates, graduation rates, alumni employment and graduate school enrolment rates, and rankings in national and international surveys of higher education institutions at UCF.

Please note: The information provided here is for general informational purposes only. We make no representations or warranties of any kind, express or implied, about the completeness, accuracy, reliability, suitability, or availability of the information. Any reliance you place on such information is strictly at your own risk.

3.3 Define effective Statements at each layer of CSSF

Defining statements at each layer of the Campus Success System Framework (CSSF) are important for several reasons. Firstly, they provide a clear and concise articulation of what success means at each level. This helps to ensure that everyone in the campus community – from faculty and staff to students and alumni – is working towards the same goals and understands how their efforts contribute to overall success.

Secondly, defining statements help to establish a framework for decision-making and resource allocation. By identifying the key factors that contribute to success at each level, campus leaders can make strategic choices about where to invest time, energy, and resources.

Finally, defining statements can help to foster a culture of accountability and continuous improvement. By establishing clear metrics for success and regularly tracking progress against those metrics, campus leaders can identify areas where improvement is needed and take action to address those areas.

For example, if a university has a defining statement for Syllabus Success that includes specific criteria for effective syllabus design and assessment, faculty can use that statement as a guide when designing their courses. The university can then collect data on student engagement, success rates, and course evaluations to assess the impact of the Syllabus Success initiative and adjust as needed. Similarly, if a university has a defining statement for Campus Success that includes metrics such as graduation rates and alumni employment rates, campus leaders can use that statement as a guide when making decisions about resource allocation and programmatic initiatives.

Overall, defining statements at each layer of the Campus Success System Framework (CSSF) are a critical component of a comprehensive approach to campus improvement. By articulating clear goals and metrics for success, universities can create a culture of accountability and continuous improvement that leads to better outcomes for students, faculty, staff, and the community as a whole.

When you look at the defining the statements at each level means the same should be effective, simple, and achievable. And hence it is imperative we define the statements after multiple brainstorming and deeper discussion as per core values of the Institute.

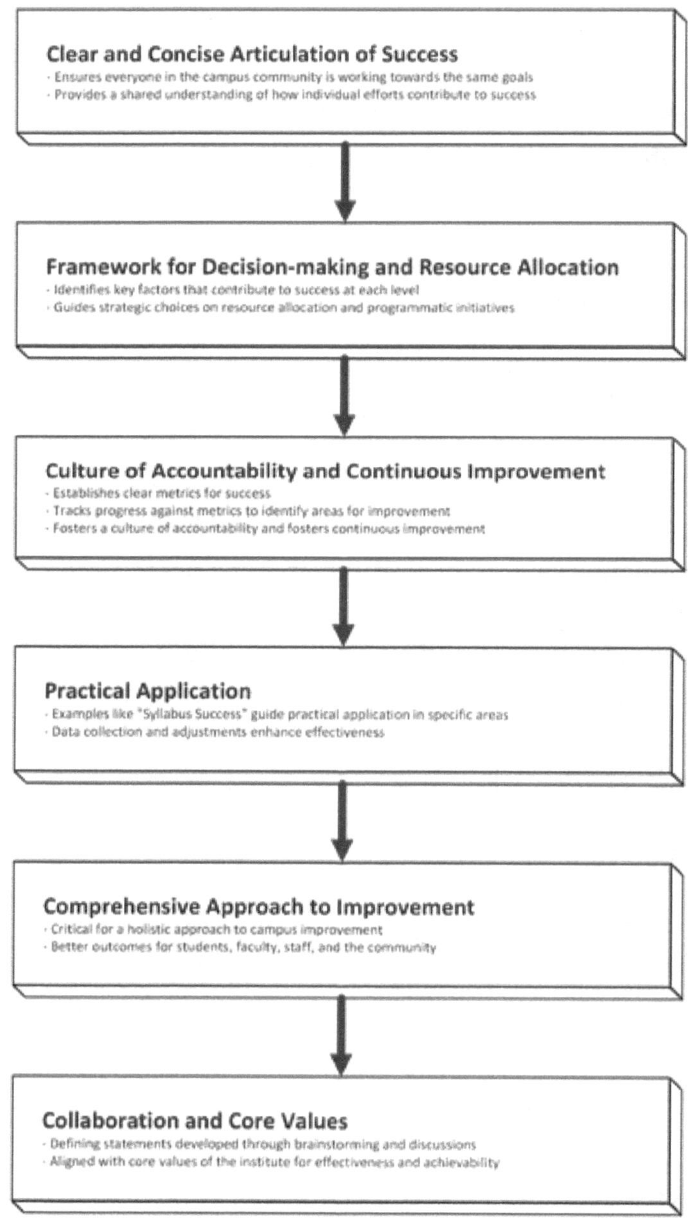

Figure 14: The Campus Success System Framework (CSSF): A Holistic Approach to Achieving Success in Higher Education

How to Define Effective Statements at Each Level of Campus Success System Framework (CSSF)

4.1 Syllabus Success

Syllabus Success can be defined as the achievement of **Effective Course Outcomes** and Learning Objectives. Effective Course Outcomes are statements that describe what students will be able to know, do, or understand as a result of completing a particular course. Learning Objectives are specific, measurable, and observable statements that describe what students are expected to achieve in terms of knowledge, skills, and attitudes by the end of a course.

To achieve Syllabus Success, faculty members must design and deliver courses that align with the learning objectives and course outcomes. This involves developing clear and specific objectives that are measurable and attainable, creating a curriculum that is aligned with those objectives, and using assessment methods that are aligned with the objectives and outcomes. By achieving Syllabus Success, universities can ensure that their courses are effective and provide students with the knowledge and skills they need to be successful in their academic and professional lives.

4.2 Graduate Success

Graduate Success can be defined as the achievement of **Effective Program Outcomes**. Effective Program Outcomes are statements that describe what students are expected to know, do, or understand at the end of a particular degree program. These outcomes should be aligned with the program's goals and objectives, and should be specific, measurable, and attainable.

To achieve Graduate Success, universities must design and deliver degree programs that align with the program outcomes. This involves developing clear and specific outcomes that are measurable and attainable, creating a curriculum that is aligned with those outcomes, and using assessment methods that are aligned with the outcomes. By achieving Graduate Success, universities can ensure that their graduates are well-prepared for their chosen careers and are able to contribute to society in meaningful ways.

4.3   Alumni Success

Alumni Success can be defined as the achievement of **Effective Program Educational Objectives**. Effective Program Educational Objectives are statements that describe what students are expected to achieve in terms of knowledge, skills, and attitudes after completing a particular degree program. These objectives should be aligned with the program's goals and outcomes, and should be specific, measurable, and attainable.

To achieve Alumni Success, universities must design and deliver degree programs that align with the program educational objectives. This involves developing clear and specific objectives that are measurable and attainable, creating a curriculum that is aligned with those objectives, and using assessment methods that are aligned with the objectives. By achieving Alumni Success, universities can ensure that their graduates are successful in their careers and are able to make a positive impact on society.

4.4   Campus Success System Framework (CSSF)

Campus Success System Framework (CSSF) can be defined as the achievement of **Effective Vision and Mission of Program**. The vision and mission of a university should provide a clear and compelling statement of the institution's purpose and goals and should be aligned with the institution's core values.

To achieve Campus Success, universities must develop and communicate a clear and compelling vision and mission for the institution. This involves engaging stakeholders from across the campus community to ensure that the vision and mission reflect the values and aspirations of the institution. By achieving Campus Success, universities can ensure that they are able to attract and retain high-quality faculty and students and are able to make a positive impact on society through their research, teaching, and service.

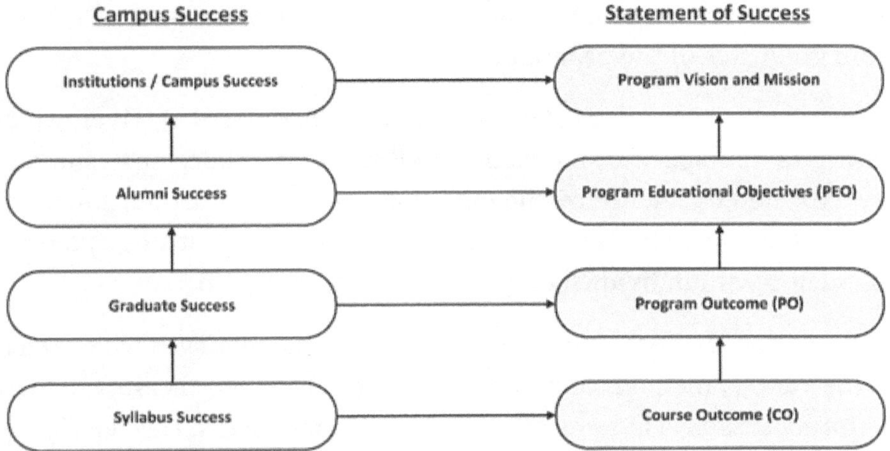

Figure 15: Defining Effective Statements for Each Level of the Campus Success System Framework (CSSF)

This diagram showcases the process of defining effective statements at each level of the Campus Success System Framework (CSSF). It highlights four key levels: Syllabus Success, Graduate Success, Alumni Success, and Campus Success. For each level, the diagram emphasizes the importance of aligning objectives, outcomes, and objectives with the respective goals and values of the institution. By defining clear and measurable statements, universities can ensure that their courses, programs, and overall mission are aligned and contribute to the success of students, graduates, and the campus community. This comprehensive approach to defining effective statements at each level helps institutions foster a culture of continuous improvement and achieve desired outcomes in higher education.

Now let's see how to define effective statements which is quantifiable and more importantly scientifically placed as per required for OBE Implementation.

4.5 Pyramid of Campus Success Statement

The layers are arranged hierarchically, starting from the Institute Vision/Mission as the foundation. The Program Vision/Mission layer sits below the Institute level, representing the specific vision and mission statements of individual programs within the institute. Moving downward, the Program Educational Objectives (PEO) layer represents the broad accomplishments and professional achievements expected from graduates of the program.

Below the PEO layer, we have the Program Outcomes (PO) layer, which describes the specific knowledge, skills, and attitudes that students are expected to acquire by the end of the program. Further down, the Course Outcomes (CO) layer represents the specific learning outcomes associated with individual courses within the program.

At the bottom of the pyramid, we have the Assessments layer, which refers to the various methods and tools used to evaluate and measure student performance and achievement of the desired outcomes at each level.

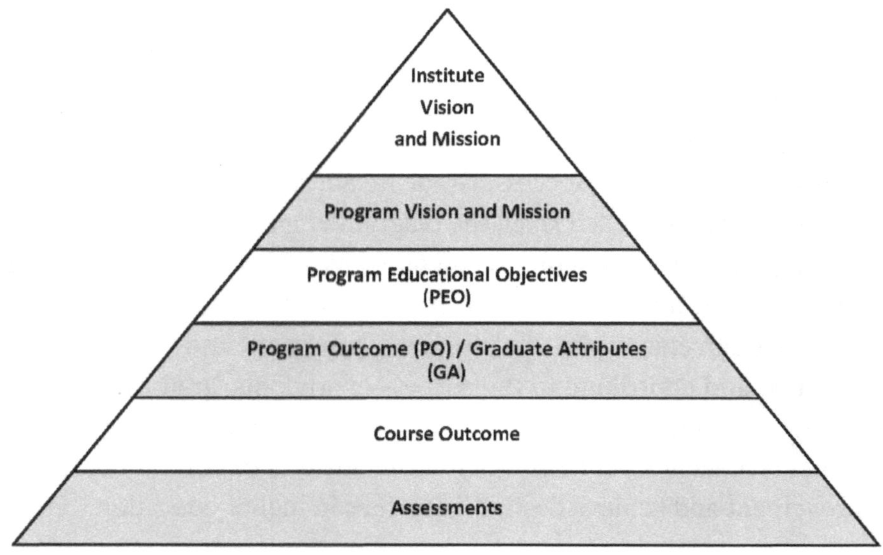

Figure 16: Pyramid of Campus Success Statements: Building a Foundation for Achievement

This pyramid representation emphasizes the nested structure of the Campus Success Statement, with each layer building upon the one below it. It illustrates how the institute's vision and mission inform the program's vision and mission, which then guide the establishment of program-level objectives, outcomes, and course-level outcomes. Finally, assessments are employed to assess and track the attainment of the desired outcomes at each level.

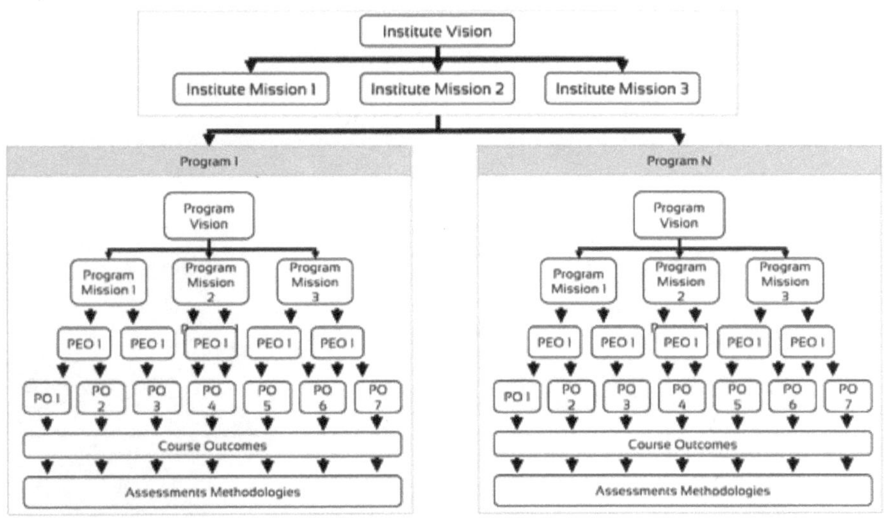

Figure 17: Pyramid of Campus Success Statements: Building a Foundation for Achievement in the Institute for Multiple Programs

This diagram illustrates the Pyramid of Campus Success Statements, which outlines the hierarchical structure of defining statements within the Campus Success System Framework (CSSF) for multiple programs in the institute where each program will have respective statements of its own. The pyramid starts with the Institute Vision/Mission as the foundation, followed by the Program Vision/Mission layer, representing the specific vision and mission statements of individual programs. Moving upwards, we have the Program Educational Objectives (PEO) layer, describing the broad accomplishments expected from graduates. Above that, the Program Outcomes (PO) layer defines the specific knowledge, skills, and attitudes students should acquire. Next, the

Course Outcomes (CO) layer outlines the learning outcomes for individual courses. At the top of the pyramid, the Assessments layer encompasses the methods used to evaluate student performance and measure the achievement of desired outcomes at each level. This pyramid structure emphasizes the importance of a strong foundation and alignment between different levels of statements to foster success in higher education institutions.

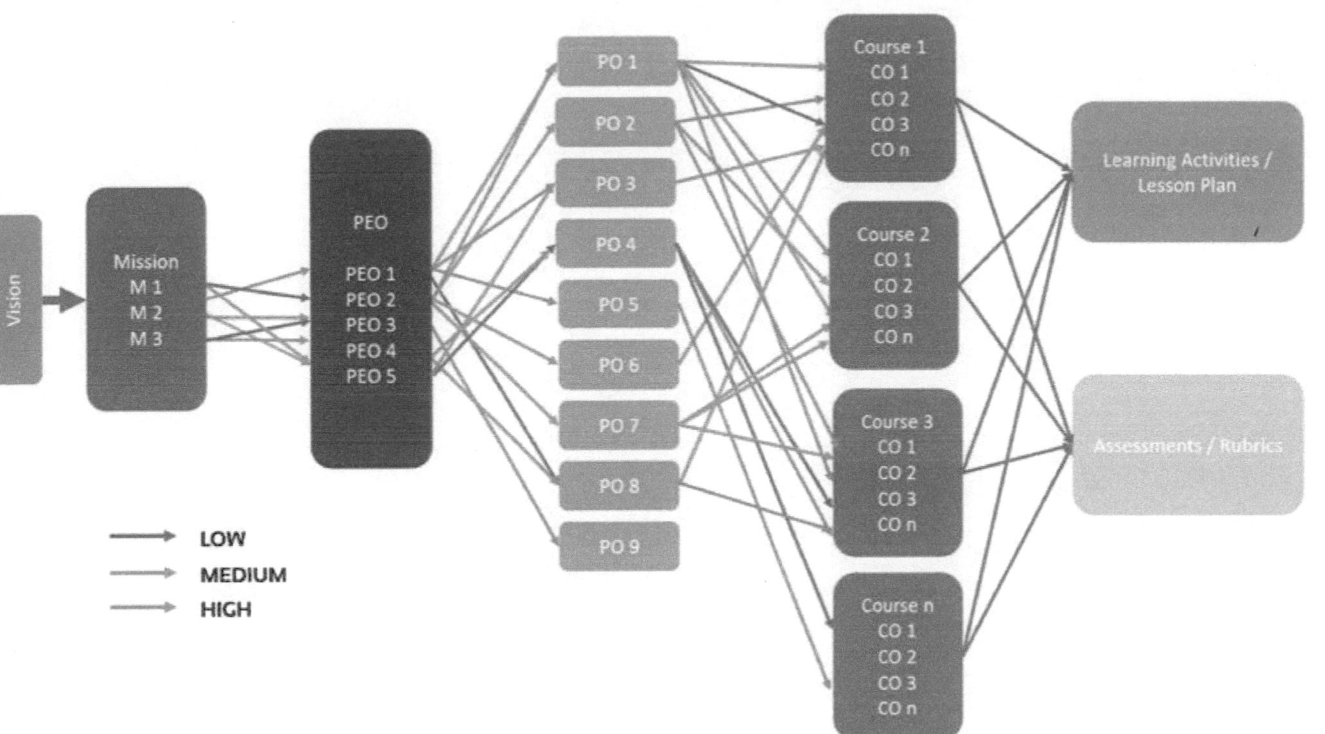

Figure 18: Marco Level View: Interlinked Magic View of your Campus Success System Framework (CSSF)

Chapter 5

Defining Vision and Mission of the Program

Before we understand how to define effective Vision and Mission for the Program, lets understand what the difference between Vision and Mission of the Institute is.

The vision and mission statements of an institute and a program serve different purposes and are developed at different levels of the organization.

The vision statement of an institute provides a long-term view of what the institution hopes to achieve in the future. It describes the ideal state that the institution wants to create and the impact it wants to have on society. The vision statement is often inspirational and aspirational, and it serves as a guide for the institution's strategic planning and decision-making processes.

The mission statement of an institute describes the purpose of the institution and the broad strategies that it will use to achieve its vision. It defines the core activities and values of the institution and provides a framework for aligning the institution's resources and activities with its goals. The mission statement is typically more specific and action-oriented than the vision statement, and it provides a basis for evaluating the effectiveness of the institution's programs and services.

On the other hand, the vision and mission statements of a program describe the goals and objectives of that specific program. The program's vision statement provides a long-term view of what the program hopes to achieve, while the mission statement describes the purpose of the program and the strategies that it will use to achieve its vision. The program's vision and mission statements provide guidance to the faculty and staff who are responsible for designing and delivering the program, as well as to the students who are pursuing the program.

In summary, the vision and mission statements of an institute provide a broad view of the institution's goals and objectives, while the vision and mission statements of a program provide a more focused view of the program's goals and objectives. Both types of statements are important for aligning an institution or program with its values and goals, and for ensuring that its activities and resources are directed towards achieving those goals.

The vision and mission statements of a program should be aligned with the overall vision and mission statements of the institution, while also reflecting the unique goals and values of the program.

The program's vision statement should be consistent with the institution's vision statement but should also express the program's specific aspirations and goals. For example, if the institution's vision is to be a leader in providing high-quality education, the program's vision might be to produce graduates who are highly skilled and knowledgeable in their field of study.

Likewise, the program's mission statement should be consistent with the institution's mission statement but should also reflect the program's unique purpose and focus. For example, if the institution's mission is to provide an excellent education to a diverse student population, the program's mission might be to provide a specialized education in a particular discipline or area of study.

In summary, the vision and mission statements of a program should be aligned with the overall vision and mission statements of the institution but should also express the unique goals and values of the program. This helps to ensure that the program is consistent with the institution's overall mission and goals, while also providing a clear and focused direction for the program's faculty, staff, and students.

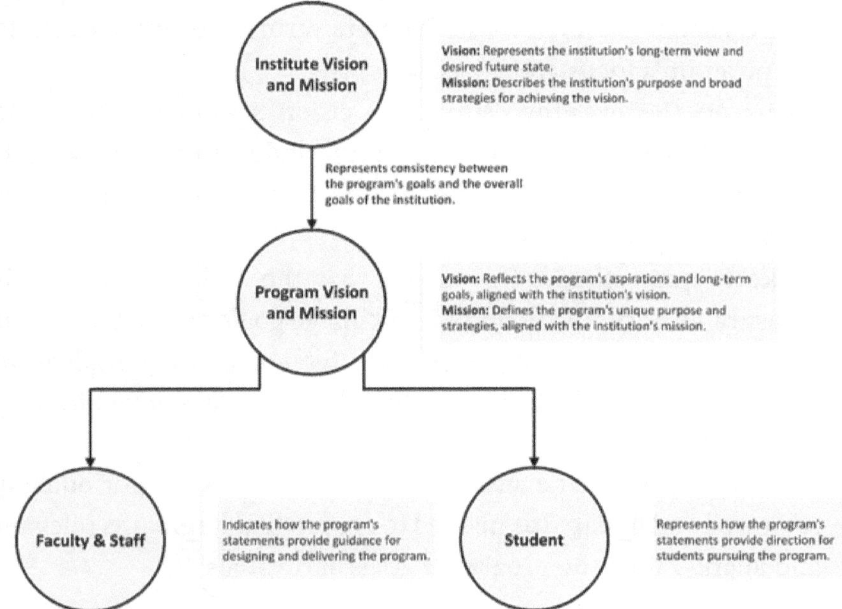

Figure 19: Aligning Vision and Mission: Institute vs Program.

5.1 Defining Vision of the Program

Here are some steps to follow when designing an effective vision statement for a program:

1. **Involve stakeholders:** Engage faculty, staff, students, and other stakeholders in the process of developing the vision statement. This helps to ensure that the vision is inclusive, reflects the values of the program, and has broad support.

2. **Review the institution's vision and mission statements:** The program's vision statement should align with the overall vision and mission statements of the institution, while also expressing the unique goals and values of the program.

3. **Be concise and memorable:** The vision statement should be short, easy to remember, and inspiring. It should capture the essence of what the program hopes to achieve and be memorable enough that stakeholders can easily recall it.

4. **Use concrete language:** Avoid vague or overly abstract language in the vision statement. Use concrete terms that are specific to the program's focus and goals.

5. **Focus on the present:** While the vision statement should be forward-looking, it should also be grounded in the present. It should describe what the program is doing now and how it is working towards achieving its vision.

6. **Make it quantifiable:** To ensure that the vision statement is measurable, it should include quantifiable goals or objectives. For example, the vision statement might include a target graduation rate or a specific number of graduates who are employed in their field of study.

7. **Keep it current:** The vision statement should be periodically reviewed and updated as needed to ensure that it remains relevant and aligned with the program's goals and values.

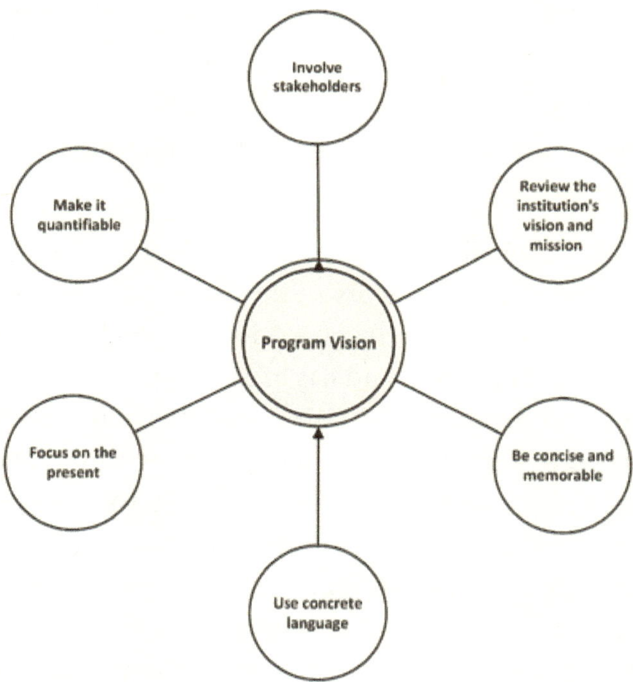

Figure 20: Steps to Designing an Effective Program Vision

The above diagram provides a step-by-step guide to defining a compelling vision statement for a program. The steps include involving stakeholders, aligning with the institution's vision and mission, ensuring conciseness and memorability, using concrete language, focusing on the present, incorporating quantifiable goals, and maintaining currency through periodic review. By following these steps, program leaders can create a vision statement that inspires and guides the program's stakeholders, reflecting its unique goals and values while aligning with the broader institutional vision.

By following these steps, program leaders can develop an effective vision statement that is aligned with the institution's overall mission and goals, while also reflecting the unique goals and values of the program.

5.2 Defining Mission of the Program

A program mission statement is typically developed by program leaders in consultation with faculty, staff, students, and other stakeholders. It should be aligned with the institution's overall mission statement and reflect the unique goals and values of the program.

An effective mission statement is practical, quantifiable, and well-aligned with the program's vision and institution's mission. It should be specific and focused, using concrete language to describe the program's goals and objectives. It should also be measurable, including quantifiable goals or objectives that can be used to evaluate the program's success.

Overall, the mission statement of a program serves as a guide for program leaders, faculty, staff, and students, providing a clear direction for the program's activities and helping to ensure that everyone is working towards the same goals and objectives.

Here are some steps to follow when designing an effective program mission statement:

1. **Involve stakeholders:** Engage faculty, staff, students, and other stakeholders in the process of developing the mission statement. This helps to ensure that the mission is inclusive, reflects the values of the program, and has broad support.

2. **Review the institution's mission statement:** The program's mission statement should align with the overall mission statement of the institution, while also expressing the unique goals and values of the program.

3. **Be concise and specific:** The mission statement should be short, focused, and specific. It should capture the essence of what the program does and what it aims to achieve.

4. **Use concrete language:** Avoid vague or overly abstract language in the mission statement. Use concrete terms that are specific to the program's focus and goals.

5. **Make it measurable:** To ensure that the mission statement is measurable, it should include quantifiable goals or objectives. For example, the mission statement might include a target graduation rate, a specific number of graduates who are employed in their field of study, or a certain level of academic excellence.

6. **Align with the program's vision:** The mission statement should be aligned with the program's vision statement, reflecting the same goals and objectives.

7. **Align with the institution's mission:** The mission statement should also align with the overall mission of the institution, reflecting its core values and priorities.

8. **Keep it current:** The mission statement should be periodically reviewed and updated as needed to ensure that it remains relevant and aligned with the program's goals and values.

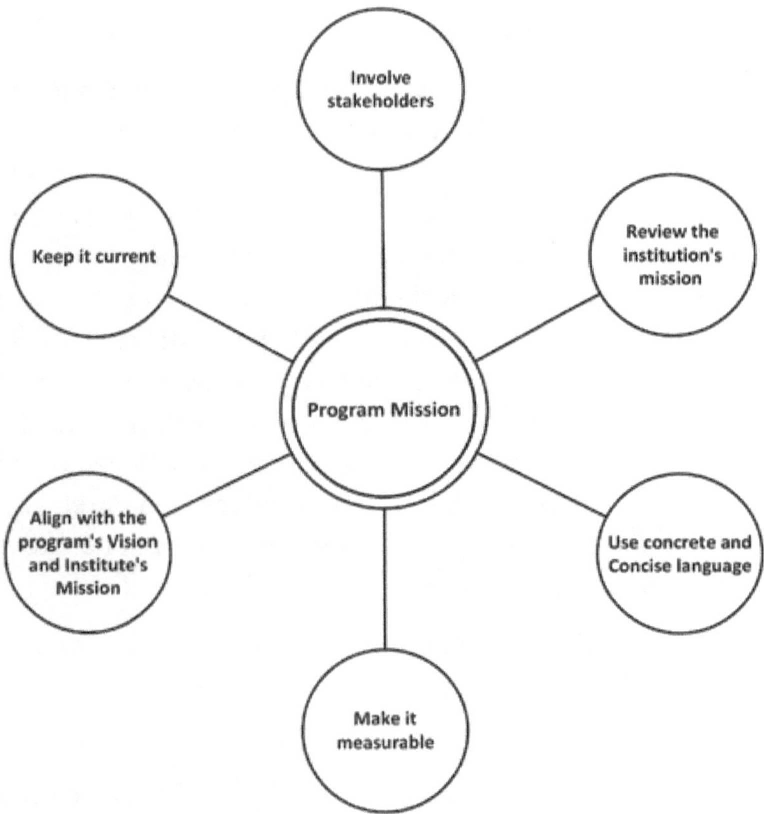

Figure 21: Steps to Crafting an Effective Program Mission

The diagram highlights the importance of stakeholder involvement, alignment with the institution's mission, conciseness, specificity, use of concrete language, measurability, alignment with the program's vision, and regular review. By following these steps, program leaders can create a mission statement that defines the program's purpose, goals, and values, and guides its activities towards success.

By following these steps, program leaders can develop an effective mission statement that is aligned with the institution's overall mission and goals, while also reflecting the unique goals and values of the program.

5.3 Formation of Committee for the Defining Effective Vision and Mission

Forming a committee to develop a program's vision and mission statements is an important step in ensuring that the program is well-aligned with institutional goals and values, and that it is positioned to achieve its strategic objectives. By involving a diverse group of stakeholders in the process, the committee can ensure that the vision and mission statements reflect the unique values and priorities of the program, and that they are well-supported by key stakeholders such as faculty, staff, students, alumni, and industry partners. Additionally, the committee's work can help to clarify the program's priorities and identify opportunities for future growth and development. Ultimately, forming a committee to develop a program's vision and mission statements is an important investment in the program's success, and can help to ensure that the program is well-positioned to achieve its goals and objectives.

Here are some steps for forming a committee to define an effective vision and mission for a program:

1. **Identify stakeholders:** Start by identifying key stakeholders who should be involved in the process. This might include program leaders, faculty, staff, students, alumni, industry partners, and other relevant parties.

2. **Set clear objectives:** Establish clear objectives for the committee's work, such as defining the program's unique value proposition, setting strategic goals, or clarifying the program's mission and vision.

3. **Choose a facilitator:** Choose a facilitator who can guide the committee through the process of defining the program's vision and mission. This might be a member of the committee, an outside consultant, or someone else with relevant expertise.

4. **Establish meeting schedule:** Set a regular meeting schedule for the committee, ensuring that all members are able to attend and participate fully.

5. **Define roles and responsibilities:** Define the roles and responsibilities of each committee member, outlining their specific tasks and expectations.

6. **Develop a process for gathering feedback:** Develop a process for gathering feedback from stakeholders, such as surveys, focus groups, or individual interviews.

7. **Use data to inform decision-making:** Use data and feedback gathered from stakeholders to inform the committee's decision-making process. For example, you might analyse student retention rates, alumni employment data, or industry trends to help guide the committee's work.

8. **Draft and revise the vision and mission:** Work together to draft and revise the program's vision and mission statements, using the feedback and data gathered from stakeholders to guide the process.

9. **Finalize the statements:** Once the statements have been drafted and revised, finalize them and ensure that they are well-aligned with the institution's overall vision and mission, as well as the program's goals and objectives.

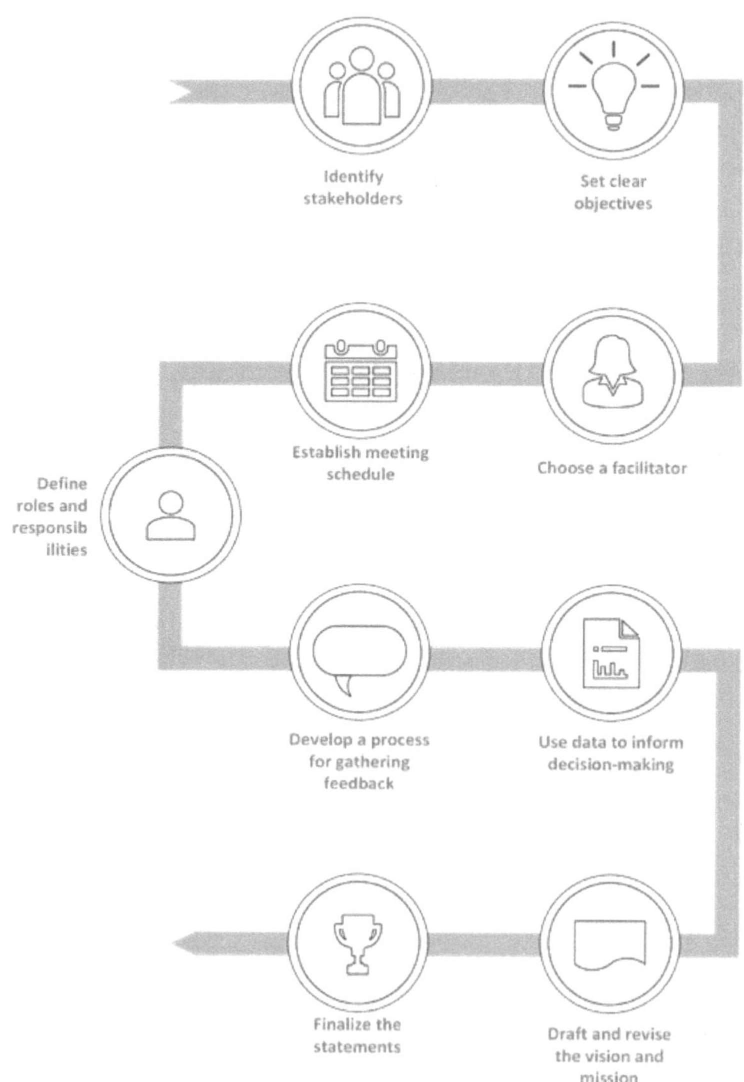

Figure 22: Steps for Forming a committee to Define Program Vision and Mission

Overall, forming a committee to define an effective vision and mission for a program is an important step in ensuring that the program is aligned with institutional goals and values, and that it is well-positioned to achieve its strategic objectives. By involving a diverse group of stakeholders in the process, and using data to guide decision-making, the committee can develop a vision and mission that reflects the unique values and priorities of the program.

5.4   Process of Defining the Vision and Mission with the Help of Committee

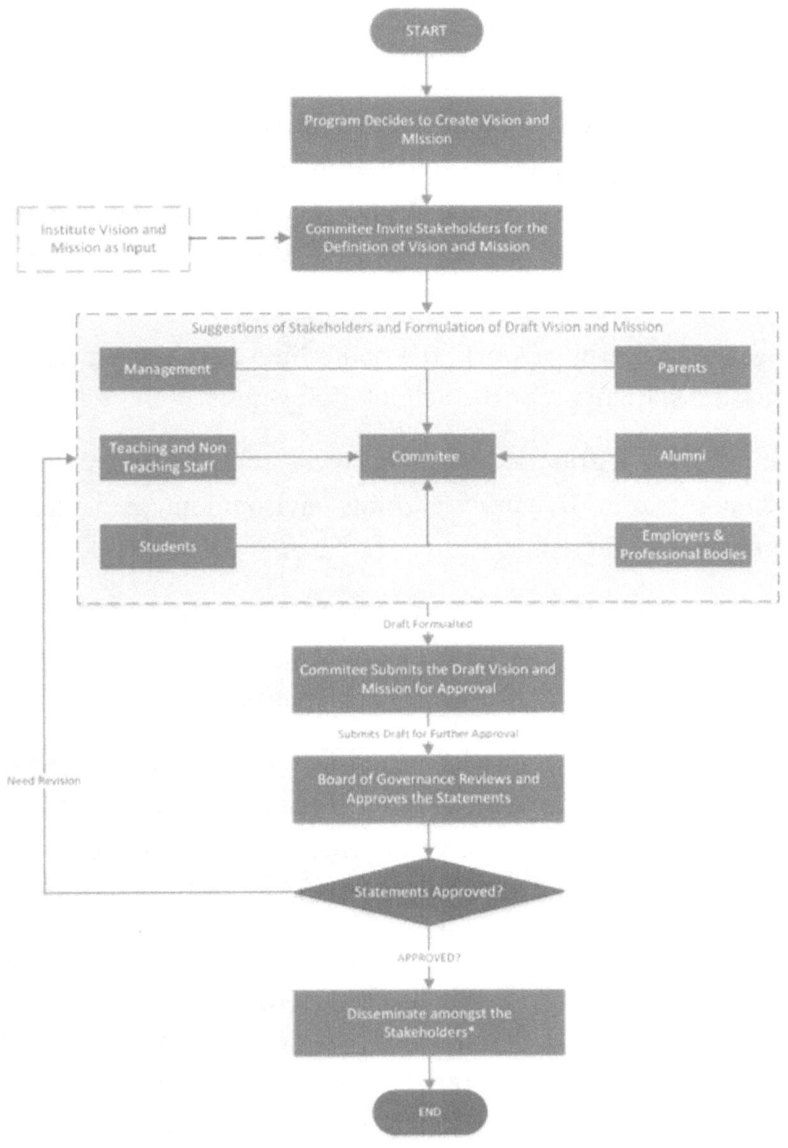

Figure 23: Process of Defining the Vision and Mission with the Help of Committee

Here is an example of a university that formed a committee to develop an effective vision and mission statement:

5.4.1 Case study: Virginia Commonwealth University (VCU)

VCU's School of Business formed a strategic planning committee to develop a new mission and vision statement for the school. The committee was made up of faculty members, staff, students, alumni, and industry partners.

The committee used a data-driven approach to guide their work, including analysing student and alumni surveys, conducting focus groups, and reviewing industry trends and best practices. They also engaged in extensive consultation with stakeholders across the university and the business community.

After several months of work, the committee developed a new vision and mission statement for the School of Business:

Vision: "To be a premier urban business school recognized for its impactful research, dynamic learning environment, and meaningful community engagement."

Mission: "To prepare students to become productive and responsible citizens who contribute to the betterment of society through successful business careers, relevant research, and engaged service."

The new vision and mission statements were well-received by stakeholders, and were seen as more focused, relevant, and aligned with the school's strategic goals and values. The committee's work also helped to clarify the school's priorities and identify opportunities for future growth and development.

Overall, VCU's School of Business is a great example of how a committee can work collaboratively to develop an effective vision and mission statement that reflects the unique values and priorities of a program.

5.5 How to Define Effective Vision and Mission when you are preparing for Accreditation

5.5.1 Define Balanced Statement Between Past, Current and Future State of the Program / Department

Ask your team to define the perfect state of being, and then write it down in the present tense. Why do you exist? What's your purpose?

Examples:

- Microsoft: "A computer on every desktop."
- Nike: "To bring inspiration and innovation to every athlete in the world."
- Apple: "A computer in the hands of everyday people."
- Charles Schwab: "Helping investors help themselves."
- Disney: "Make people happy."
- Google: "To provide access to the world's information in one click."

5.5.2 Make it Memorable

A team vision is written as a short sentence or statement. And it should inspire. It should be to the point and easy to remember.

A well-written vision can give you goose bumps.

It should be powerful and say, "We do this" – – not "We want to do this" or "We're going to do this."

5.5.3 Keep in Sync

Your vision statement should connect your department and institute vision.

It should sync well with your Institute Vision and Mission

5.5.4 Gain Consensus

One of the important things in this process is inclusion. Everybody needs to have a say and feel a sense of ownership.

Include:

- All Faculty Members
- Students
- Alumni Members
- Parents
- Employers
- Social Organizations
- Industries
- Management team

5.5.5   Make it Achievable

A great vision is achievable. But it should also cause the organization to stretch.

Avoid using 'Flowery' Words Like:

- Excellence
- Centre of Excellence
- World Class
- Global Excellence
- State of the Art

5.5.6   Make it Visible

It's your team's vision. Be proud! Make your tagline visible almost everywhere you go.

Put it Everywhere you can:

- Classroom
- Seminar Halls
- Departments
- Faculty Rooms
- Visiting Cards
- Collaterals
- Seminar Posters / Banners
- Power point presentations

- Website
- Mail Signatures
- Collage
- Etc.

5.5.7 Document the process

Document all the process for creation of Vision and Mission. Also, keep track every year through objectives and meetings.

Documents:

- Committee Appointment
- Minutes of Meetings
- Flow charts of Formation
- Annual Review Report

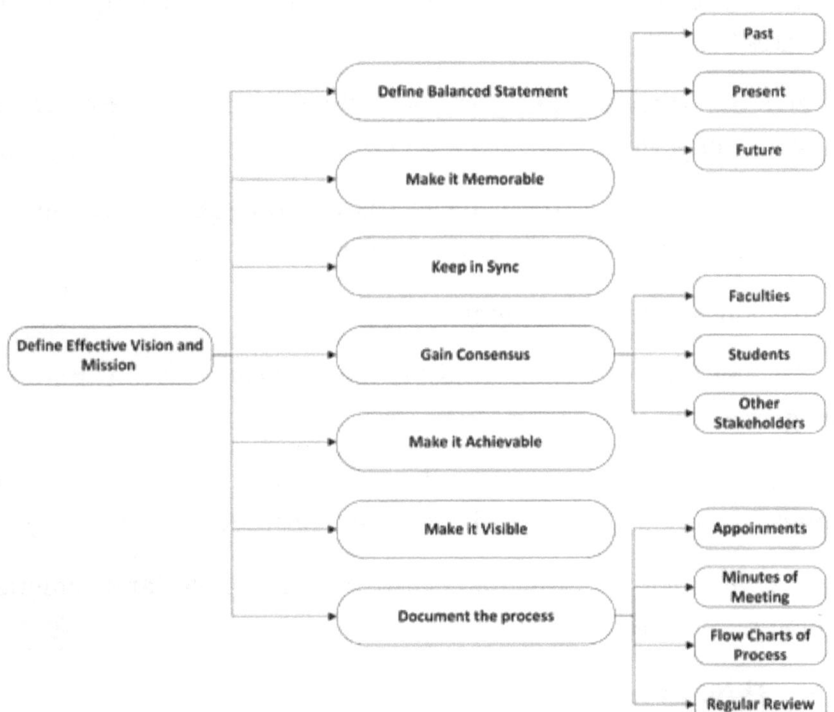

Figure 24: Steps for Defining Effective Vision and Mission for Effective Accreditation and Rankings

This diagram outlines the steps to follow when defining an effective vision and mission for a program in preparation for accreditation. It emphasizes the importance of creating a balanced statement that reflects the past, current, and future state of the program, making it memorable, ensuring alignment with the institute's vision and mission, gaining consensus among stakeholders, making it achievable yet challenging, ensuring visibility throughout the campus, and documenting the entire process. By following these steps, institutions can develop compelling and aligned vision and mission statements that support accreditation requirements and drive continuous improvement and success.

Examples of Program Vision (PGDM / MBA)

"We work hard every day to make our students the most respected business experts. "

"To create and promote employable, passionate and productive Business graduates."

"To give our students the most compelling Academic, Research, and Innovative experience. "

"To reinvent how our Graduates to share knowledge, tell stories, and inspire Industry and Society towards progress."

Example of Mission Statement

M1: To develop socially responsible and ethically driven innovative managers and future leaders.

M2: To evolve a system of quality education and research in management through sustained institutionalized efforts of students and faculty.

M3: To equip the students with contemporary and emerging developments in the field of management.

5.5.8   Flavour of Vision and Mission

Vision is Direction and Mission is Action toward that Direction. Keep only 3 Mission Statements and name them as M1, M2, M3.

Following Concepts can be used:

- Academic Process
- Research
- Innovation
- Social
- Intellectual Contributions
- Sustainability
- Career Oriented
- Specialized Skills
- Ethics

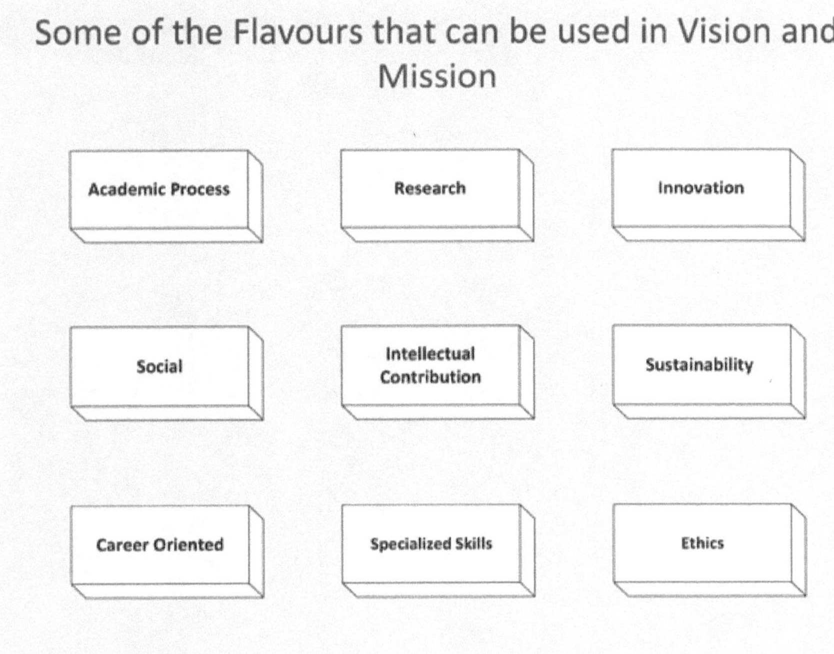

Figure 25: Flavour of Vision and Mission Statements

This above diagram highlights various concepts that can be incorporated into vision and mission statements. These concepts include academic processes, research, innovation, social impact, intellectual contributions, sustainability, career orientation, specialized skills, and ethics. By selecting and integrating these concepts into vision and mission statements, institutions can showcase their unique direction and actions toward achieving their goals and fulfilling their purpose.

Chapter 6

Data-Driven Approach to Creating Effective Program Educational Objectives (PEO)

Program Educational Objectives (PEOs) are broad statements that describe the expected accomplishments and professional achievements of graduates of a program within a few years after graduation. PEOs are typically developed through a collaborative process that involves faculty, industry representatives, alumni, and other stakeholders. They provide a clear vision of the intended outcomes of the program and help to ensure that the program is well-aligned with the needs of industry and society.

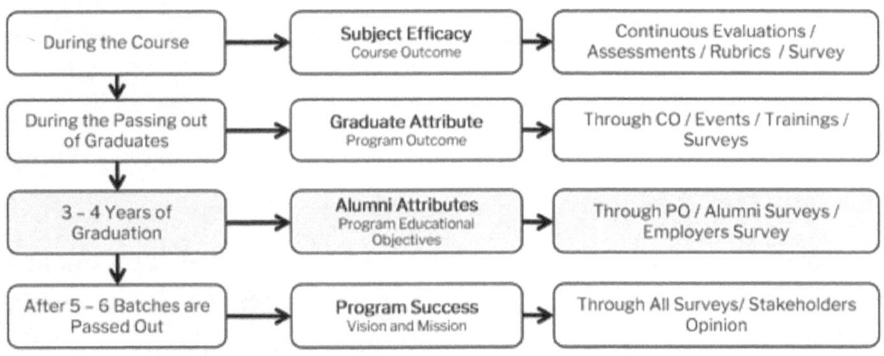

Figure 26: Program Educational Objectives (PEOs): Shaping Graduate Achievements

Program Educational Objectives (PEOs) are pivotal statements that define the expected accomplishments and professional achievements of graduates within a few years after completing a program. These objectives are collaboratively developed, involving faculty, industry representatives, alumni, and other stakeholders. PEOs provide a clear direction for the program, ensuring alignment with industry needs and societal demands. They guide curriculum design, learning experiences, and student development, shaping graduates' skills, knowledge, and competencies. By focusing on PEOs, educational institutions prepare graduates to excel in their chosen professions and contribute meaningfully to their fields of expertise.

PEOs can include a range of different outcomes, such as professional accomplishments, leadership roles, contributions to society, and lifelong learning. They are often specific to a particular program and are intended to be measurable, achievable, and relevant to the program's goals and objectives. PEOs may also be reviewed periodically to ensure that they remain relevant and aligned with the evolving needs of the program and its stakeholders.

Overall, PEOs are an important component of a program's overall assessment and evaluation process, as they provide a clear and measurable set of outcomes that the program is expected to achieve. By defining clear PEOs, programs can ensure that they are well-aligned with the needs of industry and society, and that they are well-positioned to achieve their strategic objectives.

6.5   Importance of Program Educational Objectives (PEOs)

Program Educational Objectives (PEOs) are an essential component of Outcome-Based Education (OBE) that help to define the overarching goals of a program. PEOs provide a clear and concise statement of what a graduate of the program should be able to do, know, and be, and they help to ensure that the program is aligned with the needs of industry, society, and other stakeholders.

Figure 27: The Significance of Program Educational Objectives (PEOs)

Effective PEOs should be specific, measurable, achievable, relevant, and time-bound (SMART). They should be based on input from a variety of stakeholders, including faculty, students, alumni, employers, and other members of the community. PEOs should also be reviewed and updated periodically to ensure that they remain relevant and aligned with the evolving needs of the program's stakeholders.

In practice, PEOs are often used to guide the development of program curriculum, assessments, and other educational activities. They help to ensure that graduates of the program have the knowledge, skills, and attributes that are necessary for success in their chosen careers. Effective PEOs are therefore critical for ensuring that graduates are well-prepared to make meaningful contributions to society and to the organizations that employ them.

6.2 Program Educational Objectives (PEOs) are important for several reasons

1. **Provide a clear direction for the program:** PEOs provide a clear statement of what a program aims to accomplish in terms of graduate outcomes. By defining PEOs, the program can set

clear goals and objectives that guide its curriculum, teaching methodologies, and other aspects of its educational offerings.

2. **Align the program with industry and societal needs:** PEOs are typically developed in consultation with industry representatives, alumni, and other stakeholders to ensure that the program is well-aligned with the needs of the industry and society. By focusing on PEOs, the program can ensure that it is preparing graduates who are well-equipped to meet the needs of their future employers and make positive contributions to society.

3. **Enable continuous improvement:** PEOs can serve as a basis for ongoing assessment and evaluation of the program. By regularly reviewing and measuring progress against the PEOs, the program can identify areas for improvement and make necessary changes to ensure that it is meeting its goals and objectives.

4. **Enhance program credibility:** Well-defined and measurable PEOs can enhance the credibility of a program among its stakeholders, including students, employers, and accrediting agencies. By clearly articulating the outcomes that the program aims to achieve, the program can demonstrate its commitment to excellence and accountability.

Overall, PEOs are important because they provide a clear and measurable set of outcomes that the program aims to achieve and help to ensure that the program is well-aligned with the needs of industry and society. By focusing on PEOs, programs can continuously improve and enhance their offerings, and ultimately prepare graduates who are well-equipped to make positive contributions to society.

6.3   Why we need PEO?

Whenever I talk about PEO, the common questions asked by faculty members are why we need PEO then NBA / NAAC is already providing us with PO. While this is a common question that arises when discussing Program Educational Objectives (PEOs) in relation to Program Outcomes (POs). While POs and PEOs may seem similar, they serve different purposes and are important for different reasons.

Program Outcomes (POs) (Specific Learning Outcomes)	Program Educational Objectives (PEOs) (Broad Professional Achievements)
Knowledge, skills, and attitudes students acquire by program completion	Broad accomplishments and professional achievements of graduates
Defined by faculty, industry, alumni, and stakeholders	Developed through collaboration among faculty, industry, alumni, and stakeholders
Clear and measurable set of learning outcomes for students when they graduate	Clear vision of intended outcomes of the program after 3 – 4 years of Graduation
Ensures program alignment with industry and societal needs	Ensures program alignment with industry and societal needs
Focuses on specific learning outcomes to be achieved by students	Focuses on broader professional accomplishments and achievements in graduates' careers
Assesses students' knowledge, skills, and attitudes	Assesses graduates' accomplishments and achievements in their careers
Ensures program effectiveness and student success	Ensures graduates are well-prepared, equipped, and capable of making positive contributions
Provides direction for program implementation and improvement	Provides a clear vision of expected outcomes and program goals
Measurable inside the Campus	Measurable outside the Campus

Table 1: The Difference between PO and PEO

Program Outcomes (POs) are specific statements that describe the knowledge, skills, and attitudes that students are expected to acquire by the time they complete a program. POs are typically defined by faculty in collaboration with industry representatives, alumni, and other stakeholders. They provide a clear and measurable set of learning outcomes that students are expected to achieve and help to ensure that the program is well-aligned with industry and societal needs.

Program Educational Objectives (PEOs), on the other hand, are broad statements that describe the expected accomplishments and professional achievements of graduates of a program within a few years after graduation. PEOs are typically developed through a collaborative process that involves faculty, industry representatives, alumni, and other stakeholders. They provide a clear vision of the intended outcomes of the program and help to ensure that the program is well-aligned with the needs of industry and society.

While POs focus on the specific learning outcomes that students are expected to achieve, PEOs focus on the broader professional accomplishments and achievements that graduates are expected to attain in their careers. PEOs are important because they provide a clear direction for the program and help to ensure that the program is well-aligned with the needs of industry and society. By focusing on PEOs, programs can ensure that they are preparing graduates who are well-equipped to meet the needs of their future employers and make positive contributions to society.

Overall, both POs and PEOs are important for defining the outcomes of a program and ensuring that it is well-aligned with industry and societal needs. While POs focus on the specific learning outcomes that students are expected to achieve, PEOs focus on the broader professional accomplishments and achievements that graduates are expected to attain in their careers. By defining both POs and PEOs, programs can ensure that they are well-positioned to achieve their strategic objectives and make positive contributions to society.

Effective Program Educational Objectives (PEOs) should be designed to meet the needs of all stakeholders, including students, employers, alumni, and faculty.

6.4   Broader Steps to Design an Effective PEO

Below are some key steps to defining effective PEOs:

1. **Involve stakeholders:** PEOs should be developed in consultation with key stakeholders, including industry representatives, alumni, and students. This ensures that the PEOs are well-aligned with the needs of the industry and society and that they reflect the expectations of current and future students.

2. **Be specific:** PEOs should be specific and measurable and should describe the expected accomplishments of graduates within a few years after graduation. They should clearly define what graduates are expected to know, be able to do, and understand in their professional careers.

3. **Be aligned:** PEOs should be well-aligned with the program's mission, vision, and goals, as well as with industry and societal needs. They should reflect the program's unique strengths and capabilities and should be designed to meet the changing needs of the industry and society.

4. **Be flexible:** PEOs should be flexible enough to accommodate changes in the industry and society, as well as changes in the program's offerings and curriculum. They should be regularly reviewed and updated to ensure that they remain relevant and aligned with the program's strategic objectives.

5. **Be realistic:** PEOs should be realistic and achievable, given the program's resources and capabilities. They should be designed to challenge students and prepare them for successful careers but should also be attainable for most graduates.

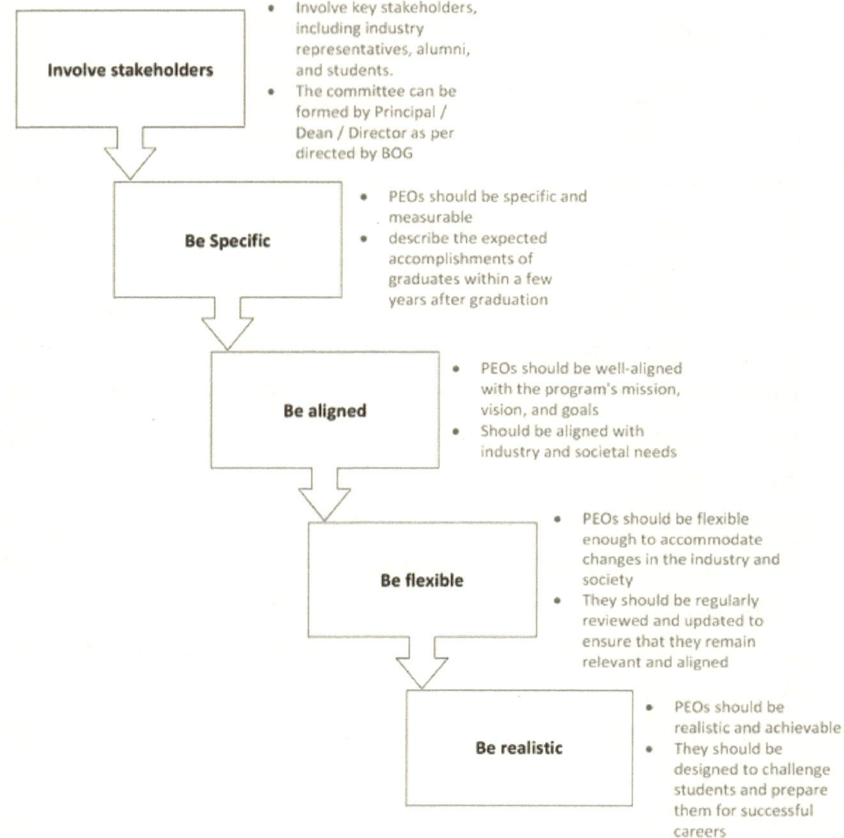

Figure 28: Key Steps to Designing Effective Program Educational Objectives (PEOs)

The above diagram illustrates, defining effective Program Educational Objectives (PEOs) involves several important steps. First, it is essential to involve stakeholders such as industry representatives, alumni, and students in the development process to ensure alignment with industry and societal needs. Second, the PEOs should be specific, measurable, and describe the expected accomplishments of graduates within a few years after graduation. Third, the PEOs should be well-aligned with the program's mission, vision, and goals, as well as flexible enough to accommodate changes in the industry and society. Lastly, the PEOs should be realistic and achievable, challenging students while remaining attainable for most graduates. By following these steps, educational institutions can design

PEOs that effectively prepare graduates for successful careers and meet the evolving demands of the professional world.

Overall, effective PEOs should be specific, measurable, and aligned with the program's mission, vision, and goals, as well as with industry and societal needs. They should be developed in consultation with key stakeholders and should be regularly reviewed and updated to ensure that they remain relevant and effective.

6.5   Process of Formation of PEO

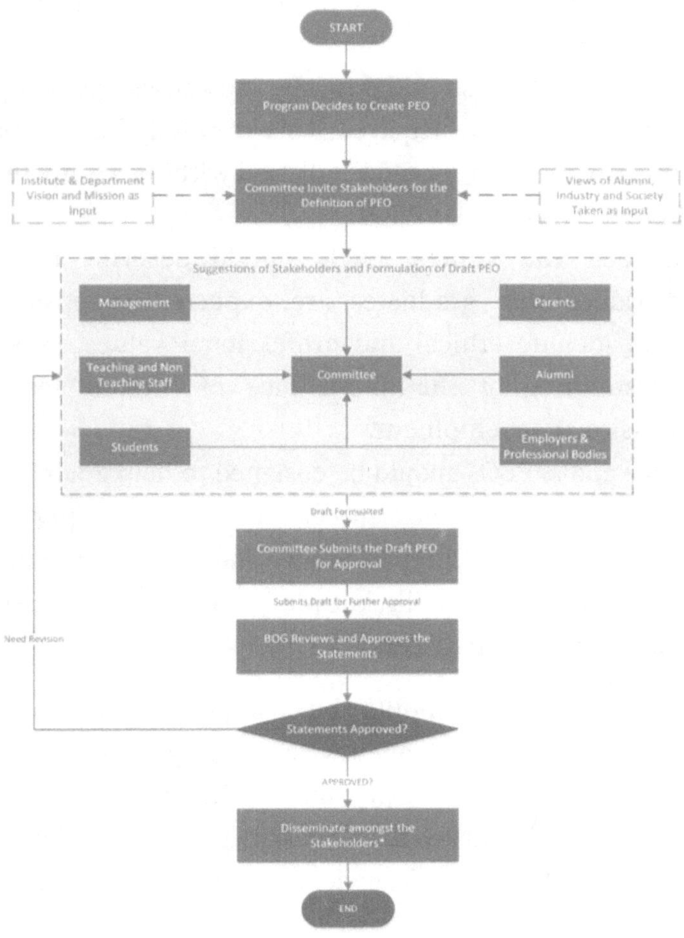

Figure 29: Process of Formation of PEO practically in the Campus

6.5.1 Key Components to be Considered in Designing PEO

Effective Program Educational Objectives (PEOs) should include the following components:

1. **Competencies:** PEOs should describe the competencies that graduates are expected to possess. These competencies should be aligned with the program's mission, vision, and goals, and should reflect the needs of the industry and society.

2. **Skills:** PEOs should describe the skills that graduates are expected to have developed. These skills should be specific and measurable and should be aligned with the competencies described in the PEOs.

3. **Knowledge:** PEOs should describe the knowledge that graduates are expected to have acquired. This knowledge should be specific to the program and should be aligned with the competencies and skills described in the PEOs.

4. **Attitudes and values:** PEOs should describe the attitudes and values that graduates are expected to possess. These should include ethical and professional values, as well as an understanding of the importance of lifelong learning and professional development.

5. **Career goals:** PEOs should be designed to help graduates achieve their career goals. They should describe the types of careers that graduates are prepared for, and should provide a clear understanding of the skills, knowledge, and competencies required for success in those careers.

Overall, effective PEOs should be comprehensive, specific, and measurable, and should be aligned with the program's mission, vision, and goals, as well as with industry and societal needs. They should be designed to prepare graduates for successful careers and should provide a clear understanding of the knowledge, skills, and attitudes required for success in those careers.

6.5.2   Case Study: Of Implementation of Effective PEO

6.5.2.1 Georgia Institute of Technology (Georgia Tech)

Georgia Tech's School of Electrical and Computer Engineering developed PEOs that focused on preparing graduates for leadership roles in industry, academia, and government. The PEOs emphasized the development of technical and professional skills, as well as a commitment to lifelong learning and professional development. As a result, Georgia Tech's graduates have been highly sought-after by employers and have gone on to successful careers in a variety of industries.

The Georgia Institute of Technology (Georgia Tech) has developed PEOs for each of its engineering programs. Here are some examples of PEOs from the School of Electrical and Computer Engineering:

1.   Graduates will be successful in professional careers in industry, government, or academia, and will demonstrate leadership, ethical behaviours, and a commitment to lifelong learning.
2.   Graduates will be able to design, analyse, and implement complex electrical and computer systems, and will have the technical and analytical skills necessary to address emerging challenges in the field.
3.   Graduates will be able to work effectively in interdisciplinary teams, communicate effectively with a variety of stakeholders, and demonstrate a commitment to diversity, equity, and inclusion.

Overall, these PEOs emphasize the development of technical and professional skills, as well as a commitment to lifelong learning and professional development. By focusing on these core competencies, Georgia Tech's graduates are well-prepared to become leaders in a variety of industries and to make meaningful contributions to society.

Please note: The information provided here is for general informational purposes only. We make no representations or warranties of any kind, express or implied, about the completeness, accuracy, reliability, suitability, or availability of the information. Any reliance you place on such information is strictly at your own risk.

6.5.2.2 **Purdue University**

Purdue University's School of Mechanical Engineering developed PEOs that focused on preparing graduates to become innovative leaders in industry, government, and academia. The PEOs emphasized the development of technical skills, as well as the ability to work effectively in teams and to communicate effectively with a variety of stakeholders. As a result, Purdue's graduates have been highly successful in a variety of industries, including aerospace, automotive, and energy.

The School of Mechanical Engineering at Purdue University has developed PEOs that emphasize the development of technical and professional skills, as well as the ability to work effectively in teams and to communicate effectively with a variety of stakeholders. Here are some examples of PEOs from the School of Mechanical Engineering:

1. Graduates will be able to apply the principles of mechanical engineering to solve complex problems in a variety of industries and will have the technical and analytical skills necessary to address emerging challenges in the field.
2. Graduates will be able to work effectively in interdisciplinary teams, communicate effectively with a variety of stakeholders, and demonstrate a commitment to diversity, equity, and inclusion.
3. Graduates will be able to apply ethical principles to their work and demonstrate a commitment to lifelong learning and professional development.

Overall, these PEOs emphasize the development of technical and professional skills, as well as the ability to work effectively in teams and to communicate effectively with a variety of stakeholders. By focusing on these core competencies, Purdue's graduates are well-prepared to become leaders in a variety of industries and to make meaningful contributions to society.

Please note: The information provided here is for general informational purposes only. We make no representations or warranties of any kind, express or implied, about the completeness, accuracy, reliability, suitability, or availability of the information. Any reliance you place on such information is strictly at your own risk.

6.5.2.3 University of California, Berkeley

The University of California, Berkeley's Department of Mechanical Engineering developed PEOs that focused on preparing graduates to become leaders in research, innovation, and entrepreneurship. The PEOs emphasized the development of technical and analytical skills, as well as the ability to work effectively in interdisciplinary teams and to communicate effectively with a variety of stakeholders. As a result, UC Berkeley's graduates have been highly successful in a variety of industries, including biotechnology, robotics, and energy.

Overall, effective PEOs can help universities to transform themselves by providing a clear understanding of the skills, knowledge, and competencies required for success in today's rapidly changing job market. By focusing on the development of technical, professional, and interpersonal skills, universities can prepare graduates to become leaders in a variety of industries and to make meaningful contributions to society.

The Department of Mechanical Engineering at the University of California, Berkeley has developed Program Educational Objectives (PEOs) that emphasize the development of technical, professional, and leadership skills. Here are some examples of PEOs from the Department of Mechanical Engineering:

1. Graduates will be able to apply the principles of mechanical engineering to solve complex problems in a variety of industries

and will have the technical and analytical skills necessary to address emerging challenges in the field.

2. Graduates will be able to communicate effectively with a variety of stakeholders, work effectively in interdisciplinary teams, and demonstrate a commitment to diversity, equity, and inclusion.

3. Graduates will have the leadership skills necessary to be effective managers and entrepreneurs and will demonstrate a commitment to ethical behaviour and lifelong learning.

Overall, these PEOs emphasize the development of technical, professional, and leadership skills, as well as a commitment to ethical behaviour and lifelong learning. By focusing on these core competencies, UC Berkeley's graduates are well-prepared to become leaders in a variety of industries and to make meaningful contributions to society.

Please note: The information provided here is for general informational purposes only. We make no representations or warranties of any kind, express or implied, about the completeness, accuracy, reliability, suitability, or availability of the information. Any reliance you place on such information is strictly at your own risk.

6.6 Effective Program Educational Objectives

In this section, we are exploring practical strategies for designing Program Educational Objectives (PEOs) that are effective, aligned with the program and scientifically sound. By taking a data-driven approach to PEO development, institutions can ensure that their objectives are both relevant and achievable. This involves establishing a diverse and inclusive committee that includes faculty members, industry experts, alumni, current students, and institutional leadership. The committee should work collaboratively to identify the skills and attributes that are most important for graduates of the program to possess, considering the needs of industry and the expectations of stakeholders. By prioritizing the development of effective PEOs, institutions can better prepare students for success in their chosen careers, while also meeting the demands of a rapidly changing job market.

6.6.1 Committee Formation for the PEO Creation

The committee responsible for defining Program Educational Objectives (PEOs) should be diverse and inclusive, with representation from all stakeholders including faculty members, industry experts, alumni, current students, and institutional leadership. Each member of the committee should bring a unique perspective and skill set that contributes to the development of effective PEOs.

The ideal number of committee members can vary based on the size and complexity of the program, but typically a committee of 8-12 members is appropriate. This allows for a diversity of viewpoints while still ensuring that the committee is manageable and able to make timely decisions.

Faculty members should be included on the committee because they have a deep understanding of the program curriculum and course outcomes and can provide insight into the skills and knowledge that graduates need to possess. Industry experts can offer a perspective on the skills and attributes that are in high demand in the job market and can provide guidance on how the program can better prepare students for careers in the field. Current students and alumni can provide feedback on the program's strengths and weaknesses and offer suggestions for improvement.

Overall, the committee should be focused on creating PEOs that are aligned with the institution's mission and goals, and that reflect the needs and expectations of the program's stakeholders. By taking a collaborative and inclusive approach to defining PEOs, the committee can ensure that the resulting objectives are relevant, effective, and achievable.

6.6.2 Creating Effective PEO

Creating effective Program Educational Objectives (PEOs) is a crucial part of implementing Outcome-Based Education (OBE) in higher education. PEOs provide a framework for aligning curriculum and learning outcomes with the needs of industry, society, and other stakeholders. To create effective PEOs, it is important to involve alumni in the process, as they can provide valuable insights into the knowledge, skills, and attributes that are necessary for success in their careers.

The first step in creating effective PEOs is to gather information from alumni about their current job roles. This can be done through surveys or other data-gathering methods. The goal is to understand the specific job roles that graduates are working in and the knowledge, skills, and attributes that are required for success in those roles.

Once the data has been gathered, the next step is to rank the most important knowledge, skills, and attributes based on the percentage of graduates who are working in each job role. This will help the committee to identify the most important traits that graduates need to be successful in their careers.

The committee can then use this information to develop a set of PEOs that are aligned with the needs of industry and society. The PEOs should be practical, measurable, and aligned with the overall mission and vision of the program.

For example, let us consider a program in Computer Science. The alumni survey reveals that most graduates are working in software development roles. Based on this information, the committee identifies the most important knowledge, skills, and attributes required for success in software development, such as programming skills, problem-solving abilities, communication skills, teamwork, and adaptability.

The committee then develops a set of PEOs that are aligned with these needs. For example, the PEOs might include:

1. Graduates will have a strong foundation in programming skills and problem-solving abilities.
2. Graduates will be able to work effectively in teams and communicate technical information to non-technical stakeholders.
3. Graduates will be able to adapt to changing technologies and environments.

By using alumni feedback to create PEOs, the program can ensure that its graduates are well-prepared for success in their chosen careers. This approach can also help to ensure that the program remains relevant and responsive to the needs of industry and society.

In Summary here is the process:

1. Conduct a job role survey of alumni to understand their current roles.
2. From the survey, identify the skills, traits, and attributes required for success in the alumni's job roles.
3. Rank the identified skills, traits, and attributes based on the percentage of alumni working in those job roles who possess them.
4. Select the top 5 skills, traits, and attributes to be included in the PEOs.
5. Work collaboratively with the committee, which includes faculty members, industry experts, alumni, current students, and institutional leadership, to refine and finalize the PEOs.
6. Communicate the PEOs to all stakeholders, including faculty members, students, industry partners, and accrediting bodies.
7. Continuously evaluate and improve the PEOs based on feedback and outcomes data.

6.6.2.1   Rank the Job profile and Attributes. Rank the top Five as per Highest Number of Alumni in the Attribute

JOB PROFILES OF ALUMNI	ATTRIBUTES OF JOB PROFILE	% OF ALUMNI	RANKING
JOB PROFILE 1	ATTRIBUTE 1	35%	1
JOB PROFLE 2	ATTRIBUTE 2	28%	2
JOB PROFLE 3	ATTRIBUTE 3	26%	3
JOB PROFLE 4	ATTRIBUTE 4	20%	4
JOB PROFLE 5	ATTRIBUTE 5	18%	5

Figure 30: Rank the Job profile and Attributes.

6.6.2.2   Attributes listed in top 5 are origins of PEO.

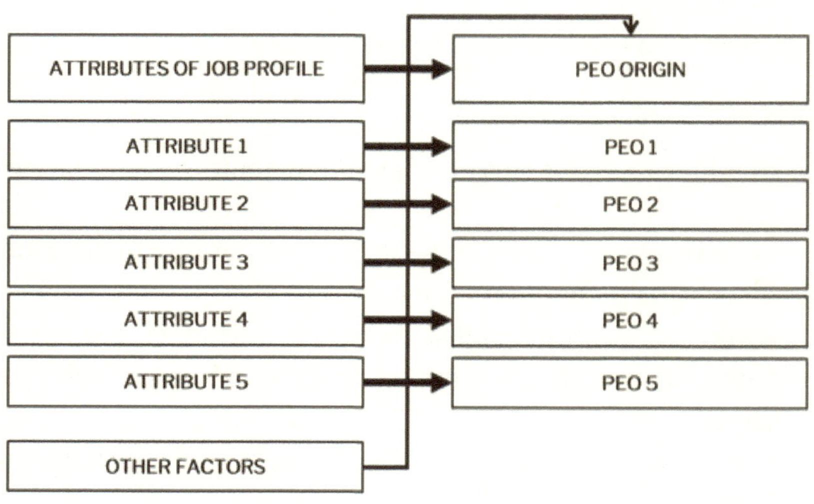

Figure 31: Attributes listed in top 5 are origins of PEO.

6.6.2.3   Example of Attributes ➔ PEO

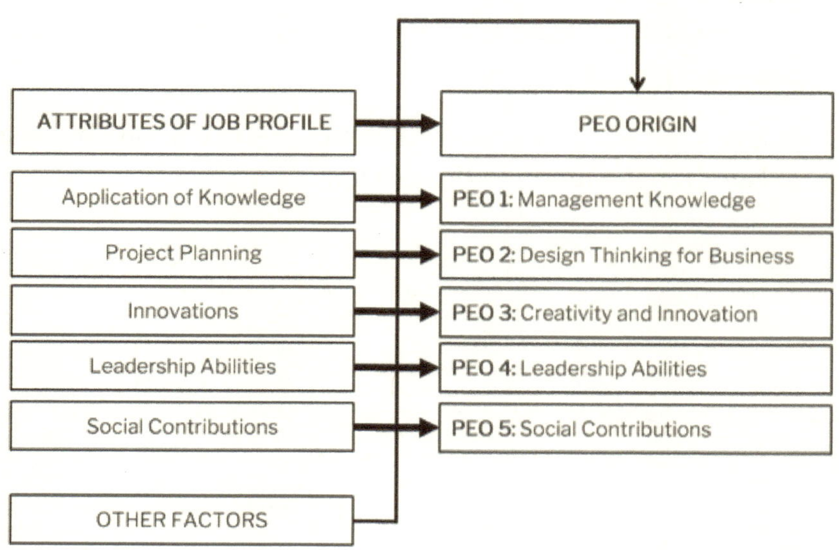

Figure 32: Example of Attributes to PEO

6.6.2.4 Example of Drafting the PEO as per above activity

The Graduate will be Able to:

PEO 1: Management Knowledge

Exhibit subject knowledge and expertise of managerial functions.

PEO 2: Design Thinking of Business

Develop critical and a holistic approach for designing and implementing solutions to problems of business, government, and society.

PEO 3: Creativity and Innovation

Nurture the spirit of innovation, creativity, and entrepreneurship in the projects they work in.

PEO 4: Leadership Abilities

Develop effective communication, interpersonal, motivational, decision making and leadership skills.

PEO 5: Social Contributions

Inculcate value-based leadership, ethical qualities, and a sense of social purpose.

Chapter 7

How to Define Effective Program Outcomes or Graduate Attributes

Program Outcomes (POs) are specific statements that describe what students should be able to do upon completing a degree program. They outline the knowledge, skills, and attitudes that students are expected to have attained by the end of the program.

POs are used to guide the curriculum development process, as well as to measure student learning and program effectiveness. They provide a framework for designing courses, assessments, and other educational experiences that are aligned with the overall goals of the program. Additionally, POs serve as a means of communication between the program and its stakeholders, including students, faculty, employers, and accrediting bodies.

POs can be developed through a collaborative process involving faculty, students, and other stakeholders. The process typically involves identifying the program's mission and goals, reviewing industry standards and best practices, and defining the knowledge, skills, and attitudes that students should acquire.

Once POs have been established, they can be used to inform the development of learning outcomes, assessments, and other program components. For example, courses can be designed to align with specific POs, and assessments can be developed to measure student mastery of POs.

Overall, POs are an essential component of program design and evaluation, providing a clear framework for ensuring that students are prepared to succeed in their chosen field upon graduation.

7.1 Origins of Program Outcomes (PO) in Higher Education

The origins of Program Outcomes (PO) can be traced back to the early 20th century when industrialization and technological advancements led to an increased demand for skilled workers. This led to the development of vocational and technical education programs that were designed to train individuals with the necessary skills to meet the demands of the workforce.

In the 1960s, the concept of PO began to gain popularity in higher education as a means of measuring the effectiveness of educational programs. The development of the Outcomes-Based Education (OBE) movement in the 1980s further emphasized the importance of PO in education.

Since then, PO has become an integral part of higher education and is widely used in the accreditation and evaluation of educational programs. In the United States, the Accreditation Board for Engineering and Technology (ABET) began requiring PO in the accreditation of engineering programs in 1997. Other accrediting bodies, such as the Accreditation Council for Business Schools and Programs (ACBSP) and the Accreditation Commission for Education in Nursing (ACEN), also require the use of PO in the accreditation process.

Overall, the use of PO has become an established practice in higher education and is seen as a valuable tool for measuring the effectiveness of educational programs in achieving their intended outcomes.

7.1.1 Here's a timeline of the application of Program Outcomes from their origin:

1980s: The concept of Program Outcomes (PO) is introduced in response to the need for quality assurance in higher education.

1990s: The Accreditation Board for Engineering and Technology (ABET) starts requiring engineering programs to develop and assess program outcomes.

2000s: Other accrediting bodies such as the Accreditation Council for Business Schools and Programs (ACBSP) and the National Association of Schools of Art and Design (NASAD) begin to require program outcomes.

2010s: The use of program outcomes becomes more widespread in higher education, with many institutions adopting them as part of their accreditation and assessment processes.

2020s: Program outcomes continue to be an important aspect of quality assurance in higher education, with an increasing focus on aligning them with workforce needs and incorporating technology and data analytics in their development and assessment.

It's worth noting that the timeline above reflects the general trends and milestones in the application of PO and may vary depending on the specific field or region.

The use of Program Outcomes is not limited to any specific country and has been implemented worldwide. Many countries and institutions have adopted POs to ensure that their educational programs are meeting specific goals and objectives. In fact, the use of learning outcomes and competency-based education has been promoted by international organizations such as the United Nations Educational, Scientific and Cultural Organization (UNESCO) and the Organisation for Economic Co-operation and Development (OECD). Countries such as Australia, Canada, the United Kingdom, and the United States have been at the forefront of implementing POs in higher education, and other countries around the world have followed suit.

7.1.2 The International Engineering Alliance (IEA)

The International Engineering Alliance (IEA) is a global network of engineering organizations that work together to promote professional engineering standards and facilitate the mobility and recognition of engineering qualifications around the world. The IEA was formed in 1993 and has since grown to include members from more than 30 countries, including the United States, Canada, Australia, Japan, and many European and Asian countries.

One of the primary objectives of the IEA is to promote the highest standards of engineering education and training. To this end, the IEA has developed a set of Graduate Attributes that define the essential knowledge, skills, and competencies that engineering graduates should possess. These Graduate Attributes are designed to ensure that engineering graduates are well-prepared to meet the challenges of the modern engineering profession and to promote the mobility and recognition of engineering qualifications across national boundaries.

The Graduate Attributes defined by the IEA are based on a set of core competencies that include the ability to apply mathematical, scientific, and engineering principles to solve complex engineering problems; the ability to communicate effectively in a variety of contexts; the ability to work effectively in teams and to manage complex projects; and the ability to adapt to new technologies and to continue learning throughout their careers.

In addition to promoting high standards of engineering education and training, the IEA also works to facilitate the mobility and recognition of engineering qualifications around the world. This is accomplished through a series of international agreements, including the Washington Accord, which provides a framework for the mutual recognition of engineering qualifications among the signatory countries.

Overall, the IEA plays a critical role in promoting the highest standards of engineering education and training and in facilitating the mobility and recognition of engineering qualifications across national boundaries.

7.1.3 The International Engineering Alliance (IEA) has signed three main accords:

- **Washington Accord:** The Washington Accord was signed in 1989 and is an international agreement among bodies responsible for accrediting engineering degree programs. The accord recognizes the substantial equivalency of accredited engineering programs in satisfying the academic requirements for the practice of engineering at the professional level. It currently has 20 signatory countries, including the United States, Australia, Canada, China, India, Japan, and the United Kingdom.

- **Sydney Accord:** The Sydney Accord was signed in 2001 and recognizes the substantial equivalency of accredited engineering technician programs in satisfying the academic requirements for the practice of engineering at the para-professional level. It currently has 13 signatory countries, including Australia, Canada, Japan, Korea, Malaysia, and the United Kingdom.

- **Dublin Accord:** The Dublin Accord was signed in 2002 and recognizes the substantial equivalency of accredited engineering technician programs in satisfying the academic requirements for the practice of engineering at the para-professional level. It currently has 17 signatory countries, including Australia, Canada, Ireland, Korea, New Zealand, and the United Kingdom.

7.1.4 The Washington Accord

The Washington Accord is an international accreditation agreement for engineering education. It was signed in 1989 by the engineering organizations of several countries, including the United States, the United Kingdom, Canada, Australia, and Japan. The Washington Accord establishes the criteria that must be met by engineering programs for them to be accredited by the signatory countries.

One of the criteria established by the Washington Accord is the requirement for engineering programs to have clearly defined program outcomes. The use of program outcomes ensures that engineering graduates are prepared to meet the needs of the profession and the expectations of the public. The Washington Accord has played a significant role in promoting the use of program outcomes in engineering education around the world.

The following are the signatory countries and territories of the Washington Accord, their respective accreditation bodies, and years of admission:

Country	Member Institution	Year of admission
Australia	Engineers Australia	1989
Canada	Engineers Canada	1989
Costa Rica	Association of Engineers and Architects of Costa Rica	2020
China	China Association for Science and Technology	2016
Hong Kong	The Hong Kong Institution of Engineers	1995
India	National Board of Accreditation	2014
Indonesia	Persatuan Insinyur Indonesia (PII)	2022
Republic of Ireland	Engineers Ireland	1989
Japan	Japan Accreditation Board for Engineering Education	2005
Malaysia	Board of Engineers Malaysia (BEM)	2009
Mexico	Consejo de Acreditación de la Enseñanza de la Ingeniería (CACEI)	2022
New Zealand	Engineering New Zealand	1989
Pakistan	Pakistan Engineering Council	2017
Peru	ICACIT	2018
Russia	Association for Engineering Education of Russia	2012
Singapore	Institution of Engineers Singapore	2006

South Africa	Engineering Council of South Africa	1999
South Korea	Accreditation Board for Engineering Education of Korea	2007
Sri Lanka	Institution of Engineers, Sri Lanka	2014
Taiwan	Institute of Engineering Education Taiwan	2007
Turkey	MÜDEK	2011
United Kingdom	Engineering Council	1989
United States	ABET	1989

Table 2: Signatory countries and territories of the Washington Accord

The following countries have provisional signatory status and may become member signatories in the future:

State	Institution
Bangladesh	Institution of Engineers, Bangladesh
Chile	Acredita.CI
Philippines	Philippine Technological Council
Myanmar	Myanmar Engineering Council
Thailand	Thailand Accreditation Board of Engineering Education
Saudi Arabia	Education and Training Evaluation Commission (ETEC)

Table 3: Countries having provisional signatory status.
Source: Wikipedia

7.2   Why we need PO?

Program outcomes (PO) are an essential part of higher education, as they help to ensure that students are well-prepared for their future careers. PO define what students are expected to know and be able to do by the end of their program of study. They provide a clear and specific set of skills, knowledge, and competencies that graduates are expected to possess, and are used as a basis for evaluating the effectiveness of a program in meeting its educational objectives.

PO help to ensure that students are prepared for the workforce by providing a clear set of expectations for their learning outcomes. This ensures that students acquire the necessary skills and knowledge needed to be successful in their chosen field and helps to bridge the gap between higher education and the workforce. PO also provide a framework for assessing program effectiveness and for making improvements to the curriculum as needed.

In addition, PO provide a basis for accreditation and quality assurance, as they are used to evaluate the effectiveness of a program in meeting its educational objectives. By defining clear PO, higher education institutions can ensure that they are meeting the needs of their students and providing them with a high-quality education that will prepare them for success in their chosen careers.

Overall, the use of PO is crucial to ensuring that higher education institutions are meeting the needs of their students and preparing them for the workforce. By defining clear PO, institutions can ensure that they are providing a high-quality education that will help students to achieve their career goals and make meaningful contributions to society.

Program Outcomes (PO) are the specific knowledge, skills, and abilities that a student is expected to demonstrate by the end of a program. POs are important in higher education because they serve as a tool to measure and communicate student learning and achievement. POs define the expected learning outcomes of a program, and they help to ensure that students are achieving the necessary competencies to succeed in their chosen career.

The components of PO may vary depending on the nature of the program. For example, the POs for an engineering program may include technical skills such as design and analysis, but also softer skills such as communication and teamwork. On the other hand, the POs for a humanities program may include critical thinking and analysis, cultural literacy, and effective written communication.

The components of PO can be broadly categorized into knowledge, skills, and attitudes. Knowledge refers to the theoretical and conceptual understanding that students should acquire in the program. Skills refer to the practical abilities that students should be able to demonstrate. Attitudes refer to the values, beliefs, and ethical principles that students should develop during the program.

The specific components of PO will depend on the goals of the program, the needs of the industry or field, and the expectations of the stakeholders. It is important to regularly review and update POs to ensure that they remain relevant and up to date with the changing needs of the industry and society.

Program Outcomes (PO)	
	Define expected learning outcomes
	Specific knowledge, skills, and abilities
	Measure and communicate student achievement
	Bridge the gap between education and the workforce
	Basis for evaluating program effectiveness
	Improve curriculum and program quality
	Basis for accreditation and quality assurance
	Ensure students are well-prepared for careers
	Varied components: knowledge, skills, attitudes
	Vary by program and stakeholder expectations
	Regular review and update for relevance

Figure 33: Diagram illustrating the importance and components of Program Outcomes (PO) in higher education.

Chapter 8

Data-Driven Approach to Defining Effective Program Outcomes (PO)

Following steps can be used to define the Program outcome:

- **Identify the program's mission statement:** The mission statement should provide a clear understanding of the program's purpose, target audience, and the intended outcomes.
- **Review program requirements and curriculum:** Program requirements and curriculum will give you an understanding of what the program is designed to teach and how it is organized.
- **Identify the intended audience:** Identify the students who are expected to complete the program and determine the knowledge, skills, and attitudes they should possess upon graduation.
- **Identify the program's goals:** Program goals represent the broad aspirations that the program aims to achieve. Goals should be aligned with the program's mission and should be stated in a way that is specific, measurable, achievable, relevant, and time bound.
- **Identify the key knowledge, skills, and attitudes (KSAs):** Identify the knowledge, skills, and attitudes that students should possess upon graduation to be successful in their careers.
- **Draft the POs:** Draft POs that clearly state the intended outcomes and are aligned with the program's mission, goals, and KSAs.
- **Revise and refine the POs:** Revise and refine the POs based on feedback from stakeholders and experts.
- **Validate the POs:** Validate the POs by ensuring that they are realistic, measurable, and achievable.

- **Implement and monitor the POs:** Implement the POs and monitor progress towards achieving them. Use the data collected to adjust and improvements as necessary.
- **Continuously improve the POs:** Continuously improve the POs by updating them as needed based on changes in the program, industry trends, and stakeholder feedback.

These steps should help you define effective POs that are aligned with your program's mission and goals, and that reflect the knowledge, skills, and attitudes that students need to succeed in their careers.

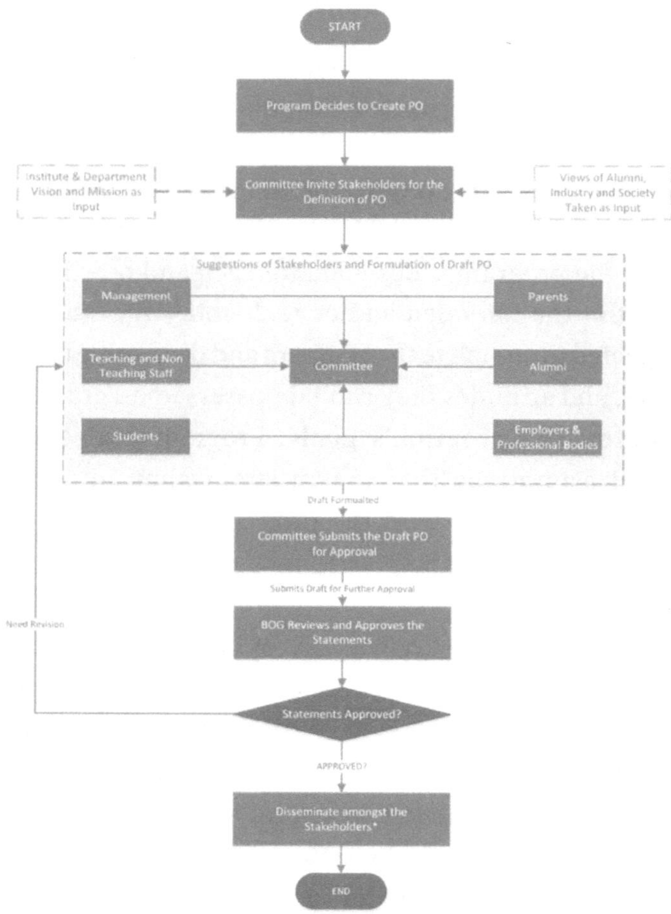

Figure 34: Data-driven and practical approach to defining effective Program Outcomes (PO) for higher education programs.

8.1 Committee to identify the Program Outcome (PO)

To form a committee to define Program Outcomes (PO), the following steps can be taken:

- **Identify stakeholders:** Identify the key stakeholders who will be involved in the process. This can include Management Representative, Regulatory body Members, faculty members, students, industry representatives, alumni, and Social Contributors.

- **Define the committee's roles and responsibilities:** Define the roles and responsibilities of each committee member. This can include setting expectations for attendance, participation, and contributions to the process.

- **Develop a timeline:** Develop a timeline for the PO definition process. This should include milestones, deadlines, and checkpoints to ensure the process stays on track.

- **Determine the scope of the PO:** Determine the scope of the PO based on the program's objectives and mission. This will help the committee define the POs that are most relevant to the program.

- **Identify the PO components:** Identify the components that should be included in the PO. This can include knowledge, skills, and abilities that graduates should possess upon completion of the program.

- **Define the PO:** Define the PO based on the components identified in step 5. This should be done in consultation with the stakeholders to ensure the PO are aligned with the program's objectives and mission.

- **Evaluate and revise:** Evaluate the PO periodically to ensure they remain relevant and effective. Revise the PO as necessary based on changes in the program's objectives and mission, industry trends, or feedback from stakeholders.

Overall, forming a committee to define PO is a collaborative effort that involves input from various stakeholders to ensure that the PO are aligned with the program's objectives and mission.

8.2 Identifying the key knowledge, skills, and attitudes (KSAs)

Identifying the key knowledge, skills, and attitudes (KSAs) required for a program's graduates is an important step in defining Program Outcomes (POs). Here are some steps to help identify these KSAs:

- **Conduct a needs assessment:** Conduct a needs assessment to identify the knowledge, skills, and attitudes that are required in the field. This can be done by reviewing job descriptions, talking to professionals in the field, and analysing industry trends.
- **Identify the program's goals:** Identify the program's goals and objectives. These should align with the needs of the field, and the KSAs required for the program's graduates should be directly related to these goals.
- **Conduct a gap analysis:** Conduct a gap analysis to determine the gap between the current state of the program and the desired state. This will help to identify the specific KSAs that need to be developed or enhanced.
- **Define the KSAs:** Define the KSAs that are required for the program's graduates. These should be specific, measurable, and achievable.
- **Engage stakeholders:** Engage stakeholders, including faculty, students, alumni, and employers, in the process of defining the KSAs. This will help to ensure that the KSAs are relevant and appropriate for the field.
- **Finalize the POs:** Finalize the POs based on the identified KSAs. The POs should be aligned with the program's goals, and should be specific, measurable, achievable, relevant, and time bound.

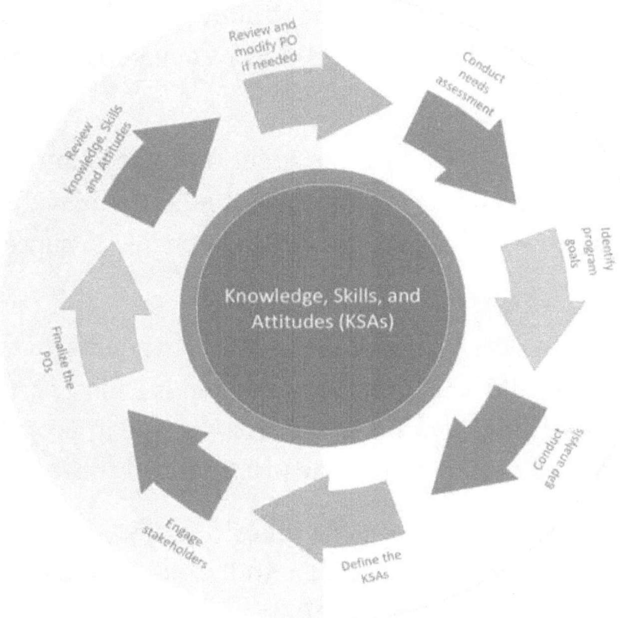

Figure 35: Continuous Improvement Process to identify key knowledge, skills, and attitudes (KSAs) for defining Program Outcomes (POs)

This diagram illustrates the steps involved in identifying the key knowledge, skills, and attitudes (KSAs) required for a program's graduates to define effective Program Outcomes (POs).

The process begins with conducting a needs assessment, which involves reviewing job descriptions, consulting professionals in the field, and analysing industry trends to identify the KSAs that are required in the field. This step helps to ensure that the POs are relevant and aligned with industry needs.

Next, the program's goals and objectives are identified, and these goals should directly relate to the KSAs required for the program's graduates. The diagram emphasizes the importance of aligning the KSAs with the program's goals to ensure that graduates are well-prepared for their future careers.

A gap analysis is then conducted to determine the gap between the current state of the program and the desired state. This analysis helps to identify the specific KSAs that need to be developed or enhanced to bridge the gap.

The KSAs are defined based on the identified needs and goals of the program. They should be specific, measurable, and achievable, ensuring that graduates possess the necessary competencies to succeed in their chosen careers.

Engaging stakeholders, including faculty, students, alumni, and employers, is crucial in this process. Their input and perspectives help to ensure that the identified KSAs are relevant and appropriate for the field, reflecting the needs of both the program and the industry.

The POs are finalized based on the identified KSAs. The POs should be aligned with the program's goals and should follow the SMART (Specific, Measurable, Achievable, Relevant, Time-bound) criteria to effectively guide the program's curriculum and assessment processes.

Overall, the process of defining POs requires a collaborative effort among stakeholders and should be an ongoing process that is regularly reviewed and updated based on feedback and changes in the field.

8.3   Case Study for successful Implementation of Program Outcome (PO)

Bachelor of Science in Electrical Engineering (BSEE) program at the University of Illinois at Urbana-Champaign

The BSEE program at the University of Illinois at Urbana-Champaign has been consistently ranked among the top engineering programs in the United States. The program was first accredited by the Engineering Accreditation Commission (EAC) of ABET in 1936 and has maintained its accreditation ever since. The program has a long history of focusing on the development of student competencies and outcomes, and the use of PO has been an important part of this focus.

In 2003, the BSEE program undertook a comprehensive review of its curriculum and outcomes. A committee was formed consisting of faculty members, industry representatives, and alumni to review and update the program's PO. The committee identified the key knowledge, skills, and attitudes (KSAs) that were necessary for BSEE graduates to be successful in their careers.

The PO were defined in terms of seven categories, which included technical knowledge, communication skills, teamwork, ethics, professional development, global awareness, and lifelong learning. Within each category, specific KSAs were identified and mapped to the courses in the curriculum. This mapping helped to ensure that the KSAs were covered in the curriculum and that the students were provided with opportunities to develop these competencies.

The program also implemented a system for assessing the PO. Surveys were sent to alumni and employers to gather feedback on the graduates' performance in the workplace. Faculty members also assessed the students' performance on the KSAs through exams, projects, and other assignments. The results of these assessments were used to make changes to the curriculum and to improve the delivery of the program.

The implementation of PO in the BSEE program has led to several positive outcomes. The program has been able to align its curriculum with the needs of the industry and to ensure that its graduates are well-prepared for their careers. The program's accreditation has been reaffirmed, and the graduates of the program have been successful in securing employment and pursuing further education. Overall, the implementation of PO has been a key factor in the success of the BSEE program at the University of Illinois at Urbana-Champaign.

Please note: The information provided here is for general informational purposes only. We make no representations or warranties of any kind, express or implied, about the completeness, accuracy, reliability, suitability, or availability of the information. Any reliance you place on such information is strictly at your own risk.

The Bachelor of Science in Electrical Engineering (BSEE) program at the University of Illinois at Urbana-Champaign had the following Program Outcomes (POs):

1. An ability to identify, formulate, and solve complex engineering problems by applying principles of engineering, science, and mathematics.
2. An ability to apply engineering design to produce solutions that meet specified needs with consideration of public health, safety, and welfare, as well as global, cultural, social, environmental, and economic factors.
3. An ability to communicate effectively with a range of audiences.
4. An ability to recognize ethical and professional responsibilities in engineering situations and make informed judgments, which must consider the impact of engineering solutions in global, economic, environmental, and societal contexts.
5. An ability to function effectively on a team whose members together provide leadership, create a collaborative and inclusive environment, establish goals, plan tasks, and meet objectives.
6. An ability to develop and conduct appropriate experimentation, analyse, and interpret data, and use engineering judgment to draw conclusions.
7. An ability to acquire and apply new knowledge as needed, using appropriate learning strategies.

These POs were designed to reflect the knowledge, skills, and attitudes that graduates of the program were expected to possess and were used to assess the effectiveness of the program in preparing students for successful careers in electrical engineering.

Please note: The information provided here is for general informational purposes only. We make no representations or warranties of any kind, express or implied, about the completeness, accuracy, reliability, suitability, or availability of the information. Any reliance you place on such information is strictly at your own risk.

8.4   Balancing Skills for Success: The Ideal Allocation of Technical and Life Skills in PEOs and POs

The allocation of skills within PEOs and POs can vary depending on the program, industry requirements, and the desired outcomes for graduates. While the 60% technical skills and 40% life skills allocation for POs and the reversed ratio for PEOs can be a common approach, it's important to note that these percentages can differ based on specific program objectives and industry demands.

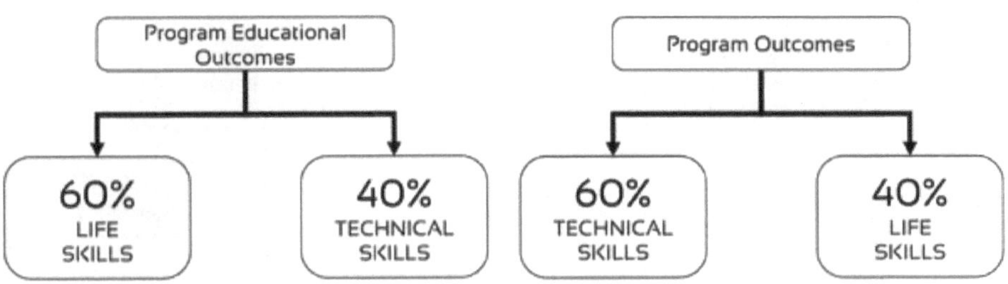

Figure 36: Balancing Technical and Life Skills in PEOs and POs

The purpose of PEOs is to focus on the broader professional achievements and accomplishments of graduates within a few years after graduation. This includes their ability to succeed in their careers, adapt to changing industry needs, and contribute effectively to society. As such, the inclusion of life skills such as communication, critical thinking, teamwork, and adaptability is essential.

On the other hand, POs primarily emphasize the specific technical knowledge, skills, and competencies that students need to acquire by the end of the program. These skills are directly related to their field of study and are critical for their success in their chosen professions.

The ideal balance between technical skills and life skills in PEOs and POs should be determined by considering factors such as industry requirements, program objectives, and the overall goals of the institution. It is important for the program to stay updated with the latest industry trends and incorporate changes in the allocation of skills as needed to ensure graduates are well-prepared for the workforce and capable of meeting the demands of their careers.

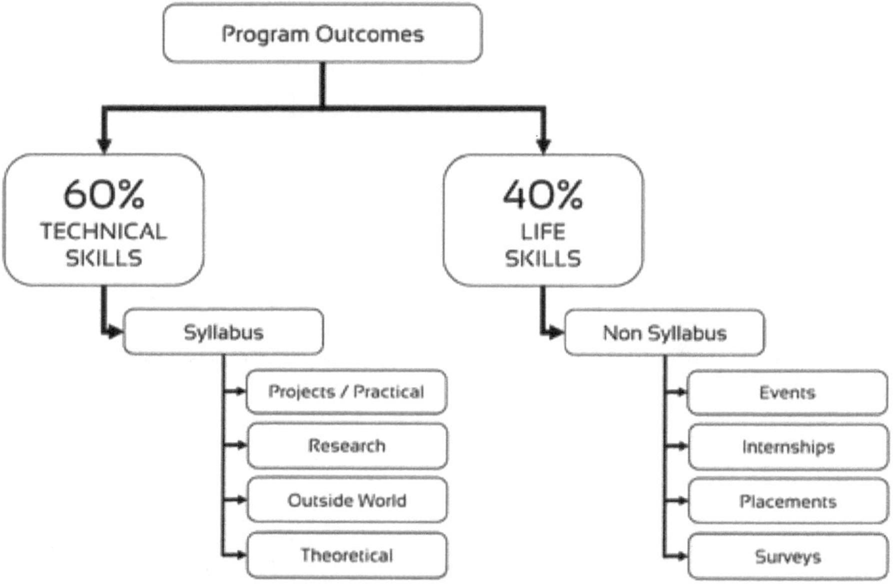

Figure 37: Balancing Technical and Life Skills with focused activities in the Campus in POs

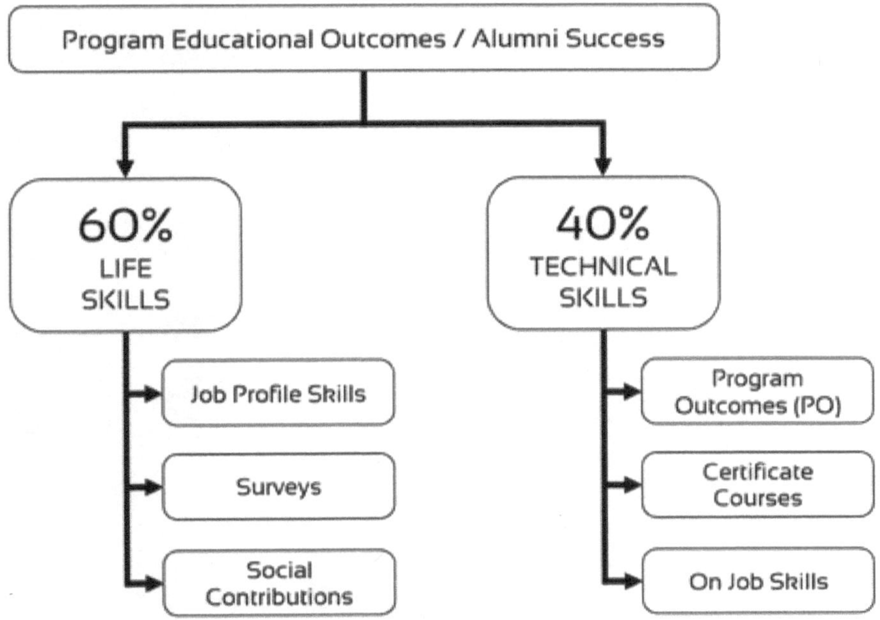

Figure 38: Balancing Technical and Life Skills with focused activities in the Campus in PEOs

Chapter 9

Understanding MOBF for Designing the Course Outcomes

Course Outcomes (CO) are specific and measurable statements that describe what a student will be able to do upon completion of a course. They are designed to align with the program outcomes and to ensure that the course is contributing to the overall goals of the program. COs are typically written in terms of the knowledge, skills, and abilities that students will gain because of taking the course.

COs should be specific and measurable, meaning that it should be clear what the student will be able to do because of completing the course, and how this will be measured. COs are typically written at a level of detail that is more specific than program outcomes and should be aligned with the overall goals of the program. They should also be developed with consideration of the needs of stakeholders such as employers, accreditation bodies, and other interested parties.

COs are usually developed by the course instructor in collaboration with the program faculty and other stakeholders, such as employers or industry professionals. They should be reviewed and updated on a regular basis to ensure that they remain relevant and aligned with the changing needs of the program and the industry.

Overall, COs help to ensure that courses are designed to meet the needs of the program and its stakeholders, and that students are equipped with the knowledge and skills needed to succeed in their future careers.

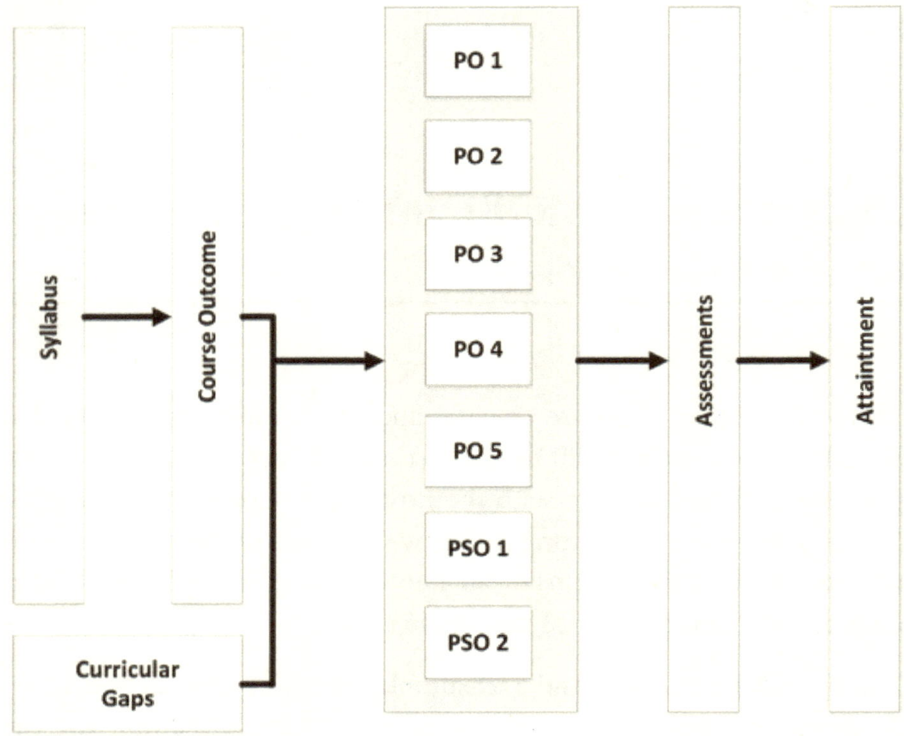

Figure 39: Course Outcomes (CO): Bridging Learning with Program Goals

The diagram illustrates the role of Course Outcomes (CO) in connecting individual courses with the overall goals of the program. COs are specific and measurable statements that describe what students will be able to do upon completing a course. They serve as a bridge between course-level learning and program-level objectives.

COs are aligned with the program outcomes to ensure that each course contributes to the overarching goals of the program. They are designed to specify the knowledge, skills, and abilities that students will acquire because of taking the course. COs are written with clarity, indicating what students will be able to do and how their achievements will be measured.

Course instructors, in collaboration with program faculty and stakeholders such as employers or industry professionals, develop COs.

These outcomes are reviewed and updated regularly to ensure their relevance and alignment with the evolving needs of the program and the industry.

By connecting course-level learning with program-level goals, COs help to ensure that courses are designed to meet the needs of the program and its stakeholders. They play a vital role in equipping students with the necessary knowledge and skills to succeed in their future careers.

Course Outcomes, also known as Course Learning Outcomes (CLOs), have been used in the field of education for several decades to assess student learning and guide course design. The roots of the concept of course outcomes can be traced back to the 1970s, when educational theorists began to emphasize the importance of defining specific learning objectives for courses and aligning those objectives with broader program and institutional goals.

In the United States, the widespread use of course outcomes can be attributed in large part to the efforts of accreditation agencies such as the Accreditation Board for Engineering and Technology (ABET), which began requiring engineering programs to establish program and course outcomes in the 1990s. As a result, course outcomes have become a standard part of curriculum design and assessment in many fields, including engineering, business, health sciences, and education.

The use of course outcomes has also been driven by broader trends in higher education, such as the shift towards outcomes-based education (OBE) and the emphasis on accountability and assessment. Course outcomes help to ensure that courses are aligned with program and institutional goals and provide a framework for assessing student learning and improving course design.

Overall, the use of course outcomes reflect a broader shift towards a more student-centered and outcomes-focused approach to education, in which the emphasis is on defining and measuring specific learning objectives and ensuring that students can demonstrate mastery of key concepts and skills.

9.1   Taxonomy Framework

The Taxonomy framework helps faculties organize and arrange three important components of education: Learnings, Objectives, and Measurements.

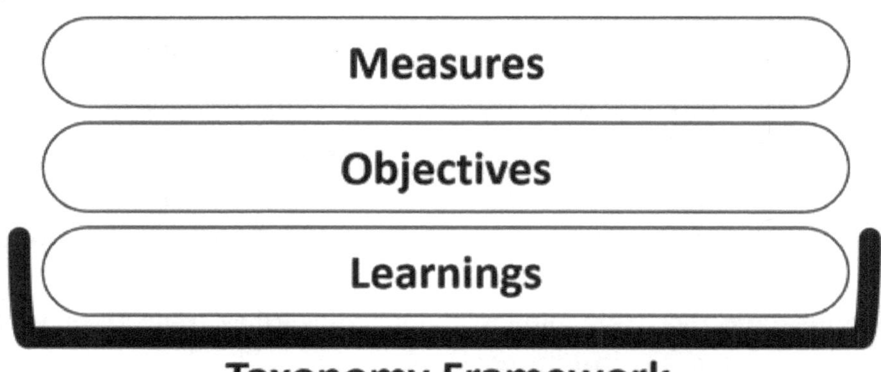

Figure 40: The Taxonomy Framework: Organizing Learnings, Objectives, and Measurements

Learnings: The Taxonomy framework provides a structured way to categorize and organize different levels of learning. It helps faculties identify the cognitive processes and skills that students need to develop. By using Bloom's Taxonomy or other similar frameworks, faculties can ensure that the learning experiences they design promote a progressive development of knowledge and skills, starting from foundational concepts and moving towards higher-order thinking and application.

Objectives: The Taxonomy framework helps faculties in setting clear and specific learning objectives. Objectives define what students should be able to accomplish or demonstrate because of their learning experiences. By aligning their objectives with the different levels of the Taxonomy framework, faculties can ensure that they cover a range of cognitive processes and provide opportunities for students to engage in critical thinking, problem-solving, and other higher-order skills.

Measurements: The Taxonomy framework also assists faculties in developing appropriate measurements and assessments to evaluate student learning. Each level of the Taxonomy corresponds to different types of assessments that align with the specific cognitive processes being targeted. For example, assessments at the Remembering level may involve simple recall or recognition tasks, while assessments at the Evaluating level may require students to analyse and evaluate information. By considering the Taxonomy framework, faculties can design assessments that align with their learning objectives and provide meaningful feedback on student progress and achievement.

Overall, the Taxonomy framework provides a systematic approach for faculties to organize and align their instruction, objectives, and assessments. It helps ensure that the learning experiences are comprehensive, progressive, and effectively measure student learning outcomes.

The statements of the Campus Success System Framework (CSSF) consist of two broad types of components: Knowledge (Noun) and Cognition (Verb). These components are essential for creating effective success statements that are measurable and impactful.

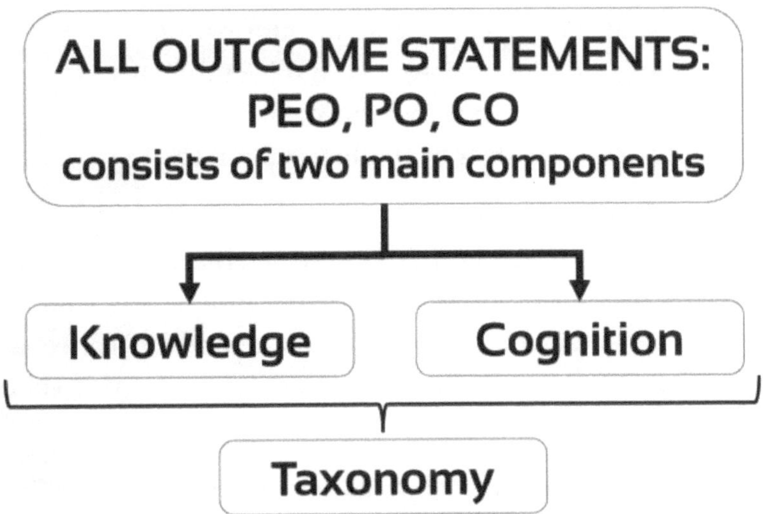

Figure 41: Components of Effective Campus Success Statements: Knowledge and Cognition

Knowledge (Noun): The Knowledge component refers to the specific information, facts, concepts, or skills that students are expected to acquire or demonstrate. It represents the content or subject matter that students need to understand or master. The Knowledge component is typically represented by nouns and describes what students should know or possess because of their educational experiences.

Examples of Knowledge components could include:

- Theoretical knowledge of key concepts in a field
- Familiarity with specific theories or models
- Understanding of historical events or significant works
- Proficiency in technical skills or tools

Cognition (Verb): The Cognition component refers to the mental processes or actions that students are expected to perform or engage in. It represents the cognitive abilities and skills that students should develop or apply. The Cognition component is typically represented by verbs and describes what students should be able to do with the knowledge they have acquired.

Examples of Cognition components could include:

- Analysing and evaluating data or information
- Applying theories or concepts to solve problems.
- Critically examining arguments or perspectives
- Communicating ideas or findings effectively

By combining the Knowledge (Noun) and Cognition (Verb) components, success statements can be created that clearly define what students are expected to know and be able to do. This combination ensures that the statements are both measurable and effective, as they encompass both the content knowledge and the cognitive skills that students need to acquire and demonstrate.

The **Taxonomy Table** is a matrix that includes different combinations of action verbs (representing cognitive processes) and nouns (representing knowledge or content areas). Each cell in the table represents a specific combination of a cognitive level and a knowledge domain.

For example, a cell in the table might include the combination "analyse concepts" or "evaluate arguments." This indicates that at a certain cognitive level, such as analysing or evaluating, the focus is on applying that cognitive process to a specific knowledge domain, such as concepts or arguments.

The Taxonomy Table allows educators to choose appropriate action verbs and knowledge domains that align with their learning objectives and instructional context. It provides a systematic way to link cognitive processes and knowledge areas, helping to guide the design of learning activities, assessments, and instructional strategies.

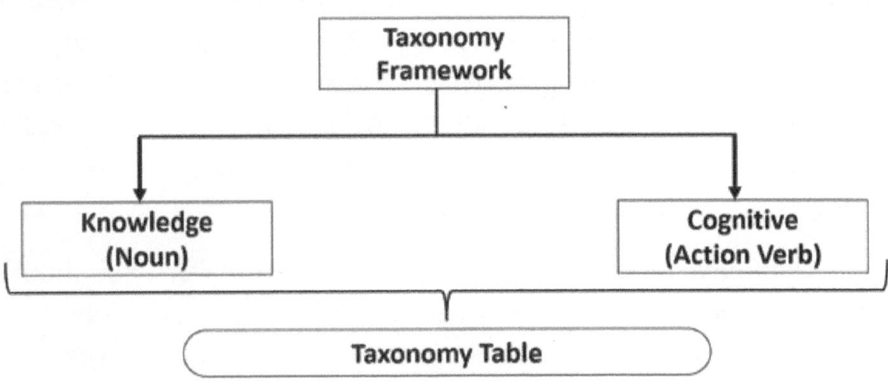

Figure 42: The Taxonomy Table: Linking Cognitive Processes and Knowledge Domains

Cognitive Processes (Action Verbs): The Taxonomy Table includes various cognitive processes, such as remembering, understanding, applying, analysing, evaluating, and creating. These action verbs represent the different levels of cognitive engagement and reflect the complexity of mental activities involved in learning.

Knowledge Domains (Nouns): The knowledge domains in the Taxonomy Table represent the specific content areas or subject matters that students engage with during their learning. These may include concepts, principles, facts, procedures, theories, models, arguments, and more. The knowledge domains provide the context for applying the cognitive processes.

Linking Cognitive Processes and Knowledge Domains: The Taxonomy Table allows educators to select appropriate action verbs and knowledge domains that align with their learning objectives and instructional context. By choosing a specific combination of a cognitive level and a knowledge area, educators can design targeted learning activities and assessments that foster the desired cognitive engagement and knowledge application.

Guiding Instructional Design: The Taxonomy Table serves as a valuable tool for instructional designers and educators to guide the design of learning experiences. It helps ensure that learning objectives are aligned with the intended cognitive outcomes and knowledge domains. Educators can use the Taxonomy Table to create well-structured lesson plans, develop appropriate assessment tasks, and select instructional strategies that promote effective learning.

The Taxonomy Table provides a systematic framework for linking cognitive processes and knowledge domains, supporting educators in designing meaningful and impactful learning experiences. By considering the combination of cognitive levels and knowledge areas, educators can facilitate deep understanding, critical thinking, and application of knowledge within their instructional contexts.

While the Taxonomy Table can be customized based on the specific needs of a subject or discipline, it typically does not have a fixed number of cells or a specific matrix size. The number of cells in the table can vary depending on the chosen cognitive levels and knowledge domains relevant to the learning context.

The Knowledge Dimension		Cognitive Process Dimension					
		1. Remember	2. Understand	3. Apply	4. Analyse	5. Evaluate	6. Create
A	Factual Knowledge						
B	Conceptual Knowledge						
C	Procedural Knowledge						
D	Meta Cognitive Knowledge						

Table 4: Examples of Taxonomy Table

9.2 Is there a difference between Learning Outcomes and Course Outcomes?

Yes, there is a difference between Course Outcomes and Learning Outcomes.

Course Outcomes are the specific knowledge, skills, and abilities that students are expected to demonstrate at the end of a course. They are usually defined by the instructor or the curriculum developer and are aligned with the program outcomes. Course Outcomes are specific to a particular course and are used to evaluate the effectiveness of the course in achieving its goals.

Learning Outcomes, on the other hand, are the broader goals that students are expected to achieve through their educational experiences. They are typically defined by the institution or program and are meant to guide the development of courses and programs. Learning Outcomes focus on the general skills and knowledge that students should acquire during their educational journey, and they are used to evaluate the overall effectiveness of the program in achieving its goals.

In summary, Course Outcomes are specific to a course and focus on the knowledge, skills, and abilities that students should acquire because of taking the course. Learning Outcomes, on the other hand, are broader and focus on the overall goals that students should achieve through their educational experiences.

9.3 Course Outcomes and Outcome Based Education

Course outcomes are a key component of outcome-based education (OBE). OBE is an educational approach that focuses on defining specific measurable outcomes for students to achieve, and then designing curricula and assessment methods to ensure that those outcomes are met. In an OBE framework, course outcomes are defined based on the program outcomes (PO) and the desired learning objectives of the course. The course outcomes provide a clear statement of what students are expected to learn and achieve in a particular course. These outcomes are typically stated in measurable terms, making it possible to evaluate whether students have met the desired learning objectives. In short, course outcomes are an essential tool for implementing OBE in the classroom.

9.4 Course Outcomes and Blooms Taxonomy

Bloom's Taxonomy is often used in conjunction with Course Outcomes as a framework to design and assess learning objectives. Course Outcomes are typically written using action verbs that align with Bloom's Taxonomy levels. For example, a course outcome that requires students to "analyse" a given problem aligns with the "analysis" level of Bloom's Taxonomy, while an outcome that requires students to "create" a solution aligns with the "creation" level.

By using Bloom's Taxonomy in conjunction with Course Outcomes, educators can design course activities and assessments that align with the desired level of learning. This ensures that students are provided with opportunities to engage in higher-order thinking and develop the necessary skills to meet the course outcomes. Additionally, it allows educators to assess student progress towards meeting the outcomes using assessment strategies that are aligned with the desired level of learning. We will discuss more about this in this chapter later. But let's first understand the basics of Blooms Taxonomy. These topics are naturally part of B.Ed., M.Ed., or Teacher Training courses. But as we faculties are trained professional and not trained teachers, we need to understand scientific relevance of Blooms Taxonomy to understand Course Outcome holistically.

9.4.1 Blooms Taxonomy

Bloom's Taxonomy is a framework that classifies learning objectives into three domains: cognitive, affective, and psychomotor. It was first introduced by Benjamin Bloom and his colleagues in 1956, with the aim of promoting higher levels of thinking in education.

The cognitive domain, which is the most well-known and widely used, includes six levels of learning objectives, arranged in a hierarchical order from lower level to higher-level thinking. These levels are:

Level 1	Remembering	The ability to recall information or previously learned concepts. Examples include recalling facts, definitions, or concepts.
Level 2	Understanding	The ability to comprehend the meaning of the information being learned. Examples include interpreting, paraphrasing, and summarizing.
Level 3	Applying	The ability to use or apply knowledge in a new or different situation. Examples include solving problems, using concepts in new situations, and applying theories.
Level 4	Analysing	The ability to break down information into smaller parts, identify patterns, and relationships. Examples include comparing, contrasting, and evaluating.

Level 5	Evaluating	The ability to make judgments or decisions based on criteria and standards. Examples include assessing, judging, and evaluating.
Level 6	Creating	The ability to use knowledge and skills to produce something new. Examples include designing, inventing, and constructing.

Table 5: Six levels of learning objectives

The affective and psychomotor domains focus on emotional and physical learning objectives, respectively. These domains are less frequently used in educational settings.

Bloom's Taxonomy has undergone several revisions since its original publication in 1956. The most recent revision, published in 2001, includes changes to the language used to describe each level of thinking and the addition of a knowledge dimension, which distinguishes between factual, conceptual, procedural, and metacognitive knowledge.

In recent years, there has been a renewed interest in Bloom's Taxonomy as a tool for designing and assessing student learning outcomes. Many educators use it to create course objectives and assessment tools that promote higher levels of thinking and deeper learning. Additionally, it has been adapted for use in online and blended learning environments, where it can be used to structure activities and assessments that promote active and engaged learning.

9.5   Addition of Knowledge Category in Blooms Taxonomy

Bloom's Taxonomy is a framework that organizes learning objectives and helps educators design effective learning experiences. While the original version of Bloom's Taxonomy only had three domains – Cognitive, Affective, and Psychomotor – a revised version added the Knowledge category as a precursor to the Cognitive domain.

he revised version of Bloom's Taxonomy, published in 2001 by a group of cognitive psychologists led by Anderson and Krathwohl, expands on the original framework by incorporating a focus on knowledge categories. The revised taxonomy includes six cognitive processes: Remembering, Understanding, Applying, Analysing, Evaluating, and Creating.

Each of these processes is further broken down into knowledge categories, including Factual Knowledge, Conceptual Knowledge, Procedural Knowledge, and Metacognitive Knowledge.

Factual Knowledge refers to basic, foundational information that students need to know to understand a subject. This includes basic facts, vocabulary, and concepts.

Conceptual Knowledge involves the understanding of how different pieces of information fit together to form a larger concept. This includes understanding the relationships between different concepts and ideas.

Procedural Knowledge refers to knowing how to do something. This includes skills such as writing, problem-solving, and performing a physical task.

Metacognitive Knowledge involves understanding how one learns and how to control and regulate one's own learning. This includes knowledge about one's own learning preferences, study skills, and strategies for self-assessment and self-improvement.

By incorporating knowledge categories into the framework, the revised taxonomy provides a more detailed and comprehensive approach to understanding the different types of knowledge and skills that students need to acquire to be successful learners.

The addition of knowledge categories in Bloom's taxonomy provides a more comprehensive and precise way of describing the different types of learning objectives that students can achieve. The original taxonomy focused primarily on the cognitive processes involved in learning, such as remembering, understanding, applying, analysing, evaluating, and creating. While these processes are still essential to understanding how students learn and develop critical thinking skills, the revised taxonomy adds an additional layer of complexity by emphasizing the different types of knowledge that underlie each cognitive process.

By including knowledge categories such as factual, conceptual, procedural, and metacognitive, the revised taxonomy encourages educators to think more deeply about the specific types of knowledge that students need to acquire to achieve mastery of a particular subject or skill. For example, a teacher who wants students to demonstrate mastery of a complex scientific concept might emphasize the conceptual knowledge category, which includes principles, theories, and models. In contrast, a teacher who wants students to learn how to perform a specific task, such as solving a mathematical equation, might emphasize the procedural knowledge category, which includes skills, algorithms, and techniques.

Level A	**Factual knowledge**	This type of knowledge includes basic information about a subject that is generally accepted as true. It is knowledge of specific details, such as dates, names, and definitions.
Level B	**Conceptual knowledge**	This type of knowledge involves understanding the relationships between different pieces of information. It includes organizing and classifying information into categories, and understanding the principles and theories that underlie a subject.
Level C	**Procedural knowledge**	This type of knowledge is about knowing how to do something and being able to demonstrate it. It involves the ability to apply concepts and principles in a practical way, and to use tools and techniques to solve problems.

Level D	Metacognitive knowledge	This type of knowledge is about understanding how one learns and how to regulate one's own thinking and learning processes. It involves knowledge of one's own cognitive processes, such as attention, memory, and problem-solving, as well as knowledge of different strategies for learning and problem-solving.

Table 6: Knowledge categories or Domain (Noun)

Overall, the addition of knowledge categories in Bloom's taxonomy helps educators to be more intentional and precise in their instructional design, assessment, and evaluation. It provides a more nuanced and detailed framework for understanding how students learn and how to design effective learning experiences that promote deep, meaningful learning.

The cognitive domain of Bloom's taxonomy is concerned with intellectual or mental skills and the development of knowledge in individuals. It is based on the premise that higher-order thinking is developed through a hierarchy of cognitive skills or abilities, which must be developed in sequence which is Remember, Understand, Apply, Analyse, Evaluate and Create. The addition of the knowledge category in the revised taxonomy emphasizes that the cognitive domain is not only concerned with mental skills, but also with the type of knowledge that is acquired and how it is organized. This helps in creating a more comprehensive framework for assessing learning outcomes, as it considers not just the ability to recall or understand information, but also the ability to apply it in various contexts, analyse it, evaluate it, and create something new from it.

There is scientific evidence that supports the cognitive domain of Bloom's taxonomy. Cognitive processes in the brain involve neural networks that are activated when a person engages in thinking, learning, and problem-solving. The development of these neural networks is influenced by environmental and social factors, as well as genetic factors.

Research in the field of neuroscience has shown that different cognitive processes are associated with different regions of the brain. For example, the prefrontal cortex is involved in executive functions such as decision-making, planning, and working memory. The hippocampus is involved in memory formation and retrieval, while the parietal lobe is involved in spatial cognition and attention.

Studies have also shown that the development of cognitive skills can be enhanced through specific training and practice. For example, cognitive training programs have been shown to improve working memory, attention, and problem-solving skills in individuals of all ages.

Overall, the scientific basis for the cognitive domain of Bloom's taxonomy lies in our understanding of the neural networks and cognitive processes that underlie thinking and learning.

Neural networks are a fundamental aspect of the brain that enable cognitive processes such as thinking and learning. These networks consist of groups of neurons that are connected by synapses, which allow them to communicate and process information. The cognitive processes involved in thinking and learning, such as attention, memory, perception, and decision-making, are believed to be based on the activity of these neural networks.

For example, attention is related to the activation of certain neural networks that help to focus our awareness on specific stimuli or information. Memory involves the encoding and retrieval of information by the brain, which is thought to rely on the formation and activation of neural networks that represent the information. Perception, or the interpretation of sensory information, is based on the activity of neural networks that are specialized for processing different types of sensory information.

Decision-making is a complex cognitive process that involves the integration of multiple sources of information, evaluation of options, and selection of a course of action. This process is thought to be based on the activity of neural networks that integrate inputs from different brain regions and allow for the weighing of different factors and outcomes.

Overall, the neural networks and cognitive processes that underlie thinking and learning are complex and interdependent, involving multiple brain regions and systems. Understanding the mechanisms underlying these processes is a key area of research in neuroscience and has important implications for education and cognitive development.

Here are a few research papers related to the neural networks and cognitive processes that underlie thinking and learning:

- Raizada, R. D. S., & Kriegeskorte, N. (2010). Pattern-information fMRI: new questions about detection, resolution, and interpretation. Frontiers in human neuroscience, 4, 34. doi: 10.3389/fnhum.2010.00034
- Norman, K. A., & O'Reilly, R. C. (2003). Modeling hippocampal and neocortical contributions to recognition memory: A complementary-learning-systems approach. Psychological review, 110(4), 611–646. doi: 10.1037/0033-295x.110.4.611
- Kiefer, M., & Pulvermüller, F. (2012). Conceptual representations in mind and brain: Theoretical developments, current evidence, and future directions. Cortex, 48(7), 805–825. doi: 10.1016/j.cortex.2011.04.006
- Van Overwalle, F. (2009). Social cognition and the brain: A meta-analysis. Human brain mapping, 30(3), 829–858. doi: 10.1002/hbm.20547
- Vaidya, C. J., & Gordon, E. M. (2013). Phenotypic variability in resting-state functional connectivity: Status. Brain connectivity, 3(2), 99–120. doi: 10.1089/brain.2012.0112

These papers provide insights into the neural mechanisms underlying cognitive processes such as recognition memory, concept formation, social cognition, and resting-state functional connectivity.

The **affective domain** in Bloom's Taxonomy refers to the emotional and social aspects of learning, including attitudes, beliefs, and values. It is concerned with the development of values, attitudes, and beliefs that will influence behaviours and guide decision-making. The affective domain is important because it helps students to develop a sense of responsibility, self-awareness, and respect for others.

The affective domain has five levels, starting from the lowest level to the highest level: receiving, responding, valuing, organizing, and characterizing. At the receiving level, the student becomes aware of the existence of the value, belief, or attitude. At the responding level, the student is willing to actively participate and engage with the value, belief, or attitude. At the valuing level, the student develops a more personal commitment to the value, belief, or attitude. At the organizing level, the student begins to integrate the value, belief, or attitude into their existing values and beliefs. At the characterizing level, the student has fully internalized the value, belief, or attitude and it has become a part of their character.

The affective domain is often seen as complementary to the cognitive domain because it addresses the development of the whole person, including their emotional and social well-being. By integrating the affective domain into teaching and learning, educators can help students to develop a deeper understanding of themselves and others, as well as a stronger sense of social responsibility and citizenship.

While the affective domain is not traditionally emphasized in classroom teaching, it can still play an important role in student learning and development. In fact, research has shown that affective factors such as motivation, attitudes, and emotions can have a significant impact on learning outcomes. Teachers can use strategies such as creating a positive learning environment, providing opportunities for student choice and autonomy, and incorporating emotional and social learning into the curriculum to help foster the development of the affective domain.

The **psychomotor domain** in Bloom's taxonomy refers to the skills and abilities that individuals acquire through physical activity and practice. These skills are related to the use of muscles and the coordination of body movements. Examples of psychomotor skills include riding a bike, typing, or playing a musical instrument.

Bloom's taxonomy categorizes psychomotor skills into seven different levels, ranging from the most basic reflex actions to the most complex movements requiring great precision and control. These levels are:

Perception – the ability to use sensory cues to guide motor activity.

Set – readiness to act; a mental, emotional, or physical predisposition to respond to a stimulus.

Guided response – the early stages of learning a complex skill, with the aid of an instructor or coach.

Mechanism – proficiency in performing a learned motor skill without hesitation or errors.

Complex overt response – the ability to perform a skill that requires a high level of coordination and control, such as dancing or playing a sport.

Adaptation – the ability to modify a learned skill to fit new situations or requirements.

Origination – the ability to create a new motor skill or combine existing skills into a new pattern or sequence.

The psychomotor domain is often associated with vocational or technical education, but it is also relevant to a wide range of fields, including sports, performing arts, and healthcare. Effective teaching in the psychomotor domain involves providing learners with opportunities to practice and receive feedback on their skills, as well as encouraging self-reflection and self-evaluation.

9.6 Knowledge Category and its Subcategories (How to Practically identify the Knowledge type in Syllabus)

As we discussed earlier, the Cognitive Domain of Blooms Taxonomy consists of six levels of thinking, from lower-order thinking skills such as remembering and understanding, to higher-order thinking skills such as analysing, evaluating, and creating. These levels can be further organized into three main categories: the Knowledge Category, the Skills Category, and the Metacognitive Category.

The Knowledge Category, as the name suggests, is concerned with the knowledge that students must acquire to be successful in a given subject.

Knowledge categories refer to the types of knowledge that learners acquire through their educational experiences. There are four main categories of knowledge: factual, conceptual, procedural, and metacognitive. Factual knowledge refers to knowledge about specific facts or information, such as dates, names, and definitions. Conceptual knowledge, on the other hand, involves understanding the relationships between ideas and the underlying concepts that connect them. Procedural knowledge is the knowledge of how to do something, such as how to solve a math problem or play a musical instrument. Finally, metacognitive knowledge is knowledge about how to learn and the processes involved in learning, such as planning, monitoring, and evaluating one's own learning strategies. Each of these knowledge categories plays an important role in learning, and understanding the subcategories and examples within each category can help educators design effective instruction to support student learning.

This knowledge can be further broken down into four subcategories, as follows:

Factual Knowledge: This is knowledge of basic facts, concepts, and information that are essential to understanding a subject. For example, in a biology class, students must learn the names and functions of various parts of a cell.

Conceptual Knowledge: This is knowledge of the underlying principles and relationships that govern a subject. For example, in a physics class, students must learn the concepts of force, mass, and acceleration.

Procedural Knowledge: This is knowledge of how to perform tasks or procedures associated with a subject. For example, in a chemistry class, students must learn how to perform titrations.

Metacognitive Knowledge: This is knowledge of one's own thinking processes and how to regulate them. For example, students must learn how to monitor their own comprehension and adjust their strategies when they encounter difficulties.

Now, let's consider how teachers can use the Knowledge Category in their teaching. One effective way to do this is to align course content with the subcategories of the Knowledge Category. For example, if you are teaching a biology class, you might start by focusing on factual knowledge, such as the names of different cell parts. As students become more proficient in this area, you can gradually introduce conceptual knowledge, such as the principles that govern cell function. Once students have mastered these concepts, you can move on to procedural knowledge, such as how to perform experiments involving cells.

To help students develop their metacognitive knowledge, teachers can encourage them to reflect on their own learning processes. For example, you might ask students to think about how they study and what strategies are most effective for them. You could also encourage students to track their progress over time and adjust their study strategies accordingly.

Overall, the Knowledge Category is a crucial component of Blooms Taxonomy and an important aspect of teaching and learning. By understanding the different subcategories of knowledge, teachers can design effective lesson plans and help students develop a deep understanding of the subject matter.

Understanding the syllabus is the first step for any faculty member. Syllabus provides the backbone for the course, and it helps the faculty member to design their course delivery plan.

One important aspect of the syllabus is identifying the type of knowledge categories present in the course. Factual knowledge, conceptual knowledge, procedural knowledge, and metacognitive knowledge are the four different types of knowledge categories that may be present in a course syllabus.

Factual knowledge refers to the basic information that students need to know to understand the course material. This type of knowledge includes things like definitions, facts, and details. For example, in a biology course, students may need to know the different types of cells that make up the human body or the stages of the cell cycle.

Conceptual knowledge refers to the understanding of broader ideas, theories, or principles that govern the subject matter. This type of knowledge involves the ability to make connections between different pieces of information and to see how they fit into larger patterns. For example, in a physics course, students may need to understand the principles of motion or the laws of thermodynamics.

Procedural knowledge refers to the ability to perform a task or solve a problem. This type of knowledge involves knowing the steps that need to be taken to complete a task or solve a problem. For example, in a chemistry course, students may need to know the steps involved in conducting a lab experiment or balancing a chemical equation.

Metacognitive knowledge refers to the awareness of one's own learning processes and strategies. This type of knowledge involves understanding how to learn and being able to reflect on one's own learning experiences. For example, in an education course, students may need to understand how to assess their own learning and identify the best learning strategies for themselves.

Once faculty members have identified the type of knowledge categories present in their syllabus, they can use this information to determine which cognitive domain to use in the topic delivery. For example, factual knowledge may be taught using the Remembering level of Bloom's Taxonomy, while conceptual knowledge may be taught using the Understanding or Analysing level. Procedural knowledge may be taught using the Applying level, while metacognitive knowledge may be taught using the Evaluating or Creating level.

By understanding the type of knowledge categories in their syllabus, faculty members can design pedagogical strategies that align with the learning outcomes of their course. For example, they can use instructional methods that facilitate the development of the appropriate cognitive skills needed for their students to successfully master the course material.

9.6.1 Factual Knowledge

Factual knowledge refers to the basic, foundational knowledge that is required to understand and recall specific pieces of information. It is the knowledge of specific details, concepts, terminology, principles, and facts that are relevant to a particular subject or domain. Factual knowledge is often considered the starting point of learning and is essential for developing higher-order thinking skills.

Factual knowledge is divided into different subcategories based on the type of information being learned. These subcategories include:

1. **Basic Terminology:** This subcategory refers to the specific vocabulary or jargon that is used in a particular field or subject. For example, a student studying biology would need to learn the basic terminology related to cells, genetics, and ecology to understand the concepts of the subject.

2. **Details:** This subcategory refers to the specific details related to a particular topic or concept. For example, in history, students would need to learn the details of specific historical events and dates.

3. **Concepts:** This subcategory refers to the specific concepts or ideas that are relevant to a particular subject. For example, in mathematics, students would need to learn the concepts of algebra, geometry, and calculus.

4. **Principles:** This subcategory refers to the specific principles or rules that govern a particular subject or domain. For example, in physics, students would need to learn the principles of Newton's laws of motion.

Factual knowledge can be acquired through various methods such as reading, lectures, discussions, and hands-on activities. Teachers can use various strategies to help students develop factual knowledge, such as providing relevant reading material, creating engaging lectures, and using visual aids like diagrams and charts to help students understand complex concepts. Additionally, teachers can use assessment tools like quizzes and tests to measure the students' acquisition of factual knowledge.

9.6.2 Conceptual Knowledge

Conceptual knowledge refers to the understanding of concepts, principles, and relationships between ideas. It involves the ability to organize and categorize information into a coherent framework that can be used to solve problems and make decisions.

The subcategories of conceptual knowledge include:

1. **Knowledge of classifications and categories:** This refers to the ability to identify and understand different groups and types of objects or ideas. For example, understanding the different categories of animals, such as mammals, birds, reptiles, etc. It is the understanding of how concepts are related to each other

in a hierarchical manner. For example, in biology, the concept of a "mammal" is a category that includes subcategories such as "carnivore", "herbivore", "omnivore", etc.

2. **Knowledge of principles and generalizations:** This refers to the ability to understand the underlying principles that govern a concept or idea. For example, understanding the laws of physics that govern the behaviour of objects in motion.

3. **Knowledge of theories and models:** This refers to the ability to understand and apply abstract models and theories to real-world situations. For example, understanding the theory of evolution and applying it to understand the diversity of life on Earth. It is the understanding of concepts in terms of metaphors or analogies. For example, the concept of "electricity" can be understood in terms of a flowing river where the flow of water represents the flow of electric charge.

4. **Knowledge of structures and systems:** This refers to the ability to understand the underlying structures and systems that make up a concept or idea. For example, understanding the structure of the human body and how it functions. It is the understanding of how concepts are related to each other in a network or web of interrelated ideas. For example, in computer science, the concept of "database" is related to other concepts such as "tables", "queries", "indexes", etc.

Conceptual knowledge is important in developing critical thinking skills and problem-solving abilities. It enables individuals to analyse and synthesize information, make connections between different ideas, and develop creative solutions to complex problems. Effective teaching strategies for developing conceptual knowledge include using graphic organizers, concept maps, and analogies to help students organize and relate new information to existing knowledge. To teach conceptual knowledge effectively, instructors should provide opportunities for students to make connections between concepts, use metaphors or analogies to explain concepts, and help students build mental frameworks to organize and represent their knowledge.

9.6.3 Procedural Knowledge

Procedural knowledge refers to knowledge about how to do something, often involving a series of steps or actions. It is the knowledge required to perform a task or skill. The subcategories of procedural knowledge are:

1. **Motor skills:** These are physical actions that require coordination and control of movement. Examples include swimming, typing, or riding a bicycle.
2. **Cognitive skills:** These are mental processes required for problem-solving and decision-making. Examples include critical thinking, analytical skills, and creativity.
3. **Perceptual skills:** These are skills related to sensory perception, such as the ability to recognize patterns, identify shapes, or discriminate between colours.
4. **Social skills:** These are skills related to interpersonal communication, such as listening, conflict resolution, and negotiation.

In teaching, procedural knowledge can be taught through a variety of methods, including demonstrations, practice exercises, and simulations. For example, a science teacher might demonstrate how to conduct an experiment, and then have students practice the steps on their own. Similarly, a language teacher might demonstrate how to form a sentence in a foreign language, and then have students practice by constructing their own sentences. By providing opportunities for students to practice and apply procedural knowledge, they can develop the skills necessary to perform tasks and solve problems effectively.

9.6.4 Meta-Cognitive Knowledge

Meta-cognitive knowledge refers to the knowledge about one's own thinking processes and the ability to regulate and control one's own thinking. It includes the ability to set goals, monitor progress towards those goals, and evaluate outcomes. The subcategories of meta-cognitive knowledge are:

1. **Declarative knowledge:** This includes knowledge about the strategies and skills needed to solve a problem or complete a task, as well as knowledge about one's own learning style and preferences.
2. **Procedural knowledge:** This includes the ability to use strategies and skills effectively to solve a problem or complete a task, as well as the ability to monitor and adjust one's use of these strategies.
3. **Conditional knowledge:** This includes knowledge about when and where to use specific strategies and skills, as well as the ability to transfer knowledge and skills to new situations.

Examples of meta-cognitive knowledge include:

- Knowing which strategies to use for different types of tasks and being able to monitor and adjust the use of those strategies as needed.
- Understanding one's own learning style and preferences and using that knowledge to select appropriate study techniques.
- Being able to set goals for learning, monitor progress towards those goals, and adjust strategies as needed to achieve those goals.
- Knowing when and where to use specific skills or strategies and being able to transfer those skills and strategies to new situations.

In the context of teaching and learning, developing meta-cognitive knowledge can help students become more effective learners by enabling them to regulate their own thinking and learning processes. Teachers can support the development of meta-cognitive knowledge by providing opportunities for students to reflect on their learning, set goals, and monitor progress towards those goals.

9.7 Cognitive Domain and its Types

The cognitive domain is a classification system for learning objectives and refers to the intellectual processes that learners use to obtain and use knowledge. It includes six main categories of learning objectives: remembering, understanding, applying, analysing, evaluating, and creating. Each category represents a different level of cognitive processing, from basic memory recall to the ability to generate new ideas and solutions.

Remembering involves the ability to recall previously learned information, such as facts or definitions. Understanding involves comprehension of the meaning of that information. Applying involves using that information to solve a problem or complete a task. Analysing involves breaking down complex information into smaller parts and examining relationships among those parts. Evaluating involves making judgments about the value or quality of information. Finally, creating involves generating new ideas or solutions based on previously learned information.

In the context of teaching and learning, the cognitive domain is often used to help educators design curriculum and assessments that support student learning at each level of cognitive processing. For example, a teacher might design a lesson plan that focuses on helping students remember key facts and definitions, or they might design an assessment that asks students to analyse and evaluate information to make a decision or solve a problem. By understanding the cognitive domain and its categories, educators can better support student learning and promote deeper understanding of the material being taught.

9.7.1 Remembering

Remembering is the first and simplest level of cognitive processing according to Bloom's Taxonomy. It is the ability to recall previously learned material, facts, or knowledge.

It involves the retrieval of information from long-term memory, such as names, dates, places, and definitions. Remembering can be further divided into four subcategories:

1. **Recognizing:** Identifying or selecting previously learned material from a given set of options. For example, recognizing the correct answer from a list of options.

2. **Recalling:** Retrieving previously learned information from memory without any cues or prompts. For example, recalling a phone number without looking it up.

3. **Reproducing:** Reproducing previously learned information in its original form. For example, writing a sentence from memory.

4. **Repeating:** Reproducing previously learned information in a new form. For example, summarizing a passage in one's own words.

Remembering is an essential building block for higher order thinking skills. It is important for students to have a solid foundation of facts and knowledge before moving on to more complex cognitive processes such as analysis, evaluation, and creation. Teachers can help students develop their remembering skills by providing opportunities for repetition, practice, and retrieval of previously learned material. They can also use various techniques such as mnemonics, acronyms, and visual aids to aid in memory retention.

9.7.2 Understanding

Understanding is the second level in the cognitive domain of Bloom's Taxonomy. At this level, the learner is expected to comprehend the meaning of the information provided and demonstrate the ability to explain it in their own words.

The subcategories of understanding include interpretation, categorization, summarization, comparison, and explanation:

1. **Interpretation:** Interpretation involves understanding and explaining the meaning of information, such as a chart or graph. For example, a student can interpret a graph that shows the correlation between two variables by explaining how the variables are related.

2. **Categorization:** Categorization involves grouping information based on common characteristics. For example, a student can categorize different types of animals based on their physical characteristics.

3. **Summarization:** Summarization involves identifying the main idea of a piece of information and presenting it in a concise and clear manner. For example, a student can summarize a complex article by highlighting the main points in a few sentences.

4. **Comparison:** Comparison involves identifying similarities and differences between pieces of information. For example, a student can compare and contrast two different political systems by identifying their similarities and differences.

5. **Explanation:** Explanation involves demonstrating understanding by providing reasons or evidence to support a claim. For example, a student can explain how a particular scientific phenomenon occurs by providing evidence from research studies.

In teaching and learning, the understanding level is important because it helps learners connect new information with their prior knowledge and experiences. Teachers can facilitate understanding by providing opportunities for learners to explain concepts in their own words, compare and contrast ideas, and summarize key points. Examples of teaching strategies that promote understanding include concept mapping, brainstorming, and discussions.

9.7.3 Applying

Applying cognition involves the ability to use learned material in new situations, to solve problems that have not been encountered before.

According to Bloom's Taxonomy, there are three types of Applying Cognition:

1. Applying to Familiar Situations: In this type of applying, learners apply the knowledge or skill they have learned in a familiar context. For example, a student who has learned how to solve a quadratic equation applies this knowledge to solve similar equations.

2. Applying to Unfamiliar Situations: In this type of applying, learners apply the knowledge or skill they have learned to a new

and unfamiliar situation. For example, a student who has learned how to solve a quadratic equation applies this knowledge to solve an equation that has more than one variable.

3. Analysing and Synthesizing: In this type of applying, learners take the knowledge or skill they have learned and use it to analyse and synthesize information. For example, a student who has learned about different literary devices applies this knowledge to analyse and synthesize a complex literary text.

This involves taking knowledge and using it in a practical or real-world context. Examples of applying cognition include:

1. Using mathematical formulas to solve problems in physics or engineering.
2. Applying programming concepts to develop software applications.
3. Using knowledge of anatomy and physiology to diagnose and treat patients.
4. Applying knowledge of historical events to analyse current events and make predictions for the future.
5. Using knowledge of business principles to develop a new business strategy.
6. Applying knowledge of cooking techniques and ingredients to create a new recipe.

Let's take an example of a history class where students have learned about different historical events. Applying this knowledge would mean that they can analyse how these events led to a particular outcome, and how they can apply these insights to understand current events in their society.

Another example could be of a chemistry lab where students have learned about chemical reactions. Applying this knowledge would mean that they can perform experiments to synthesize new compounds and apply this knowledge to real-life situations like pollution control or drug discovery.

In all these examples, the individual must take the knowledge that they have learned and apply it to a new and unique situation. This requires a deeper understanding of the material, as well as the ability to analyse and synthesize information to find a solution to the problem at hand.

Teaching strategies for applying cognition often involve real-world scenarios, case studies, and problem-based learning. By presenting students with problems to solve or situations to analyse, they can apply their knowledge and develop a deeper understanding of the material. Instructors can also encourage students to ask questions, test hypotheses, and experiment with different approaches to problem-solving.

Teachers can promote applying cognition by providing students with opportunities to practice using their knowledge in real-life situations. This can include lab experiments, simulations, case studies, and problem-solving activities that require students to apply their knowledge and skills in new and unfamiliar situations.

9.7.4 Analysing

Analysing cognition in Bloom's Taxonomy refers to the ability to break down complex concepts into smaller parts and identify the relationships and patterns between those parts. This involves examining information critically and methodically, identifying cause-and-effect relationships, and distinguishing between fact and opinion.

In the analysing stage, learners are expected to go beyond simply understanding concepts and begin to deconstruct and evaluate them. Some key skills involved in analysing include:

1. **Differentiating**: Breaking down complex concepts into smaller parts and identifying the relationships between them.
2. Example: Analysing a literary work and identifying the themes and motifs used by the author.
3. **Comparing**: Identifying similarities and differences between two or more concepts.

4. Example: Comparing two different models of a machine to determine their respective strengths and weaknesses.

5. **Contrasting**: Identifying the differences between two or more concepts.

6. Example: Contrasting two different theories in psychology to better understand the differences between them.

7. **Classifying**: Grouping concepts or ideas into categories based on their shared characteristics.

8. Example: Categorizing different types of animals based on their physical features and behaviours.

9. **Organizing**: Identifying relationships between concepts and organizing them in a logical way.

10. Example: Creating an outline for a research paper to organize the main ideas and supporting evidence.

By engaging in analysing cognition, learners develop critical thinking skills and the ability to evaluate information independently. These skills are essential for success in academic and professional contexts.

9.7.5 Evaluating

Evaluating is the fourth level in the cognitive domain of Bloom's taxonomy, and it refers to the ability to make judgments based on criteria and standards. At this level, students can assess the value or quality of ideas, materials, or work based on a set of criteria. It involves making informed judgments about the worth, validity, or effectiveness of something, and it requires students to use critical thinking skills and knowledge of the subject matter.

There are two types of evaluating: formative evaluation and summative evaluation:

1. **Formative evaluation:** Formative evaluation involves providing feedback to students during the learning process to help them improve their understanding or performance. This type of evaluation can be informal, such as verbal feedback during a

classroom discussion, or more formal, such as a written evaluation of a student's work.

2. **Summative evaluation:** Summative evaluation, on the other hand, is used to assess student learning at the end of a unit, course, or program. This type of evaluation is often more formal and can take the form of exams, papers, or projects.

Examples of activities that involve evaluating cognition include:

1. Assessing the validity of an argument or the credibility of a source
2. Judging the effectiveness of a solution to a problem
3. Evaluating the accuracy of a scientific claim based on evidence.
4. Critiquing a work of art or literature based on established standards.
5. Judging the impact of a historical event or policy on society and making a review out of it.

To develop evaluating skills in students, teachers can create activities and assessments that require students to apply critical thinking skills and make informed judgments based on established criteria. They can also provide feedback and opportunities for reflection to help students understand how to improve their evaluation skills.

9.7.6 Creating

Creating is the highest level of the cognitive domain in Bloom's Taxonomy. It involves the ability to use knowledge and skills to create something new, to combine information in a unique way, or to produce an original product. This level requires not only the application of knowledge and skills, but also the use of critical thinking, problem solving, and creativity.

There are several subcategories of creating cognition:

Designing: This involves creating a plan or blueprint for a project or product. For example, a student may be asked to design a marketing campaign for a new product.

Constructing: This involves building or putting together something new. For example, a student may be asked to construct a model of a bridge or a machine.

Inventing: This involves creating something new that has never been seen before. For example, a student may be asked to invent a new product that solves a specific problem.

Composing: This involves creating something new that is artistic or expressive. For example, a student may be asked to compose a song or write a poem.

Generating: This involves coming up with new ideas or solutions to a problem. For example, a student may be asked to generate new ideas for reducing carbon emissions.

Planning: This involves creating a detailed plan for a project or product. For example, a student may be asked to plan a community service project.

Examples of activities that promote creating cognition include developing a new software program, designing a building or bridge, composing a song, or writing a novel, creating a work of art, or developing a new business idea.

Creating cognition is an important skill in today's world as it encourages innovation and problem solving. It allows individuals to think outside the box and come up with new solutions to complex problems. By fostering the ability to create, individuals are better equipped to adapt to the ever-changing demands of the world.

9.8 Why Course Outcomes are important component of Successful OBE Implementation?

Course outcomes are an essential aspect of outcome-based education because they provide a clear picture of what students are expected to achieve in a particular course. Course outcomes are specific statements that describe the expected learning outcomes of a course. They are based on the overall program outcomes and define the specific knowledge, skills, and attitudes that students should possess upon completing the course.

By defining course outcomes, educators can ensure that the course content and instructional strategies are aligned with the intended learning outcomes. It helps in establishing clear expectations for both the instructors and students and enables better communication of learning goals. With a clear understanding of what is expected, students can focus their efforts on achieving the desired learning outcomes and assess their progress towards achieving them. Course outcomes also provide a framework for assessing student learning and evaluating the effectiveness of the course and instructional strategies.

Overall, course outcomes play a critical role in ensuring that the curriculum is designed to meet the course outcome and in providing a clear framework for both teaching and assessing student learning.

1. Study conducted by Ncube et al. (2017) titled "Assessment of Student Learning Outcomes in an Outcome-Based Education Environment": This study was conducted in South Africa and involved 350 students. The researchers implemented course outcomes and assessed the student learning outcomes using rubrics. They found that the students performed better on the learning outcomes that were clearly defined and assessed using rubrics. The researchers reported that the use of course outcomes helped to focus the teaching and learning process, leading to improved student performance.

2. Study conducted by DiCicco and Enderle (2019) titled "The Impact of Course-Level Outcomes Assessment on Student Learning": This study was conducted in the United States and involved 435 students. The researchers implemented course outcomes and assessed the student learning outcomes using a pre-test and post-test design. They found that the students who were

taught using course outcomes showed significant improvement in their learning outcomes. The researchers reported that the use of course outcomes helped to clarify expectations for students, leading to improved student performance.

All these studies show that the implementation of course outcomes can lead to improved student performance. The methods used to analyse the performance include t-tests, ANOVA, and pre-test and post-test designs. The improvements in student performance ranged from 18.5% to significant improvements, depending on the study and the specific outcome measures used.

9.9 Writing Effective and scientific Course Outcomes

Outcome-based education is a student-centered approach to teaching and learning that focuses on achieving specific learning outcomes. Course outcomes are the building blocks of outcome-based education that provide a clear understanding of what students are expected to learn and achieve in a particular course. It helps faculty members and syllabus creators to develop measurable and quantifiable learning objectives for students. An effective course outcome enables students to achieve desired learning outcomes, and it also helps faculty members to measure student performance accurately. In this context, it is important to understand the process of creating course outcomes. In this section, we will discuss the step-by-step process of creating effective course outcomes.

The approach which I devised which I call it as Modular Outcome Based Framework (MOBF), as per my experience in training thousands of faculties, mentioned for creating effective course outcomes is scientific, quantifiable, replicable, and easy to implement in a university or college. It provides a step-by-step process for faculty and syllabus creators to develop measurable and quantifiable learning objectives for students.

By breaking down the syllabus into modules and teachable topics and creating a lesson plan based on them, faculty can ensure that each module has a specific learning outcome. The columns in the lesson plan, such as pedagogy type, cognition, and knowledge type, make it easier to assess the effectiveness of the teaching and learning process.

Furthermore, by combining the highest cognition and knowledge type, faculty can create course outcomes that are specific, measurable, achievable, relevant, and time-bound (SMART). This approach enables faculty to identify gaps in teaching and learning and make necessary adjustments to improve student performance.

Moreover, the approach is replicable and easy to implement across various subjects and courses, making it a valuable tool for universities and colleges to improve learning outcomes. It also enables faculty to track student progress and assess the effectiveness of the teaching and learning process.

9.10 Modular Outcome Based Framework (MOBF)

Modular Outcome Based Framework (MOBF) is a method created to help faculty and syllabus creators in designing effective course outcomes. The MOBF approach emphasizes the importance of breaking down the syllabus into modules and then breaking each module into teachable topics. This process enables the faculty to create a detailed lesson plan that includes columns such as Sr. No, Topic Name, Module Number, No of Hours Required, Pedagogy Type, Cognition, Knowledge Type, Mapped to Which CO, Assessment Planned (if any), Assessment Type, and Actual Hours Taken. By focusing on each module, MOBF ensures that each course outcome is clear, specific, measurable, and attainable. MOBF approach makes the entire process of designing course outcomes more scientific, quantifiable, replicable, and easy to implement in a university or college. This approach is a valuable tool for educators looking to improve their teaching practices and create effective learning outcomes.

Let's look at this framework in detail:

Creating effective course outcomes is a crucial aspect of outcome-based education. It enables faculty and syllabus creators to develop measurable and quantifiable learning objectives for students. There are ten steps to create effective course outcomes:

9.10.1   Step 1: Review the Syllabus

Review the syllabus to understand the overall objectives and topics covered. Reviewing the syllabus is the first step in the Modular Outcome Based Framework (MOBF) method of creating effective course outcomes. In this step, the faculty should thoroughly review the syllabus to gain an understanding of the course objectives and the topics covered in the curriculum. The syllabus should include details such as course title, description, credit hours, prerequisites, and learning outcomes. The faculty should carefully analyse the syllabus to ensure that it aligns with the overall learning objectives of the program and meets the needs of the students. They should also identify any gaps in the syllabus that need to be addressed and make changes if necessary. This step is essential to ensure that the course outcomes are aligned with the overall goals of the program and that the course meets the needs of the students.

9.10.2   Step 2: Break Down the Syllabus into Modules

If the syllabus is not already broken down into modules by the Board of Studies or the university, faculty should break it down into 5-6 modules. Breaking down the syllabus into modules is an important step in the Modular Outcome Based Framework (MOBF) for designing effective course outcomes. Modules are units of study that represent different sections of the course. Each module should have a specific theme or focus and should be self-contained so that students can easily understand the material. Ideally, the number of modules in a course should be limited to 5-6 to ensure that students can understand and absorb the material effectively.

The process of breaking down the syllabus into modules involves analysing the content of the course and identifying the major themes or topics that will be covered. This can be done by reviewing the course objectives, reading through the textbooks and other materials that will be used, and consulting with other faculty members or subject matter experts. Once the major themes or topics have been identified, they can be grouped together into modules based on their similarities or relationships.

Each module should have a clear title or label that describes its focus. The titles should be concise and descriptive and should accurately reflect the content of the module. For example, if a module focuses on the principles of marketing, the title might be "Marketing Principles and Practices". Additionally, the modules should be organized in a logical sequence so that students can build upon their knowledge as they progress through the course.

Breaking down the syllabus into modules helps to make the course more manageable for both the faculty and the students. By focusing on specific themes or topics, faculty can design effective course outcomes and assessment strategies that are aligned with the content of each module. Students can also benefit from a modular approach because they can better understand the material and retain the information more effectively when it is presented in smaller, more manageable units.

9.10.3 Step 3: Break Down Each Module into Teachable Topics

Breaking down each module into teachable topics is an important step in the Modular Outcome Based Framework (MOBF) for designing effective course outcomes. Once the modules are identified, they should be broken down further into smaller, manageable topics that can be taught within a specific period. This helps in creating a clear roadmap for the instructor to follow and ensures that all topics are covered in a structured and organized manner.

When breaking down each module, faculty should identify the key concepts, skills, and knowledge that students need to acquire to achieve the desired learning outcomes. These can be identified by analysing the module content, course objectives, and the expectations of the industry or profession for which the course is intended. Once these key concepts are identified, they should be divided into smaller, teachable topics that can be covered in a single class session.

It is important to ensure that the topics are sequenced logically so that they build upon each other and provide a comprehensive understanding of the module. Faculty should also ensure that the topics are relevant, current, and aligned with the course objectives.

In summary, breaking down each module into teachable topics helps to create a clear and structured framework for delivering the course content. It ensures that all key concepts are covered in a logical sequence, making it easier for students to understand and apply what they have learned.

9.10.4   Step 4: Create a Lesson Plan Based on the Defined Topics

Creating a lesson plan based on the defined topics is a crucial step in the Modular Outcome Based Framework (MOBF). After breaking down each module into teachable topics, the next step is to create a detailed lesson plan for each topic. The lesson plan should include all the necessary information to deliver the topic effectively, such as learning objectives, teaching strategies, learning activities, and assessments.

The first step in creating a lesson plan is to define the learning objectives. These objectives should be specific, measurable, achievable, relevant, and time-bound (SMART). They should also align with the course outcomes and the highest level of cognition identified for the module. Once the learning objectives are defined, the next step is to select appropriate teaching strategies and learning activities. The teaching strategies and learning activities should be aligned with the learning objectives and the cognition level.

The third step is to design the assessments. The assessments should be aligned with the learning objectives and the cognition level. There are different types of assessments, such as formative assessments, summative assessments, and authentic assessments. Faculty should select the appropriate type of assessment based on the learning objectives and the cognition level.

After designing the assessments, the next step is to define the resources required for delivering the lesson. These resources may include textbooks, handouts, multimedia materials, and equipment. Faculty should ensure that all the resources are available before delivering the lesson.

Finally, faculty should define the expected outcomes of the lesson and evaluate the effectiveness of the lesson plan. Faculty should assess the extent to which the learning objectives were achieved and identify areas for improvement. By creating a lesson plan based on the defined topics, faculty can ensure that all the necessary information is included and that the lesson is delivered effectively.

9.10.5   Step 5: Ensure the Lesson Plan Contains the Following Columns

To create effective course outcomes, it is important to ensure that the lesson plan contains certain columns. These columns provide a structured and organized approach to teaching and learning. The following is a detailed explanation of each column:

1. **Sr No:** This column denotes the serial number of the topic in the lesson plan.
2. **Topic Name:** This column includes the name of the topic to be covered in the class.
3. **Module Number:** This column denotes the module number to which the topic belongs.
4. **No of Hours Required:** This column specifies the number of hours required to cover the topic.

5. **Pedagogy Type:** This column includes the type of teaching method that will be used to teach the topic.

6. **Cognition:** This column denotes the type of cognitive domain that the topic belongs to. Cognition can be Remembering, Understanding, Applying, Analysing, Evaluating, and Creating.

7. **Knowledge Type:** This column denotes the type of knowledge category that the topic belongs to. Knowledge can be Factual, Conceptual, Procedural, and Meta-Cognitive.

8. **Mapped to Which CO:** This column denotes the course outcome that the topic is mapped to. This column can be left blank to be filled later.

9. **Assessment Planned:** This column includes the name of the assessment that will be used to evaluate students' learning.

10. **Assessment Type:** This column denotes the type of assessment that will be used. For example, it can be a formative assessment or a summative assessment.

11. **Actual Hours Taken:** This column can be left blank to be filled later. It denotes the actual number of hours taken to cover the topic.

By ensuring that the lesson plan contains these columns, faculty can create structured and effective course outcomes that help students achieve desired learning outcomes.

9.10.6   Step 6: Create One Course Outcome per Module

Creating one course outcome per module is an essential step in the Modular Outcome-Based Framework (MOBF) for developing effective course outcomes. The process involves identifying the key concepts and skills that students should be able to demonstrate by the end of each module. This helps to ensure that the module is focused and organized around a specific set of learning outcomes.

To create one course outcome per module, faculty should review the lesson plan and identify the most important concept or skill that students should be able to demonstrate by the end of the module. This outcome should be clear, concise, and measurable. The outcome should also be aligned with the overall learning objectives of the course.

Creating one course outcome per module allows faculty to track student progress and assess the effectiveness of their teaching. It also provides students with clear expectations of what they should be able to demonstrate at the end of each module. This approach helps to increase student engagement and motivation, as they are more likely to stay focused and on track when they have a clear understanding of what is expected of them.

Overall, creating one course outcome per module is a critical step in designing a course that is aligned with the desired learning outcomes and is an effective way to ensure that students are prepared for success in their future academic and professional endeavours.

9.10.7   Step 7: Determine the Highest Cognition

Determining the highest cognition refers to identifying the highest level of thinking required for a particular topic or module in the lesson plan. It involves categorizing the cognitive domain of the learning outcome based on Bloom's Taxonomy, which consists of six levels of cognitive thinking: Remembering, Understanding, Applying, Analysing, Evaluating, and Creating.

For example, if the topic is about Newton's laws of motion, the highest cognition required could be "Analysing" since it involves breaking down complex ideas into smaller parts and understanding the relationship between them. An example of a learning outcome that falls under this category could be "Analyse the relationship between force, mass, and acceleration in Newton's laws of motion."

Faculty can determine the highest cognition level by reviewing the content of the lesson plan and identifying the type of thinking skills required to master the topic. This information can then be used to develop course outcomes that align with the highest level of cognitive thinking required for each module or topic.

Refer below Cognition applicable words table to understand what corresponding words you can use for respective Cognition.

9.10.8 Step 8: Determine the Highest Knowledge Type

Determining the highest knowledge type is an important step in the process of creating effective course outcomes using the Modular Outcome Based Framework (MOBF). In this step, faculty or syllabus creators need to review the lesson plan for each module and identify the type of knowledge that is being taught. The four categories of knowledge types are factual, conceptual, procedural, and meta-cognitive.

To determine the highest knowledge type, faculty should first identify the specific topics being taught in the module. Then, they should consider the type of knowledge that is required for students to understand those topics. For example, if the topic is about the process of photosynthesis, then procedural knowledge would be the highest type of knowledge required, as students need to understand the steps involved in the process.

Similarly, if the topic is about the different types of governments in the world, then conceptual knowledge would be the highest type of knowledge required, as students need to understand the different concepts and theories related to governments.

In some cases, multiple knowledge types may be required for a particular topic. In such cases, faculty should determine the highest knowledge type that is required for students to understand the topic at a deeper level.

By determining the highest knowledge type for each module, faculty can ensure that the course outcomes are aligned with the learning objectives and that students are able to develop the necessary knowledge and skills to succeed in their academic and professional pursuits.

9.10.9 Step 9: Combine the Highest Cognition and Knowledge Type

Combining the highest cognition and knowledge type is a critical step in creating effective course outcomes. Once the highest cognition and knowledge type have been identified for each module, they need to be combined to create a concise and clear course outcome.

For example, let's say that the highest cognition identified in a module is "applying" and the highest knowledge type is "procedural." The course outcome could be something like "Students will be able to apply procedural knowledge to solve real-world problems."

It is important to ensure that the sentence created by combining cognition and knowledge type is not more than 20 words. The sentence should clearly and concisely communicate what the students will be able to do after completing the module.

By combining the highest cognition and knowledge type, faculty and syllabus creators can create effective course outcomes that align with the learning objectives and help students achieve desired learning outcomes.

9.10.10   Step 10: Repeat Steps 6-9 for Each Module

After creating one course outcome per module, the next step in the Modular Outcome Based Framework (MOBF) is to repeat Steps 6-9 for each module in the syllabus or lesson plan. This involves analysing the lesson plan for each module to identify the highest cognition and knowledge type, and then combining them to create a course outcome that is specific, measurable, and achievable.

For example, if the module is about "Introduction to Biology," and the highest cognition identified in the lesson plan is "Understanding," and the highest knowledge type is "Conceptual," the course outcome could be: "By the end of the module, students will be able to demonstrate an understanding of the key concepts and principles of biology."

It is important to ensure that the course outcomes for each module align with the overall learning outcomes of the course and are relevant to the needs and goals of the students. By repeating Steps 6-9 for each module, faculty and syllabus creators can create a cohesive and comprehensive set of course outcomes that reflect the intended learning objectives of the course.

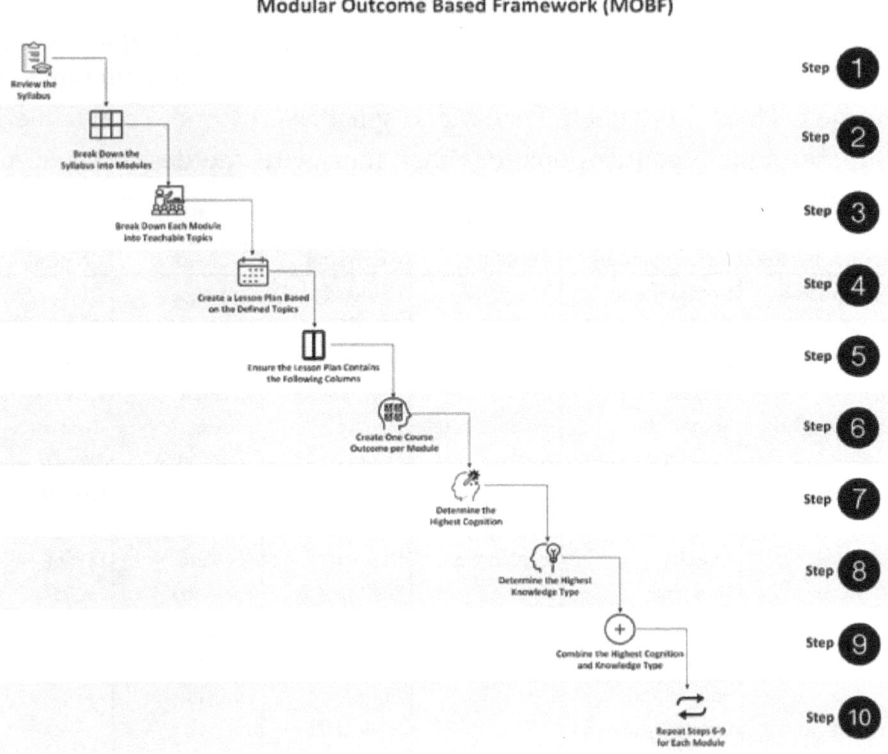

Figure 43: Modular Outcome Based Framework (MOBF): Designing Effective Course Outcomes

By following these ten steps, faculty and syllabus creators can create scientific and quantifiable course outcomes that help students achieve desired learning outcomes.

9.11 Cognition applicable words table

The six levels of cognition, namely remembering, understanding, applying, analysing, evaluating, and creating, each have their own set of words that can be used to frame course outcomes. For remembering, words such as identify, define, list, and recall can be used. For understanding, words such as explain, summarize, illustrate, and compare can be used. For applying, words such as use, demonstrate, apply, and implement can be used. For analysing, words such as analyse, differentiate, compare, and investigate can be used. For evaluating, words such as assess, critique, justify, and evaluate can be used. Finally, for creating, words such as design, invent, compose, and generate can be used. These words help faculty and syllabus creators to create clear and measurable course outcomes that align with the desired level of cognitive development.

Remembering	Understanding	Applying	Analysing	Evaluating	Creating
Recognize	Comprehend	Apply	Categorize	Appraise	Design
Recall	Explain	Implement	Classify	Critique	Compose
Identify	Interpret	Execute	Compare	Judge	Develop
Name	Paraphrase	Use	Contrast	Evaluate	Formulate
Define	Summarize	Demonstrate	Debate	Assess	Construct
List	Translate	Apply	Deduce	Determine	Devise
Memorize	Predict	Employ	Determine	Estimate	Generate
Repeat	Categorize	Practice	Differentiate	Justify	Plan
Reproduce	Classify	Implement	Discern	Validate	Invent
Retrieve	Compare	Operate	Distinguish	Prioritize	Imagine
	Contrast	Utilize	Examine	Decide	
	Demonstrate		Identify	Select	
	understanding.		Infer	Defend	
	Identify the main		Inspect		
	idea.		Investigate		
	Draw		Organize		
	conclusions.		Relate		
	Distinguish		Select		
	between		Separate		
	Infer		Subdivide		
	Relate		Synthesize		
	Synthesize				
	Differentiate				

Table 7: Applicable words that can be used for Cognition.

9.12   Examples of well-written learning outcomes

For simplicity I am presenting here only 3 – 4 CO for each subject. You are recommended to create at least 5 CO but restrict to only 6.

1. Subject: Introduction to Psychology

   a. CO1: Apply understanding of the principles of psychological research to critically evaluate research studies.
   b. CO2: Analyse the effects of various psychological theories on human behaviour.
   c. CO3: Create a research proposal that outlines the components of a sound empirical study.

2. Subject: Digital Marketing

   a. CO1: Understand the fundamental concepts of digital marketing and the impact on business.
   b. CO2: Apply various digital marketing techniques to develop a marketing plan.
   c. CO3: Analyse the performance of digital marketing campaigns and adjust strategies accordingly.

3. Subject: Financial Accounting

   a. CO1: Understand the basic principles of financial accounting and the role of accounting in business.
   b. CO2: Apply accounting concepts to record financial transactions and prepare financial statements.
   - CO3: Analyse financial statements and interpret financial data to make informed business decisions.

4. Subject: Human Resource Management

   a. CO1: Understand the role of HR management in organizational performance.
   b. CO2: Apply various HR techniques to manage recruitment, selection, and retention processes.
   c. CO3: Evaluate the effectiveness of HR strategies and adjust them accordingly.

5. Subject: Environmental Science

   a. CO1: Understand the concepts of environmental science and their relationship to sustainable development.

b. CO2: Apply scientific methods to analyse environmental problems and develop solutions.

c. CO3: Evaluate the impact of human activities on the environment and propose strategies for minimizing that impact.

6. Subject: English Literature

a. CO1: Understand the literary devices and techniques used in literature to convey meaning.

b. CO2: Apply close reading strategies to interpret and analyse literary texts.

c. CO3: Create written responses that demonstrate critical engagement with literary texts.

7. Subject: Web Design

a. CO1: Understand the principles of web design and the user experience.

b. CO2: Apply various design techniques to create effective websites.

c. CO3: Analyse the performance of websites and adjust design strategies accordingly.

8. Subject: Microeconomics

a. CO1: Understand the basic concepts of microeconomics and their application to business.

b. CO2: Apply economic models to analyse market behaviour and the decision-making of firms.

c. CO3: Analyse economic data to make informed business decisions.

9. Subject: Organizational Behaviour

a. CO1: Understand the basic concepts of organizational behaviour and their application to workplace dynamics.

b. CO2: Apply various organizational behaviour theories to analyse and address organizational problems.

c. CO3: Evaluate the effectiveness of organizational behaviour strategies and adjust them accordingly.

9.12.1 Templates for writing learning outcomes

Here are some templates for writing course outcomes as per MOBF:

Template 1:

Upon completion of [Course Name], students will be able to [Action Verb] [Knowledge Type] through [Knowledge Type].

Example: Upon completion of Biology 101, students will be able to:

Explain the basic concepts of ecology through the study organisms and how they interact with the environment around them.

Template 2:

Upon completion of [Course Name], students will be able to [Action Verb] [Knowledge Type].

Example: Upon completion of English Literature 201, students will be able to:

Evaluate the literary elements of a novel and author's intended meaning.

9.13 Representing Course Outcome in the Taxonomy Table

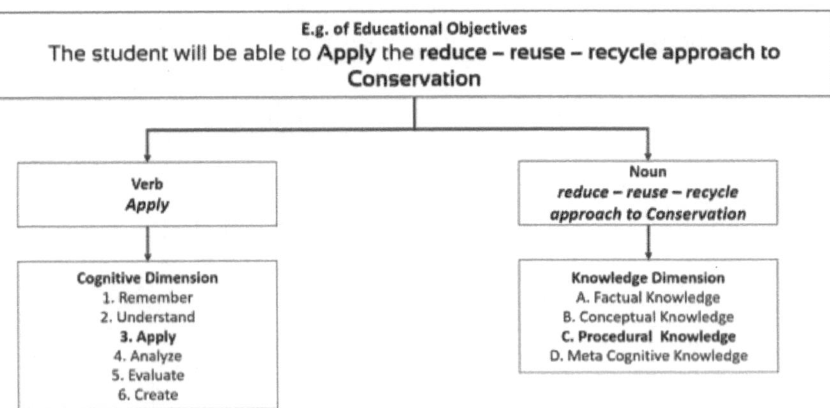

Figure 44: Example of Course Outcome and how it contains both Knowledge (Noun) and Cognition (Verb)

The Knowledge Dimension		Congnitive Process Dimension					
		1. Remember	2. Understand	3. Apply	4. Analyse	5. Evaluate	6. Create
A	Factual Knowledge						
B	Conceptual Knowledge						
C	Procedural Knowledge			✖			
D	Meta Cognitive Knowledge						

Table 8: Representing the Course Outcome in Taxonomy Table

Chapter 10

Effective Pedagogy Implementation

Pedagogy refers to the methods, practices, and techniques used in teaching and education. It encompasses the strategies and approaches used by educators to facilitate learning, promote critical thinking, and engage students in the learning process. Pedagogy is not a static concept, but rather an evolving one that has transformed over time in response to changing educational needs and goals.

Historically, pedagogy in higher education was largely centered around lectures, memorization, and rote learning. The teacher was seen as the primary source of knowledge, and the student's role was to passively absorb information. However, as education has evolved, so has pedagogy, and new approaches have emerged that prioritize student-centered learning and active engagement.

Today, pedagogy in higher education is increasingly focused on promoting critical thinking, creativity, and problem-solving skills. Educators are encouraged to incorporate active learning techniques, such as group work, discussions, and project-based assignments, that allow students to engage with the material and apply their learning in real-world contexts.

In addition, the rise of technology and online learning has led to new opportunities for pedagogical innovation, such as blended learning models that combine in-person and online instruction, and flipped classroom models that reverse the traditional lecture and homework structure.

Overall, the evolution of pedagogy in higher education has been driven by a desire to better meet the needs of today's learners and prepare them for success in a rapidly changing world.

Pedagogy plays a crucial role in outcome-based education (OBE) because it provides a framework for designing instruction that aligns with the intended learning outcomes. Pedagogy encompasses a wide range of teaching practices and strategies that are used to engage students, promote learning, and achieve desired outcomes. By selecting and applying appropriate pedagogies, instructors can create an effective learning environment that fosters the development of skills and knowledge required by the learning outcomes.

In OBE, pedagogy is used to design and deliver instruction in a way that ensures that students achieve the desired learning outcomes. This involves selecting appropriate instructional methods and materials that are aligned with the specific outcomes and the desired levels of cognition and knowledge type. Pedagogy also involves creating opportunities for students to engage in active learning and to receive feedback on their progress towards achieving the learning outcomes.

The use of pedagogy in OBE is essential for ensuring that students can acquire the necessary knowledge, skills, and competencies that are required for success in their chosen field. Effective pedagogy supports student-centered learning, encourages critical thinking, and fosters creativity and innovation. It is essential for instructors to continually assess and evaluate their pedagogical practices to ensure that they are effective in achieving the desired outcomes.

10.1   Types of Pedagogy

Pedagogy refers to the various teaching styles, methods, and strategies employed by educators to facilitate learning in their students. **There are several different types of pedagogy, each with its own strengths and weaknesses. Here are some of the most common types of pedagogy:**

1. **Lecture-Based Pedagogy:** This is the most traditional form of pedagogy, where the teacher delivers lectures on the subject matter to the students, and students take notes and ask questions. This pedagogy is often used in larger classes, where interaction with students can be limited.

2. **Inquiry-Based Pedagogy:** This type of pedagogy focuses on encouraging students to ask questions and actively engage in the learning process. The teacher acts as a facilitator, guiding students towards discovering the answers to their questions through independent research, experimentation, and analysis.

3. **Problem-Based Pedagogy:** This type of pedagogy is based on the premise that students learn best by solving real-world problems. The teacher presents a problem or challenge to the students, who work together in groups to find a solution. This pedagogy is often used in fields such as engineering, medicine, and law.

4. **Project-Based Pedagogy:** Like problem-based pedagogy, project-based pedagogy involves students working together in groups to complete a project or task. The focus is on hands-on, practical learning, with students applying what they have learned to a real-world scenario.

5. **Collaborative Pedagogy:** This type of pedagogy emphasizes collaboration and teamwork among students. The teacher serves as a guide or facilitator, and students work together to complete tasks and assignments.

6. **Experiential Pedagogy:** This type of pedagogy involves students learning through first-hand experience. This can include field trips, laboratory experiments, and other hands-on activities that allow students to apply what they have learned in the classroom to real-world situations.

Each type of pedagogy has its own strengths and weaknesses, and it is up to educators to determine which approach will work best for their students and learning outcomes. The above are just examples for discussion and you will find there many more examples available but the above are mostly used by faculties.

10.2 Frequently used Pedagogy List

There are many different pedagogical approaches that can be used in higher education to promote learning and engagement among students. Some approaches are more traditional, such as lectures and tutorials, while others are more innovative and involve the use of technology and collaborative learning. Each approach has its own strengths and limitations, and the choice of which approach to use will depend on several factors, including the goals of the course, the subject matter being taught, and the needs and preferences of the students. In this section, we will explore some of the most common pedagogical approaches used in higher education, along with their key characteristics, benefits, and challenges.

Here is a list of some commonly used pedagogies in higher education:

1. **Lectures:** Lectures are one of the oldest and most traditional forms of pedagogy. In a lecture, the instructor presents information to students in a one-way communication. This can be useful for conveying large amounts of information in a relatively short amount of time.

2. **Discussions:** Discussions are a form of active learning in which students engage in conversation with each other and the instructor. This can help students to think critically and develop communication skills.

3. **Case Studies:** Case studies are a form of problem-based learning in which students analyse real-world situations and develop solutions to problems. This can help students to develop critical thinking and problem-solving skills.

4. **Flipped Classroom:** In a flipped classroom, students are responsible for reviewing course materials before class, and class time is used for discussion, activities, and group work. This can help students to develop a deeper understanding of the material.

5. **Project-Based Learning:** In project-based learning, students work on a project over an extended period, often with a team. This can help students to develop collaboration and communication skills.

6. **Inquiry-Based Learning:** Inquiry-based learning involves students exploring a topic or question on their own, often with guidance from the instructor. This can help students to develop research and critical thinking skills.

7. **Service Learning:** Service learning involves students working on a project that benefits the community. This can help students to develop a sense of social responsibility and civic engagement.

8. **Simulations and Games:** Simulations and games can be used to simulate real-world situations and allow students to practice skills in a safe environment. This can help students to develop problem-solving skills and improve their ability to work in teams.

9. **Online Learning:** Online learning involves the use of technology to deliver course materials and facilitate communication between students and instructors. This can provide flexibility and accessibility for students but requires careful design to ensure engagement and interaction.

These are just a few examples of the many different pedagogies that can be used in higher education. The choice of pedagogy will depend on factors such as the learning goals, the subject matter, and the preferences and abilities of the instructor and students.

10.3 Cognition-Knowledge-Pedagogy Mapping Framework (CKPMF)

The biggest challenge for faculty is selecting the appropriate pedagogy based on the identified cognition and knowledge type for each lesson. As we have already discussed how to identify the ideal cognition and knowledge type, let's now focus on mapping the pedagogy against each planned topic.

Mapping the appropriate pedagogy to the identified cognition and knowledge type in the lesson plan can help faculty design a more effective and engaging lesson plan. When faculty use the appropriate pedagogy for the specific cognitive and knowledge type, it can help students learn more effectively and efficiently. By using a scientific approach to pedagogy selection, faculty can ensure that they are using evidence-based practices that have been shown to be effective for specific learning outcomes.

For example, if the identified cognition and knowledge type is "applying" and the topic is "solving mathematical problems," the appropriate pedagogy might be problem-based learning or case-based learning. This approach can help students develop critical thinking and problem-solving skills in a real-world context, rather than simply memorizing formulas.

By using a scientific approach to pedagogy selection, faculty can create a more engaging and effective learning environment for their students. This can lead to better learning outcomes, increased student engagement, and a more successful academic experience for all.

To use this approach, faculty should first identify the desired learning outcomes for each lesson or module, as well as the cognition and knowledge types required to achieve those outcomes. Next, they should consider the various pedagogical approaches available and select the one that aligns best with the identified cognition and knowledge types. This approach can help ensure that the selected pedagogy is tailored to the specific needs of the students and the learning objectives of the course.

By using an evidence-based approach to pedagogy selection, faculty can also improve student engagement and motivation. When students are engaged in the learning process and feel that the course content is relevant to their goals and interests, they are more likely to be motivated to learn and to apply what they have learned in future contexts.

Overall, using a scientific approach to pedagogy selection can help faculty to design lesson plans that are effective, engaging, and tailored to the needs of their students. This, in turn, can lead to improved learning outcomes and student success.

10.3.1   Cognition-Knowledge Type-Pedagogy Matrix

This scientific approach to pedagogy selection helps faculty to design a lesson plan that is tailored to their students' specific learning needs. By matching the appropriate pedagogy with the identified cognition and knowledge type, faculty can create engaging and interactive learning experiences that enable students to achieve the desired learning outcomes. This approach ensures that the learning experience is not only effective but also efficient, as it focuses on the use of evidence-based practices that have been shown to work. Moreover, it empowers faculty to be more intentional and purposeful in their teaching, allowing them to maximize their impact on student learning.

This section provides a clear introduction to the "Cognition-Knowledge Type-Pedagogy Matrix" and how it can be used as a helpful tool for faculty to design lesson plans that align with specific learning outcomes. It also mentions the range of pedagogies included in the matrix for each combination of cognition and knowledge type, from traditional methods such as lectures and quizzes to more interactive approaches like problem-based learning, case studies, and reflection activities.

The matrix is designed to provide a comprehensive overview of pedagogies that are best suited for specific learning outcomes. It can also help faculty to determine the appropriate pedagogy for a particular topic or learning objective by considering the combination of cognition and knowledge type. This can ensure that faculty are using evidence-based practices that have been shown to be effective in supporting student success. Additionally, the matrix can be used as a starting point for faculty to explore and experiment with different pedagogies that may be suitable for their teaching context and student population.

By using the Cognition-Knowledge Type-Pedagogy Matrix, faculty can design lesson plans that are more aligned with their intended learning outcomes. This can lead to more effective teaching and learning, as well as better documentation for accreditation purposes. Faculty can document their selection of pedagogies in their course files, showing how they have chosen specific approaches to align with specific learning outcomes. This not only demonstrates a thoughtful and evidence-based approach to teaching, but also provides documentation for accreditation and evaluation purposes. Additionally, by using the matrix, faculty can demonstrate that they are using a variety of pedagogies to address different types of learning, which is often a requirement for accreditation. Overall, the **Cognition-Knowledge Type-Pedagogy Matrix** is a valuable tool for faculty as they seek to improve their teaching practices and support student success, while also meeting accreditation requirements.

Cognition/Knowledge Type	Pedagogy
Factual/Remembering	Lecture, demonstration, drill and practice, memorization, quizzes, and tests
Factual/Understanding	Lecture with examples, problem-based learning, case studies, concept maps, mind mapping, and analogies
Factual/Applying	Problem-based learning, case studies, simulations, projects, and portfolios
Factual/Analysing	Case studies, problem-based learning, simulations, debates, and discussions
Factual/Evaluating	Debates, discussions, case studies, and problem-based learning
Factual/Creating	Projects, design challenges, and creativity exercises
Conceptual/Remembering	Drill and practice, memorization, and quizzes
Conceptual/Understanding	Lecture with examples, problem-based learning, case studies, concept maps, mind mapping, and analogies
Conceptual/Applying	Problem-based learning, case studies, simulations, projects, and portfolios
Conceptual/Analysing	Case studies, problem-based learning, simulations, debates, and discussions

Conceptual/Evaluating	Debates, discussions, case studies, and problem-based learning
Conceptual/Creating	Projects, design challenges, and creativity exercises
Procedural/Remembering	Drill and practice, memorization, and quizzes
Procedural/Understanding	Lecture with examples, problem-based learning, case studies, and simulations
Procedural/Applying	Problem-based learning, case studies, simulations, and projects
Procedural/Analysing	Case studies, problem-based learning, simulations, and discussions
Procedural/Evaluating	Debates, discussions, and case studies
Procedural/Creating	Projects and design challenges
Meta-cognition/Remembering	Reflection, journaling, and self-assessment
Meta-cognition/Understanding	Reflection, journaling, and self-assessment
Meta-cognition/Applying	Reflection, journaling, and self-assessment
Meta-cognition/Analysing	Reflection, journaling, and self-assessment
Meta-cognition/Evaluating	Reflection, journaling, and self-assessment
Meta-cognition/Creating	Reflection, journaling, and self-assessment

Table 9: Cognition-Knowledge Type-Pedagogy Matrix

10.3.2   Toolkit you can carry

Below table you can take a photograph and keep with as ready reckoner:

Cognition	Knowledge Type	Pedagogy you can use
Remembering	Factual	Lecture, demonstration, drill and practice, memorization, quizzes, tests
Understanding	Factual	Lecture with examples, problem-based learning, case studies, concept maps, mind mapping, analogies

Applying	Factual	Problem-based learning, case studies, simulations, projects, portfolios
Analysing	Factual	Case studies, problem-based learning, simulations, debates, discussions
Evaluating	Factual	Debates, discussions, case studies, problem-based learning
Creating	Factual	Projects, design challenges, creativity exercises
Remembering	Conceptual	Drill and practice, memorization, quizzes
Understanding	Conceptual	Lecture with examples, problem-based learning, case studies, concept maps, mind mapping, analogies
Applying	Conceptual	Problem-based learning, case studies, simulations, projects, portfolios
Analysing	Conceptual	Case studies, problem-based learning, simulations, debates, discussions
Evaluating	Conceptual	Debates, discussions, case studies, problem-based learning
Creating	Conceptual	Projects, design challenges, creativity exercises
Remembering	Procedural	Drill and practice, memorization, quizzes
Understanding	Procedural	Lecture with examples, problem-based learning, case studies, simulations
Applying	Procedural	Problem-based learning, case studies, simulations, projects
Analysing	Procedural	Case studies, problem-based learning, simulations, discussions
Evaluating	Procedural	Debates, discussions, case studies
Creating	Procedural	Projects, design challenges
Remembering	Meta-cognition	Reflection, journaling, self-assessment

Understanding	Meta-cognition	Reflection, journaling, self-assessment
Applying	Meta-cognition	Reflection, journaling, self-assessment
Analysing	Meta-cognition	Reflection, journaling, self-assessment
Evaluating	Meta-cognition	Reflection, journaling, self-assessment
Creating	Meta-cognition	Reflection, journaling, self-assessment

Table 10: Cognition, Knowledge Type, and respective Pedagogy you can use.

Chapter 11

Effective Assessments Implementation

Assessment is an integral part of outcome-based education as it helps measure student learning and progress towards achieving course outcomes. Direct assessment measures student learning by evaluating their performance on specific learning outcomes through tests, projects, assignments, or other forms of evaluations. Indirect assessment measures student learning through surveys, interviews, focus groups, or other forms of feedback from students or other stakeholders.

In the Indian context of higher education, the definitions of direct and indirect assessment can vary depending on the interpretation of the terms. Therefore, it is important to have a clear understanding of these terms at all levels of education. The type of assessment used in outcome-based education depends largely on the pedagogical approach adopted by the teacher.

Designing effective assessments is crucial to ensure that they align with the course outcomes and measure student learning accurately. There are various types of assessments such as formative assessment, summative assessment, criterion-referenced assessment, norm-referenced assessment, and performance-based assessment. It is important for teachers to choose the appropriate type of assessment based on the course outcomes, pedagogical approach, and the level of education.

There are various nomenclatures used in the Assessment types and Assessment Management. But we will keep it simple for the sake of effective and efficient implementation.

Let's first understand what broadly Direct and Indirect Assessments is and then we will dig deeper into different types of Assessments available with the faculty.

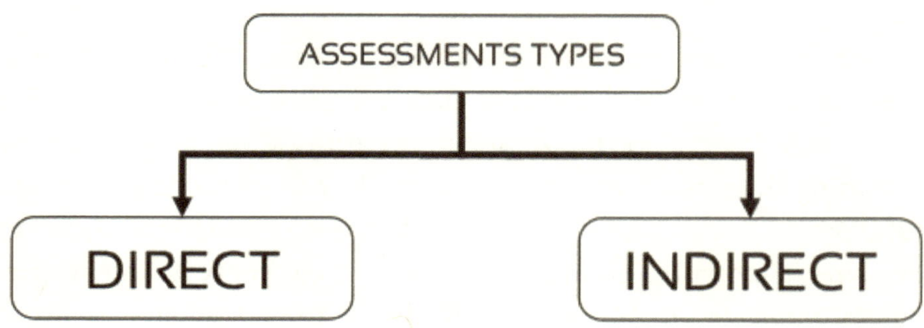

Figure 45: Assessment are of two broad types – Direct and Indirect

Direct assessment refers to the assessment of student learning outcomes that are demonstrated through actual student performance. It involves assessing student performance using various methods such as exams, quizzes, assignments, projects, and presentations. Direct assessment provides a clear measure of student achievement and is often used to measure summative outcomes, such as grades and final exams.

Indirect assessment, on the other hand, refers to the assessment of student learning outcomes through methods that are not based on actual student performance. Examples of indirect assessment methods include surveys, interviews, and focus groups. Indirect assessment provides insights into student perceptions, attitudes, and beliefs related to the learning outcomes, but it does not provide a clear measure of student achievement.

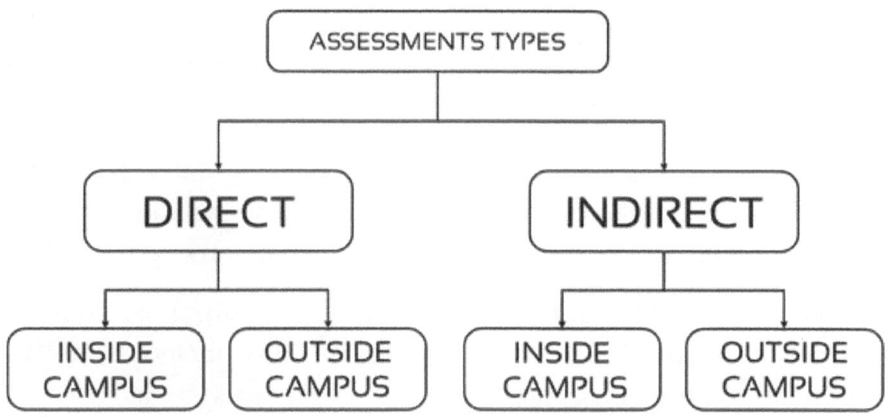

Figure 46: Assessment can be conducted either inside campus or outside Campus.

In the context of outcome-based education, both direct and indirect assessments play a crucial role in determining whether students have achieved the desired learning outcomes. It is important for faculty to use both types of assessments to get a complete picture of student learning and to make informed decisions about curriculum design and instruction.

11.1   Three-Dimensional Assessment Framework (TDAF)

The Three-Dimensional Assessment Framework (TDAF) was developed by me to simplify and clarify the assessment process for faculty. The idea for this framework came from years of experience in training faculties, teaching and developing assessments and realizing the need for a structured approach to assessment design and implementation.

The framework has been used successfully in various educational institutions to guide faculty in creating effective assessments that align with their learning outcomes and goals. By using the Three-Dimensional Assessment Framework (TDAF), faculty can ensure that their assessments are comprehensive, relevant, and meaningful for both the students and the institution.

the Three-Dimensional Assessment Framework (TDAF) is a framework that helps educators and faculty members design and implement effective assessment strategies. It is based on three dimensions: type, context, and level.

The first dimension, type, refers to the different types of assessments that can be used to evaluate student learning. These include direct and indirect assessments, as well as formative and summative assessments.

The second dimension, context, refers to the different contexts in which assessments can be conducted. This includes in-class assessments, online assessments, and real-world assessments.

The third dimension, level, refers to the different levels at which assessments can be conducted. This includes individual, group, and program level assessments. The assessment can be at the level of Course Outcomes (CO), Program Outcomes (PO), or Program Educational Objectives (PEO).

Three-Dimensional Assessment Framework (TDAF)		
The first dimension (Type)	**The second dimension (Context)**	**The third dimension (Level)**
Direct assessments	In-class assessments	Course Outcome Level
Indirect assessments	Online assessments	Program Outcome Level
Formative assessments	Real-world assessments	Program Educational Objective Level
Summative assessments		

Table 11: Three-Dimensional Assessment Framework (TDAF)

By considering these three dimensions, educators and faculty members can design and implement assessments that align with their learning outcomes and goals. The Three-Dimensional Assessment Framework (TDAF) framework can also help identify gaps in assessment strategies and ensure that they are assessing student learning effectively at all levels.

By considering these three dimensions, faculty can design and implement assessments that align with their learning outcomes and goals. This framework can also help faculty to identify gaps in their assessment strategies and ensure that they are assessing student learning effectively at all levels.

11.1.1 Second and third dimension of Three-Dimensional Assessment Framework (TDAF)

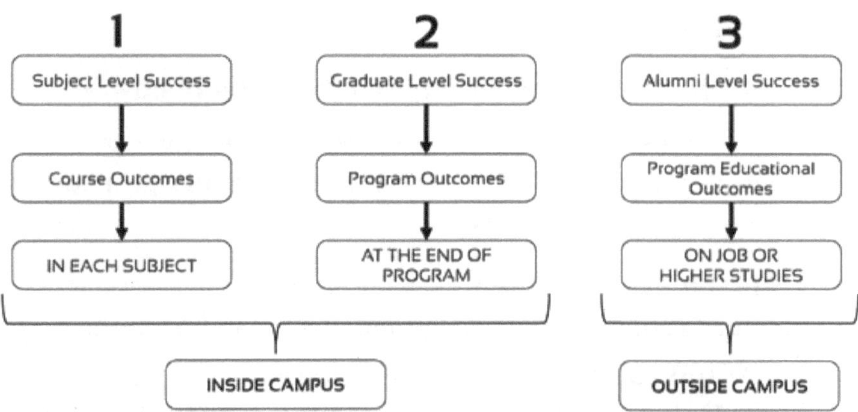

Figure 47: 3 Level / Dimensional Assessment Planning for Campus Success

As shown above in the diagram Assessment can be conducted at three levels:

1. **For Subject Level Success** – To be Conducted at Course Outcome Level and conducted Inside Campus
2. **For Graduate Level Success** – To be Conducted at Program Outcome Level and conducted Inside Campus
3. **For Alumni Level Success** – To be Conducted at Program Educational Objective Level and Conducted outside Campus

The second dimension of the Three-Dimensional Assessment Framework (TDAF) is the context in which the assessment is conducted. This can vary depending on the type of assessment being conducted and the goals of the assessment. Assessments can be conducted in-class, online, or in a real-world setting. The context can also determine the type of data that is collected and the methods that are used to collect it.

The third dimension of the Three-Dimensional Assessment Framework (TDAF) is the level at which the assessment is conducted. As mentioned earlier, assessments can be conducted at the individual, group, or program level. This dimension is closely related to the campus success statements, which can be at the course outcome level, program outcome level, or program educational objective level. It is important to consider the level at which the assessment is conducted as it can impact the type of data that is collected, the methods used to collect it, and the interpretation of the results.

11.1.2   Methods of Assessments that can be used

There are various tools and techniques that faculty can use for assessment, depending on the learning outcomes and goals of their course. Here are some examples:

1. **Tests and Exams:** These are traditional forms of assessment that measure a student's knowledge and understanding of the subject matter through written or oral questions.
2. **Projects and Assignments:** These assessments can take many forms, such as research papers, presentations, or group projects. They allow students to demonstrate their understanding and apply their knowledge to real-world situations.
3. **Portfolios:** Portfolios are collections of student work that demonstrate their progress over time. They can include a variety of assessment artifacts such as written assignments, projects, and reflections.
4. **Rubrics:** Rubrics are tools that help faculty to evaluate student work against a set of criteria or standards. They can be used for both formative and summative assessments and provide students with clear expectations for their work.
5. **Peer Reviews:** Peer reviews involve students providing feedback to each other on their work. This type of assessment helps students to develop critical thinking skills and provides them with an opportunity to learn from their peers.

6. **Course Evaluations or Course Exit Feedbacks:** Course evaluations are surveys that students complete at the end of a course to provide feedback on their learning experience. They can help faculty to understand what worked well in their course and areas for improvement.

7. **Capstone projects:** Capstone projects are typically done at the end of a program and involve a significant research or practical project that demonstrates the student's learning and abilities.

8. **Surveys and questionnaires:** Surveys and questionnaires can be used to gather feedback from students about their learning experiences. They can include questions about course content, teaching methods, and overall satisfaction.

These are just a few examples of the many tools and techniques that faculty can use for assessment. The key is to choose the right tool for the learning outcomes and goals of the course, and to use assessment results to improve teaching and learning.

11.1.3   Representing Three-Dimensional Assessment Framework (TDAF)

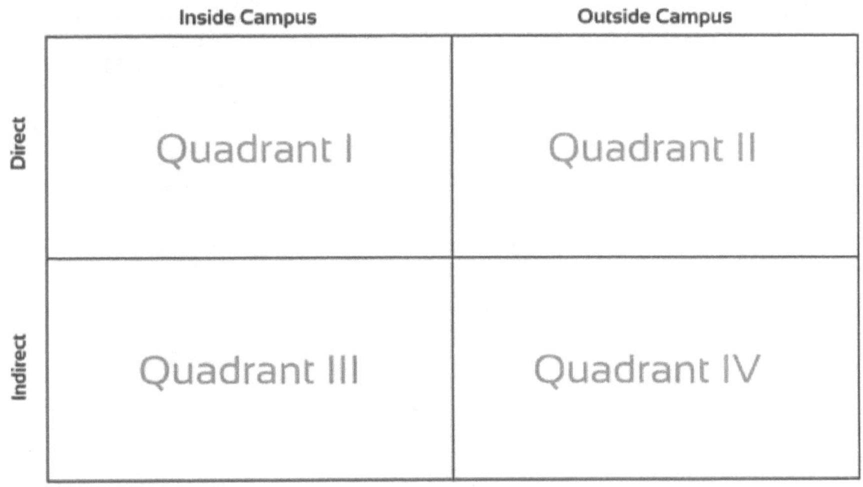

Figure 48: Representing Three-Dimensional Assessment Framework (TDAF) in four Quadrants

In this format, the X-axis represents the type of assessment, with Direct Assessment on the left and Indirect Assessment on the right. The Y-axis represents the context of assessment, with In-Class Assessment at the top and Real-World Assessment at the bottom.

Quadrant I represent Direct In-Class Assessment, such as quizzes, exams, or homework assignments that are completed in the classroom.

Quadrant II represents Indirect In-Class Assessment, such as classroom discussions or peer evaluations that are used to assess student learning.

Quadrant III represents Direct Real-World Assessment, such as capstone projects or internships that involve real-world application of knowledge and skills.

Quadrant IV represents Indirect Real-World Assessment, such as alumni surveys or employer feedback that are used to assess the effectiveness of the program in preparing students for the real world.

Here's a list of possible assessments in each quadrant and their explanations with examples:

	Inside Campus	Outside Campus
Direct	Class test (CO) Assignments (CO) Seminar /Paper Writings (CO / PO) Paper Presentation (CO / PO) Quiz (CO) Semester End Exams (CO) Rubrics (CO / PO) Demonstrations / Lab Work (CO / PO)	Placement Standard (PO) Eligibility for Higher Studies (PO) Salary Comparisons (PO) Student Admission Quality (PO)
Indirect	Course Exit Survey (CO) Program Exit Survey (PO) Facility Survey (GENERAL) Experience Survey (PO / GEN) Faculty Feedbacks (PO / GENERAL)	Alumni Survey (PEO / PO) Employers Survey (PEO / PO) Organizational Survey (MISSION) General Surveys External Entity Polls (MISSION / PEO / PO)

Figure 49: List of possible assessments in each quadrant

Quadrant I: Direct Assessment in In-Class Context

Traditional exams: This includes tests and exams that are administered in a classroom setting and assess the knowledge and skills of students in a particular subject area. For example, a midterm exam in a biology class.

Performance tasks: These assessments require students to demonstrate their learning by completing a task or project. For example, a presentation on a historical event in a history class.

Observations: This type of assessment involves observing a student's behaviour or performance in a specific situation. For example, observing a student's behaviour during a group activity in a communication skills class.

Portfolios: These assessments involve a collection of a student's work overtime. For example, a writing portfolio that contains samples of a student's written work from throughout the semester.

Quadrant II: Indirect Assessment in In-Class Context

Surveys: This type of assessment involves collecting feedback from students on their learning experience. For example, a survey on the effectiveness of a teaching method in a psychology class.

Self-reflection: This involves students reflecting on their own learning and assessing their progress. For example, a written reflection on a student's learning goals and progress in a writing class.

Quadrant III: Direct Assessment in Real-World Context

Capstone projects: These assessments involve students applying their knowledge and skills to a real-world project. For example, a marketing campaign for a local business in a marketing class.

Internships: This type of assessment involves students completing an internship and applying their learning to a real-world situation. For example, an internship in a law office in a pre-law program.

Quadrant IV: Indirect Assessment in Real-World Context

Alumni surveys: This type of assessment involves collecting feedback from alumni on their learning experience and how it has helped them in their careers. For example, a survey on how a business program has prepared alumni for their current job roles.

Employer feedback: This involves collecting feedback from employers on the skills and knowledge of graduates from a particular program. For example, feedback from employers on the effectiveness of a computer science program in preparing graduates for industry roles.

11.2 Cognition-Knowledge Type-Pedagogy-Assessment Matrix

The **Cognition-Knowledge Type-Pedagogy-Assessment Matrix** is a comprehensive framework that provides guidance to educators in designing effective lesson plans and assessments. The matrix is designed to help faculty match the appropriate pedagogy and assessment to the specific combination of cognition and knowledge type required for a given topic. It is a valuable tool for faculty who seek to align their teaching strategies with their learning outcomes and support student success.

The matrix presents a table that outlines the different pedagogies that are best suited for specific combinations of cognition and knowledge types, ranging from factual/remembering to meta-cognition/creating. The pedagogies listed in the table include lectures, demonstrations, problem-based learning, case studies, and reflection activities, among others.

In addition to pedagogies, the matrix also includes a column for assessment types that are appropriate for each combination of cognition and knowledge type. These assessment types can include quizzes, tests, projects, portfolios, and self-assessment, among others.

Using the matrix, faculty can select appropriate pedagogies and assessments that are evidence-based and effective for specific learning outcomes. By doing so, they can design lesson plans that are engaging and effective for their students. This can also help faculty to document their teaching strategies and student learning outcomes more scientifically and convincingly for any accreditations.

Cognition	Knowledge Type	Pedagogy	Assessment Types
Remembering	Factual	Lecture, demonstration, drill and practice, memorization, quizzes, tests	Written exams, multiple choice questions, short answer questions
Understanding	Factual	Lecture with examples, problem-based learning, case studies, concept maps, mind mapping, analogies	Case studies, essays, research papers, concept maps
Applyin g	Factual	Problem-based learning, case studies, simulations, projects, portfolios	Group projects, simulations, case studies, portfolios
Analysing	Factual	Case studies, problem-based learning, simulations, debates, discussions	Analytical essays, research papers, group debates and discussions
Evaluating	Factual	Debates, discussions, case studies, problem-based learning	Essays, research papers, presentations
Creating	Factual	Projects, design challenges, creativity exercises	Creative projects, design prototypes, artistic works
Remembering	Conceptual	Drill and practice, memorization, quizzes	Written exams, multiple choice questions, short answer questions

Understanding	Conceptual	Lecture with examples, problem-based learning, case studies, concept maps, mind mapping, analogies	Essays, research papers, concept maps
Applying	Conceptual	Problem-based learning, case studies, simulations, projects, portfolios	Group projects, simulations, case studies, portfolios
Analysing	Conceptual	Case studies, problem-based learning, simulations, debates, discussions	Analytical essays, research papers, group debates and discussions
Evaluating	Conceptual	Debates, discussions, case studies, problem-based learning	Essays, research papers, presentations
Creating	Conceptual	Projects, design challenges, creativity exercises	Creative projects, design prototypes, artistic works
Remembering	Procedural	Drill and practice, memorization, quizzes	Written exams, multiple choice questions, short answer questions
Understanding	Procedural	Lecture with examples, problem-based learning, case studies, simulations	Skill tests, lab exams, simulations
Applying	Procedural	Problem-based learning, case studies, simulations, projects	Lab reports, group projects, simulations
Analysing	Procedural	Case studies, problem-based learning, simulations, discussions	Analytical essays, research papers, group debates and discussions
Evaluating	Procedural	Debates, discussions, case studies	Essays, research papers, presentations

Creating	Procedural	Projects, design challenges	Creative projects, design prototypes
Remembering	Meta-cognition	Reflection, journaling, self-assessment	Self-assessment, reflective writing
Understanding	Meta-cognition	Reflection, journaling, self-assessment	Self-assessment, reflective writing
Applying	Meta-cognition	Reflection, journaling, self-assessment	Self-assessment, reflective writing
Analysing	Meta-cognition	Reflection, journaling, self-assessment	Self-assessment, reflective writing
Evaluating	Meta-cognition	Reflection, journaling, self-assessment	Self-assessment, reflective writing
Creating	Meta-cognition	Reflection, journaling, self-assessment	Self-assessment, reflective writing

Table 12: Cognition-Knowledge Type-Pedagogy-Assessment Matrix

In conclusion, the **Cognition-Knowledge Type-Pedagogy-Assessment Matrix** provides a valuable resource for faculty in designing effective lesson plans and assessments that align with their learning outcomes. By using evidence-based pedagogical practices that are tailored to specific combinations of cognition and knowledge type, faculty can create a more engaging and impactful learning experience for their students. Additionally, by documenting their use of these pedagogies and assessments in their course files, faculty can provide compelling evidence of their teaching effectiveness for accreditation and other purposes. Ultimately, the use of this matrix can help faculty to better support student success and foster a culture of continuous improvement in higher education.

11.3   Creating Assessment Rubrics

Assessment rubrics are a valuable tool for faculty to use when evaluating student work. Rubrics provide a clear set of criteria for evaluating student performance and ensure that faculty are grading assignments consistently and fairly. Rubrics can be used for a wide range of assessments, including essays, presentations, projects, and even class participation.

To create an effective assessment rubric, follow these steps:

Determine the learning outcomes: Identify the specific learning outcomes that the assignment is designed to assess. These outcomes should be measurable and aligned with the course objectives. This are already identified when you define the course outcome and design your lesson plan as per

Define the criteria: Determine the criteria that will be used to evaluate student performance. These criteria should be based on the learning outcomes and should be specific, observable, and measurable.

Determine the levels of performance: Define the levels of performance that will be used to evaluate student work. These levels should be clearly defined and should provide a range of performance from excellent to poor.

Create the rubric: Create a rubric that clearly outlines the criteria and levels of performance. The rubric should be easy to read and understand and should be provided to students before the assignment is due.

Evaluate the rubric: Test the rubric by using it to evaluate a sample of student work. Revise the rubric as needed to ensure that it is effective and accurately measures student performance.

Overall, creating an assessment rubric is an important step in ensuring that faculty are evaluating student work consistently and fairly. By following these steps, faculty can create effective rubrics that help to improve student learning and achievement.

11.3.1 Why assessment rubrics are important in Outcome Based Education

Assessment rubrics are important in Outcome Based Education (OBE) because they provide a clear and transparent way of evaluating student learning outcomes. Rubrics outline the criteria and performance levels that are expected of students for each learning outcome, making it easier for faculty to assess and provide feedback on student work. Rubrics also help students understand what is expected of them and provide them with a roadmap for achieving success in their coursework. By using rubrics, faculty can ensure that their assessments are aligned with the learning outcomes of the course and that they are providing students with meaningful feedback on their progress towards achieving those outcomes. Additionally, rubrics can help ensure that the assessment process is fair and consistent, as they provide clear guidelines for evaluating student work. Overall, assessment rubrics are an essential tool for faculty in implementing OBE and ensuring that students are meeting the expected learning outcomes.

Examples of rubrics for different types of assessments

here are some examples of rubrics for different types of assessments:

Essay writing rubric:

Thesis statement: Clearly states the topic and main argument.

Organization: Well-structured and easy to follow

Evidence: Relevant and supports the argument

Analysis: Demonstrates a deep understanding of the topic

Conclusion: Summarizes key points and provides a clear ending

Mechanics: Free of grammatical, spelling, or punctuation errors

Oral presentation rubric:

Organization: Clear introduction, body, and conclusion

Content: Covers all important points and demonstrates knowledge of the topic

Delivery: Confident, clear, and easy to understand

Visual aids: Effective and relevant to the topic

Time management: Stays within allotted time.

Audience engagement: Maintains audience interest and interacts with them.

Group project rubric:

Organization: Clearly defined roles and responsibilities

Collaboration: Demonstrates effective communication and teamwork

Content: Demonstrates a deep understanding of the topic and covers all important points

Creativity: Offers unique and creative ideas

Quality of work: Shows a high level of effort and attention to detail.

Presentation: Clear, organized, and easy to follow

Lab report rubric:

Introduction: Clearly states the purpose and background information

Hypothesis: Clearly states the hypothesis and how it will be tested

Methodology: Describes the experimental design and procedures

Results: Presents data and observations clearly and accurately

Analysis: Demonstrates a clear understanding of the results and draws appropriate conclusions

Discussion: Analyses the results and relates them back to the hypothesis

Conclusion: Summarizes the key findings and implications

Mechanics: Free of grammatical, spelling, or punctuation errors

These are just a few examples, but rubrics can be created for any type of assessment to ensure consistency and fairness in grading.

11.4 Mapping Questions to Course Outcomes in Formative Assessments

When faculty members conduct formative assessments such as class tests, assignments, or quizzes, it is important to ensure that these assessments align with the course outcomes. This can help faculty members to assess student learning effectively and provide students with clear feedback on their progress towards achieving the learning outcomes.

To map questions to course outcomes, faculty members can follow a few steps. First, they need to identify the course outcomes that will be assessed in the formative assessment. This can be done by reviewing the course syllabus and identifying the relevant outcomes that align with the assessment.

Next, faculty members can develop questions or tasks that assess the identified course outcomes. These questions should be designed to test student understanding and application of the course content related to the learning outcomes. It is important to ensure that the questions are clear, concise, and well-structured to help students understand what is being asked of them.

Finally, faculty members can map each question or task to the relevant course outcome. This can be done by clearly indicating which outcome(s) the question is assessing. By doing this, faculty members can ensure that the formative assessment is aligned with the course outcomes and is an effective tool for assessing student learning.

In conclusion, mapping questions to course outcomes can help faculty members to design effective formative assessments that assess student learning and provide clear feedback to students. By following the steps outlined above, faculty members can ensure that their formative assessments are aligned with the course outcomes and are a valuable tool for promoting student success.

To design effective assessments that align with pedagogical approaches and cognition/knowledge types, faculty should consider the following steps:

1. Identify the pedagogical approach and the corresponding cognition/knowledge type that will be addressed in the assessment.
2. Determine the learning outcome(s) that the assessment will measure.
3. Draft potential questions that align with the identified pedagogy and cognition/knowledge type.
4. Evaluate the potential questions to ensure that they are aligned with the learning outcome(s) and appropriate for the identified pedagogy and cognition/knowledge type.
5. Revise and refine the questions as needed.
6. Map the questions to the relevant course outcome(s) to ensure that they are measuring the desired learning outcomes.

By following these steps, faculty can ensure that their assessments are aligned with their pedagogical approaches and cognition/knowledge types and effectively measure the desired learning outcomes.

After identifying the appropriate pedagogy and cognition/knowledge type, faculty can draft potential questions that align with the chosen pedagogy and intended learning outcomes. The questions should be designed to assess the specific knowledge or skill that the pedagogy targets. For example, if the chosen pedagogy is problem-based learning and the intended learning outcome is for students to apply factual knowledge, the questions should focus on real-world scenarios that require the application of factual knowledge.

Faculty can also consider using Bloom's Taxonomy to guide their question development. Bloom's Taxonomy provides a framework for categorizing learning objectives and developing questions that align with different levels of cognitive complexity. This can help faculty to ensure that they are designing questions that accurately assess the course outcome and target the appropriate level of cognitive complexity.

Overall, by drafting potential questions that align with the identified pedagogy and cognition/knowledge type, faculty can ensure that their assessments are closely tied to their course outcome and are effective at measuring student progress.

Bloom's Taxonomy is a framework that can be used to design questions that align with the desired level of cognition and knowledge. The framework consists of six levels, starting with lower-order thinking skills like remembering and understanding, and moving up to higher-order thinking skills like applying, analysing, evaluating, and creating.

By using Bloom's Taxonomy, faculty can ensure that their questions are appropriately aligned with the course outcomes and the level of cognitive complexity expected from students. For example, if the desired course outcome is for students to be able to apply their knowledge, then the questions should be designed to require students to apply their knowledge to real-world scenarios or problems.

In addition to using Bloom's Taxonomy, faculty can also consider the types of questions they ask, such as multiple-choice, short-answer, or essay questions, as well as the level of difficulty of the questions. By designing questions that align with the pedagogy and cognition/ knowledge type, faculty can provide students with meaningful and effective formative assessments that support their learning and progress towards course outcomes.

11.4.1 Cognitive-Pedagogical Framework for Designing Formative Assessment Questions

Cognitive-Pedagogical Framework table presents a comprehensive framework for designing effective formative assessments that align with the desired learning outcomes of a course. The framework is based on three key dimensions: cognition/knowledge type, pedagogy, and question type. By considering these dimensions together, faculty can ensure that their assessments are aligned with the specific learning objectives of their course, and that they use evidence-based teaching strategies that have been shown to be effective for different types of learning outcomes. This resource can be a valuable tool for faculty as they seek to design and implement effective formative assessments that support student success. This table, titled "Framework for Aligning Questions with Pedagogy, Cognition, and Knowledge Type," provides a useful tool for faculty to design effective questions for formative assessments. By considering the pedagogy being used, the type of cognition and knowledge being assessed, and the corresponding question types, faculty can ensure that their assessments align with course outcomes and support student learning.

The table includes a range of question types that align with each combination of pedagogy, cognition, and knowledge type. For example, if a faculty member is using problem-based learning to assess students' understanding of conceptual knowledge, they might consider using open-ended questions that require students to apply their understanding in a real-world scenario. Similarly, if a faculty member is using memorization drills to assess factual knowledge, they might consider using multiple-choice or fill-in-the-blank questions.

Overall, this framework serves as a valuable tool for faculty to create assessments that are aligned with their teaching strategies and support student success.

Pedagogy	Cognition	Knowledge Type	Question Type
Lecture	Remembering	Factual	Recall, recognition, multiple-choice, fill-in-the-blank, matching
Lecture	Understanding	Factual	Concept explanation, examples, case studies, analogies
Problem-Based Learning	Applying	Factual	Problem-solving, simulations, case studies, projects, portfolios

Case Studies	Analysing	Factual	Analysing situations, evaluating evidence, comparing perspectives
Debate	Evaluating	Factual	Evaluating perspectives, defending a position, analysing data
Design Challenge	Creating	Factual	Generating novel ideas, prototyping, testing, evaluating
Lecture	Remembering	Conceptual	Definition, identification, matching, short answer, true/false
Lecture	Understanding	Conceptual	Examples, elaboration, interpretation, summarization, comparison
Problem-Based Learning	Applying	Conceptual	Applied problem-solving, case studies, examples
Case Studies	Analysing	Conceptual	Analysing relationships, patterns, themes, structure
Debate	Evaluating	Conceptual	Critiquing, evaluating, defending positions, analysing alternatives
Design Challenge	Creating	Conceptual	Designing, creating, prototyping, evaluating
Lecture	Remembering	Procedural	Steps, procedures, rules, definitions, key terms
Lecture	Understanding	Procedural	Examples, case studies, concept mapping, mind mapping, analogies
Problem-Based Learning	Applying	Procedural	Applied problem-solving, simulations, case studies, projects
Case Studies	Analysing	Procedural	Analysing process, steps, procedures, decision-making

Debate	Evaluating	Procedural	Evaluating process, procedures, decision-making
Design Challenge	Creating	Procedural	Creating, prototyping, testing, refining
Reflection	Remembering	Meta-cognition	Recall, self-reflection, journaling, self-assessment
Reflection	Understanding	Meta-cognition	Analysis, evaluation, self-reflection, journaling, self-assessment
Reflection	Applying	Meta-cognition	Synthesis, self-assessment, goal setting, planning
Reflection	Analysing	Meta-cognition	Self-reflection, self-evaluation, analysis of thinking processes
Reflection	Evaluating	Meta-cognition	Self-evaluation, goal setting, planning
Reflection	Creating	Meta-cognition	Planning, goal setting, creating action plans, self-assessment

Table 13: Cognition-Knowledge Type-Pedagogy-Assessment Matrix and Question Type

Note: This table is a framework and not exhaustive. The types of questions listed are examples and not comprehensive.

11.4.2 Mapping Questions to Course Outcomes

As a faculty, it is important to help faculty understand the importance of mapping questions to course outcomes (COs). This process helps to make COs quantifiable at the course level or even the student level and provides a clear understanding of what knowledge and skills students are expected to gain from the course.

By mapping questions to COs, faculty can ensure that they are assessing the learning outcomes they intended to teach, and that the assessment is aligned with the course objectives. This approach also helps in creating meaningful assessments that evaluate higher-order thinking skills and facilitate deeper learning, rather than just memorization of facts.

To map questions to COs, faculty should follow a few guidelines. First, they should identify the specific COs that each assessment question is targeting. This can be achieved by breaking down each CO into its specific components and aligning each question to those components.

It is important to note that the cognitive level of the CO need not be the same as the cognitive level of the questions. Questions should cover different levels of cognition, from lower-order to higher-order thinking skills, and cover different aspects of the CO. This can be achieved by using Bloom's Taxonomy or other frameworks that categorize cognitive skills.

Once the questions have been mapped to the COs, faculty can evaluate the effectiveness of their teaching and assessment strategies by analysing student performance on each CO. This information can be used to identify areas where students are struggling and adjust teaching methods accordingly.

Overall, mapping questions to COs is a powerful tool for faculty to ensure that their assessments are aligned with the course outcome of the course, and to facilitate deeper and more meaningful learning among students.

Some steps to map questions to course outcomes:

1. **Identify the course outcomes:** Before mapping questions to course outcomes, you need to clearly identify the course outcomes. These should be specific and measurable statements that describe what students should be able to do after completing the course.

2. **Determine the appropriate cognitive level:** Once you have identified the course outcomes, you need to determine the appropriate cognitive level for each outcome. This will help you to identify the types of questions that will best assess the outcome.

3. **Choose assessment methods:** Based on the cognitive level of each outcome, you need to choose appropriate assessment methods. For example, if the outcome requires students to apply their knowledge, you might choose to use case studies or projects to assess their understanding.

4. **Create questions:** After choosing assessment methods, you can start to create questions that align with each course outcome. Be sure to include a variety of question types, such as multiple choice, short answer, and essay questions.

5. **Align questions with outcomes:** Once you have created questions, you need to align them with the appropriate course outcome or cognition of Topic in the Lesson plan as per we discussed in Modular Outcome based Framework (MOBF). This will help you to ensure that each outcome is being adequately assessed.

6. **Review and revise:** After mapping questions to course outcomes, it is important to review and revise the questions as necessary. This will help you to ensure that the questions accurately assess the intended course outcomes.

By following these steps, you can effectively map questions to course outcomes, which can help you to create a more effective and meaningful assessment strategy.

Once the faculty has identified the cognition level of a topic in the lesson plan using the Modular Outcome Based Framework, they can determine the appropriate cognition level for the questions by considering the course outcomes (CO) associated with that topic. The COs define what students are expected to know and be able to do upon completion of the course.

The faculty should review each CO and determine the appropriate cognitive level for the associated questions. This process helps to ensure that the questions are aligned with the course outcome and that the assessment accurately measures student achievement.

In some cases, the faculty may need to adjust the cognitive level of the questions to ensure that they are appropriately challenging for the students. For example, if the CO specifies that students should be able to apply the knowledge, the questions should be designed to require application rather than just recall of information.

To map questions to course outcomes, the faculty can follow these steps:

1. Review the course outcomes associated with the topic.
2. Determine the appropriate cognitive level for the questions based on the course outcomes.
3. Draft potential questions that align with the identified cognitive level and the pedagogy used
4. Review and refine the questions to ensure they are appropriately challenging and aligned with the intended learning outcomes.
5. Assign **point values*** to each question based on the level of cognitive demand and the importance of the associated course outcome.

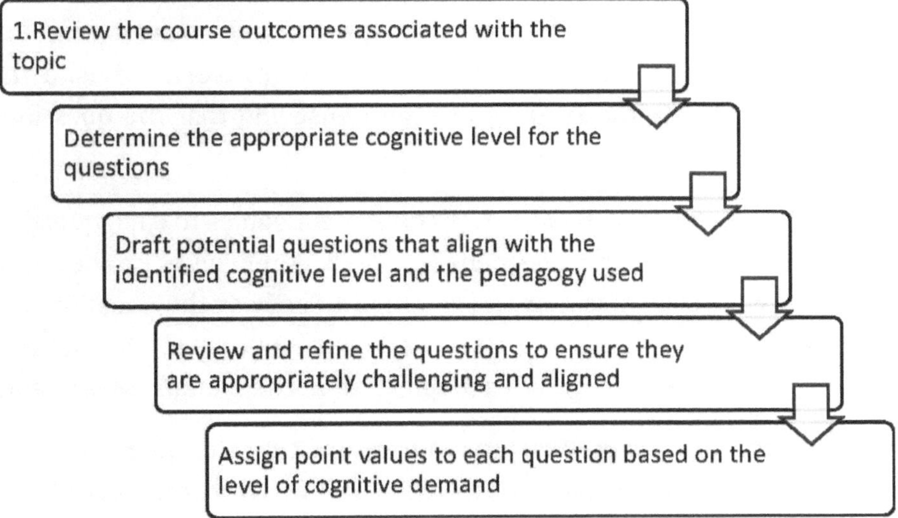

Figure 50: Mapping Questions to Course Outcomes: Steps for Faculty

When mapping questions to course outcomes, faculty can follow a series of steps to ensure alignment between the questions and the intended learning outcomes of the course.

Step 1: Review Course Outcomes – Faculty should review the course outcomes associated with the specific topic or lesson for which questions are being developed. This provides a clear understanding of the knowledge, skills, or competencies that students are expected to acquire.

Step 2: Determine Cognitive Level – Based on the course outcomes, faculty need to determine the appropriate cognitive level for the questions. This could range from simple recall or understanding to higher-order thinking skills such as application, analysis, evaluation, or creation.

Step 3: Draft Questions – Faculty can then draft potential questions that align with the identified cognitive level and the pedagogical approach used in the course. The questions should assess students' understanding and application of the course content and skills.

Step 4: Review and Refine – Faculty should review and refine the drafted questions to ensure they are appropriately challenging and aligned with the intended learning outcomes. This involves revising the wording, clarifying the instructions, and ensuring that the questions effectively assess the desired knowledge or skills.

Step 5: Assign Point Values* – Assigning point values to each question is an important step for assessment purposes. Point values can be based on the level of cognitive demand required to answer the question and the relative importance of the associated course outcome. This helps in determining the weightage of each question in the overall assessment.

By following these steps, faculty can ensure that the questions they develop align with the course outcomes and effectively assess students' mastery of the intended learning outcomes. This supports the alignment between teaching, assessment, and the achievement of the course goals.

By mapping questions to course outcomes, the faculty can ensure that the assessment is aligned with the course outcome and accurately measures student achievement. This approach can also help to identify areas where students may be struggling and inform future instructional decisions.

***Point Values**

- L1 – Remembering
- L2 – Understanding
- L3 – Applying
- L4 – Analysing
- L5 – Evaluating
- L6 – Creating

Designing and Quantifying Effective Outcome-Based Assessments for Campus Success

In the previous section, we explored how to create effective PEOs, POs, COs, and assignments using the Campus Success Statement Framework (CSSF), Modular Outcome-Based Framework (MOBF), and Three-Dimensional Assessment Framework(TDAF). In this section, we will discuss how to quantify these statements and measure our campus success. This is like having a rocket system, but now we need to fuel it to reach our desired destination – the implementation and quantifiability of Outcome-Based Education. To achieve this, we will use a simple framework to design the quantifiability of assessments and, in turn, all our campus success statements.

As we have seen in the Three-Dimensional Assessment Framework, there are three dimensions to assessment design:

1. **Type** – what type of assessment to use based on cognition and knowledge type.
2. **Context** – where or in what scenario the assessment needs to be used.
3. **Level** – at which level the assessments are to be created.

Evaluation of outcome-based education (OBE) is crucial to ensure that it is effective in achieving its intended goals. Here are the steps evaluate OBE:

1. **Alignment:** One of the primary ways to evaluate OBE is to check whether the curriculum, teaching, and assessment are aligned with the course outcome (COs). This can be done by reviewing the course materials and assessing whether they align with the COs. This we have already done in previous sections.

2. **Assessment:** Assessment is an integral part of OBE, and evaluating the quality of assessment is critical to the success of OBE. Evaluating the quality of assessment involves assessing whether the assessment tools and rubrics align with the COs and whether they accurately assess the students' learning. This we have already done in previous sections.

3. **Feedback:** Another way to evaluate OBE is to assess the quality and effectiveness of feedback given to students. Feedback should be aligned with the COs and should help students improve their learning.

4. **Student achievement:** Measuring student achievement is a keyway to evaluate the effectiveness of OBE. This can be done by assessing student performance on assessments, measuring retention rates, and evaluating graduation rates.

5. **Stakeholder feedback:** Gathering feedback from stakeholders such as students, faculty, and employers can also be valuable in evaluating the effectiveness of OBE. This feedback can be used to make improvements and ensure that OBE is meeting the needs of all stakeholders.

Overall, evaluating OBE is important to ensure that it is effective in achieving its intended goals and improving student learning outcomes. By focusing on alignment, assessment, feedback, student achievement, and stakeholder feedback, institutions can evaluate the effectiveness of their OBE programs and make improvements as needed.

In this section we will go next level and empower this assessment to make it quantitative. First Let's understand how to make our CO quantifiable.

12.1 Understanding Key Terms in the Computation of Attainment in Outcome-Based Education

Before we dive into how to compute attainment, it's important to understand some key terms that are used in the process:

1. **Correlation Level:** Correlation Level is a measurement tool that is used to map the CO to the PO and understand the extent to which the CO aligns with the PO. The Correlation level can be mapped at four levels:

   - 0: No Correlation, meaning the CO cannot contribute to the respective PO.
   - 1: Low Correlation, meaning the CO is related to or can contribute to the respective PO, but can only contribute around 20% – 50% of the PO statement.
   - 2: Medium Correlation, meaning the CO is related to or can contribute to the respective PO, but can only contribute around 50% – 65% of the PO statement.
   - 3: High Correlation, meaning the CO is related to or can contribute to the respective PO, and can contribute around 65% – 100% of the PO statement.

2. **Attainment Level:** Attainment Level is a measurement tool that is used to understand the level of attainment for campus success statements. Attainment levels are measured using four values:

   - 0: No Attainment or Zero Attainment.
   - 1: Attainment at Level 1 (Low Attainment).
   - 2: Attainment at Level 2 (Medium Attainment).
   - 3: Attainment at Level 3 (High Attainment).

3. **Attainment Slab:** Attainment Slab is a measurement tool that is used to understand at what level the class has performed in a particular Level (CO, PO, PEO) of Context based on Class performance. Attainment Slab levels are measured using four values:

   - 0: No Attainment or Zero Attainment.
   - 1: Attainment at Level 1 (Low Attainment).
   - 2: Attainment at Level 2 (Medium Attainment).
   - 3: Attainment at Level 3 (High Attainment).

4. **Attainment Target:** Attainment Target is a target that is set by faculty based on various factors such as Class Intelligence, past performance of the subject, etc. The attainment target is based on the Attainment Slab for the respective academic year. Attainment Target levels are measured using four values:

   - 0: No Attainment or Zero Attainment.
   - 1: Attainment at Level 1 (Low Attainment).
   - 2: Attainment at Level 2 (Medium Attainment).
   - 3: Attainment at Level 3 (High Attainment).

Understanding these terms is crucial for computing attainment, which we will explore in the next section.

12.2 Steps to Compute Attainment at CO Level in Outcome-Based Education

The computation of attainment is a crucial aspect of Outcome-Based Education (OBE) that allows educators to measure the extent to which students are achieving the desired learning outcomes. To compute attainment, it's important to first understand some key terms and concepts.

One important concept is the Correlation Level, which is used to measure the alignment between Course Outcomes (COs) and Program Outcomes (POs). Correlation levels can range from 0 to 3, with 0 indicating no correlation and 3 indicating high correlation. A CO with a high correlation level is one that can contribute to 65% to 100% of a given PO statement, while a CO with low correlation can only contribute around 20% to 50%.

Another important concept is Attainment Level, which is used to measure the level of attainment for campus success statements. Attainment levels can also range from 0 to 3, with 0 indicating no attainment and 3 indicating high attainment. It's important to note that attainment levels can be measured at different levels, such as CO, PO, or Program Educational Objective (PEO).

To compute attainment at the CO level, there are several steps to follow. The first step is to map the CO to questions or criteria of the rubrics, using the Three-Dimensional Assessment Framework (TDAF). Next, it's important to define the Attainment Slab, which is used to determine the level of attainment based on class performance. The Attainment Slab also ranges from 0 to 3, with 0 indicating zero attainment and 3 indicating high attainment.

Once the Attainment Slab has been defined, the next step is to plan and conduct assessments based on the Cognition-Knowledge-Pedagogy Mapping Framework (CKPMF). These assessments should be conducted according to the exam policy of the institute or department. After conducting the assessments, the answers should be evaluated by faculty members using an answer key.

Once the assessments have been evaluated, the next step is to enter the marks at the question or criteria level. Finally, the attainment can be computed based on the Student Average Attainment method. This method involves calculating the average attainment level for each CO, and then calculating the average attainment level for all COs. This gives an overall attainment level for the subject at the CO level.

By following these steps, educators can effectively compute attainment and measure the success of their OBE implementation.

Summary below of the Steps as per Discussed above:

1. Map the Course Outcomes (COs) to questions or rubrics criteria as per the Three-Dimensional Assessment Framework (TDAF).

2. Define the Attainment Slab based on the expected level of attainment for the COs.

3. Plan and design the assessments as per the Cognition-Knowledge-Pedagogy Mapping Framework (CKPMF).

4. Conduct the assessments following the exam policy of the institute or department.

5. Evaluate the assessments according to the answer key provided by the faculty.

6. Enter the marks obtained by students at the question or rubric criteria level.

7. Calculate the Attainment Level using the Student Average Attainment Method.

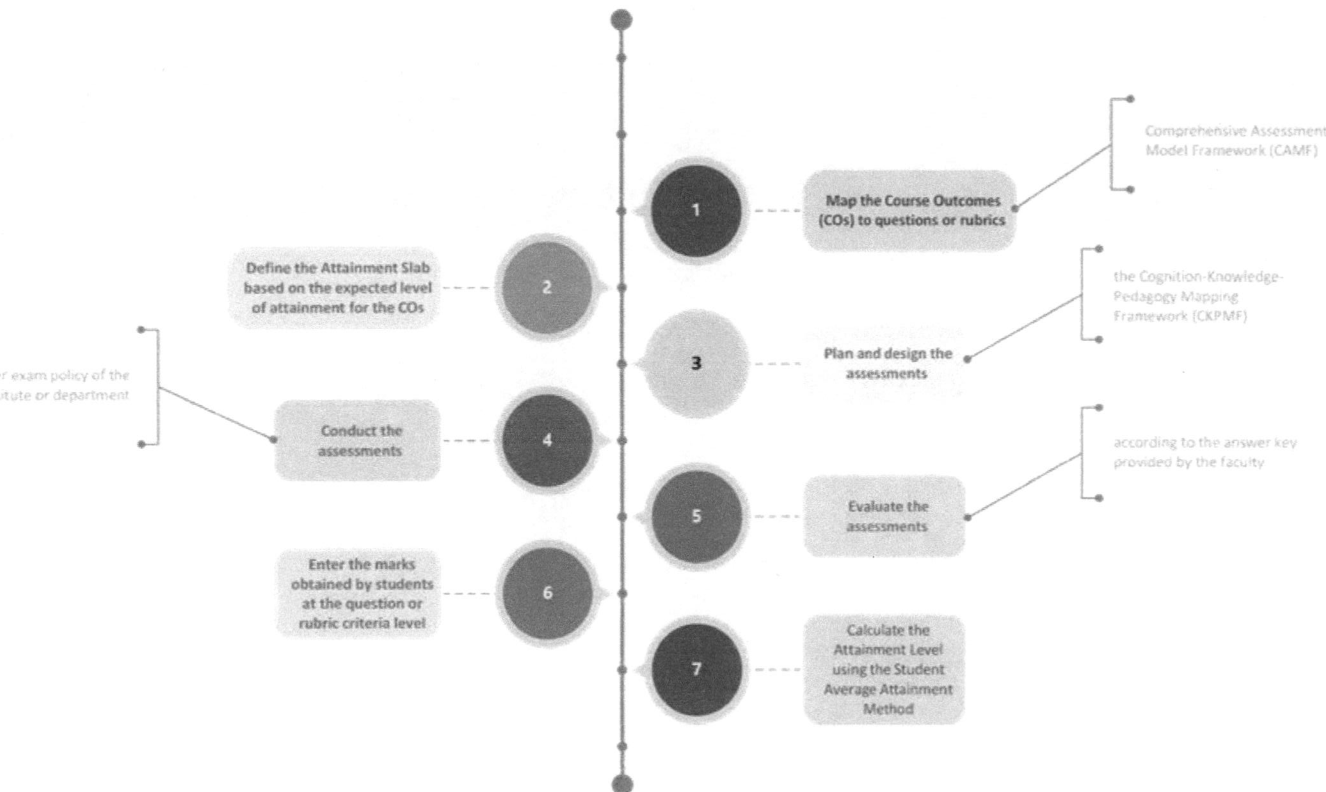

Figure 51: Steps to Compute Attainment at CO Level in Outcome-Based Education

Chapter 13

Steps for Computation of Attainment for CO and PO

These are the steps to design an effective Course File. By following these steps, faculty members can ensure that they have all the necessary information to effectively teach their courses and assess student learning outcomes. The first step is to define the course outcomes based on Revised Bloom's Taxonomy, giving them a unique course outcome code. Next, map the course outcomes to program outcomes and plan lessons and assessments accordingly. It is also important to define the attainment slab based on the target set for the course, and to map course outcomes to assessments either directly or indirectly through rubrics. Finally, enter the marks at the question level, compute the class averages, compare them to the attainment slab and target, and justify any deviations from the target. To further aid in understanding these steps, we will provide a practical example later in this book.

1. Define the Bright Students and Average Students as per the syllabus, past performance of the students and other factors.
2. Define the Course Outcomes as per Revised Bloom's Taxonomy. Name the course outcome code as per the Course Code.

Course Outcome Code	Course Outcome Statement	Cognition Level
COURSECODE.1		
COURSECODE.2		
COURSECODE.3		
COURSECODE.4		
COURSECODE.5		

Table 14: Define the Course Outcomes as per Revised Bloom's Taxonomy

3. Map the Course Outcomes to Program Outcome either no Correlation, Low Correlation, Medium Correlation or High Correlation.

Course Outcome Code	PO1	PO2	PO3	PO4	PO5	PO6	PO7	PO8	PO9	PO10	PO11	PO12
COURSECODE.1												
COURSECODE.2												
COURSECODE.3												
COURSECODE.4												
COURSECODE.5												
COURSECODE AVG												

Table 15: Map the Course Outcomes to Program Outcome

4. Plan the Lesson as per Syllabus.

Sr No	Planned Date	Topic Planned	Teaching Method	No of Hrs.	Cognition Level	Course Outcome

Table 16: Lesson Plan

5. Plan the Assessment for the whole Term of the course and as per Syllabus.

Sr No	Assessment	Assessment Type (Assignment/ Class Test / University)	Course Outcome Addressed	Maximum Marks	Assessment Method (DIRECT / INDIRECT)

Table 17: Assessment Plan

6. Define the Attainment Slab as per the Target to be set.

Method 1

Target	Attainment Level
If YY% of Student achieves XX% of Class Average	1
If YY% of Student achieves XX% of Class Average	2
If YY% of Student achieves XX% of Class Average	3

Table 18: Attainment Slab

7. Set the target for the Current Batch or Academic Year.

Course Outcome Code	Target	Justification
COURSECODE.1	2	
COURSECODE.2	1	
COURSECODE.3	3	
COURSECODE.4	2	
COURSECODE.5	1	
COURSECODE AVG	**1.8**	

Table 19: Set target for Course Outcome (CO)

8. **Map the Course outcomes to Assessments.**

8.1 DIRECT – Map questions to Course Outcomes.

Q No.	Question	Marks	Mapped CO
1	Question Statement	XX	CO1, CO2, ...
2	Question Statement	XX	CO1, CO2, ...
3	Question Statement	XX	CO1, CO2, ...
4	Question Statement	XX	CO1, CO2, ...
5	Question Statement	XX	CO1, CO2, ...

Table 20: Map Questions to applicable Course Outcomes (CO)

8.2 INDIRECT – Map the Rubrics to Course Outcomes/ Program Outcomes.

Sr No	Criteria	CO Mapped	Rating Scale	Rating Scale	Rating Scale

Table 21: Map the Rubrics to Course Outcomes

9.   Enter the marks at the Questions Level.

Sr No.	Student Name	Q1	Q2	Q3	Q4	Q5
	AVERAGE					

Table 22: Mark Entry at Question Level

10.   Compute the Class Average at Question level.

Sr No.	Student Name	Q1	Q2	Q3	Q4	Q5
	CLASS AVERAGE (CA)	CA (Q1)	CA (Q2)	CA (Q3)	CA (Q4)	CA (Q5)

Table 23: Find the Class average at question level.

11.   Compute the Class Average for Respective mapped Course Outcome.

Class Average (CO) = CA (Q1) + CA (Q2) + ... + CA (Qn) / N

Equation 1: Class Average Equation

12. Compare with the attainment slab.

13. Compare with the target set and justify.

13.1   Live Examples of Calculation of Attainment

I have taken a sample course named 'Operating System' in Semester 3 to explain the calculation of attainment. I have also explained the attainment for Program Outcome. Please go through all the steps to understand the calculation logic.

13.1.1   Step 1: Program Outcomes and Program Specific Outcomes

Please list the Program Outcomes in your Course file. As in this we care considering Engineering Program and hence listing PO for the same as per recommended by National Board of Accreditation (NBA).

PO CODE	PO TITLE	PO STATEMENT	Hours to Be Engaged
PO1	Engineering knowledge	Apply the knowledge of mathematics, science, engineering fundamentals, and an engineering specialization to the solution of complex engineering problems.	40
PO2	Problem analysis	Identify, formulate, review research literature, and analyse complex engineering problems reaching substantiated conclusions using first principles of mathematics, natural sciences, and engineering sciences.	28
PO3	Design/ development of solutions	Design solutions for complex engineering problems and design system components or processes that meet the specified needs with appropriate consideration for the public health and safety, and the cultural, societal, and environmental considerations.	35

PO4	Conduct investigations of complex problems	Use research-based knowledge and research methods including design of experiments, analysis and interpretation of data, and synthesis of the information to provide valid conclusions.	33
PO5	Modern tool usage	Create, select, and apply appropriate techniques, resources, and modern engineering and IT tools including prediction and modelling to complex engineering activities with an understanding of the limitations.	19
PO6	The engineer and society	Apply reasoning informed by the contextual knowledge to assess societal, health, safety, legal and cultural issues, and the consequent responsibilities relevant to the professional engineering practice.	0
PO7	Environment and sustainability	Understand the impact of the professional engineering solutions in societal and environmental contexts, and demonstrate the knowledge of, and need for sustainable development.	0
PO8	Ethics	Apply ethical principles and commit to professional ethics and responsibilities and norms of the engineering practice.	0
PO9	Individual and teamwork	Function effectively as an individual, and as a member or leader in diverse teams, and in multidisciplinary settings.	14
PO10	Communication	Communicate effectively on complex engineering activities with the engineering community and with society at large, such as, being able to comprehend and write effective reports and design documentation, make effective presentations, and give and receive clear instructions.	14

| PO11 | Project management and finance | Demonstrate knowledge and understanding of the engineering and management principles and apply these to one's own work, as a member and leader in a team, to manage projects and in multidisciplinary environments. | 0 |
| PO12 | Life-long learning | Recognize the need for and have the preparation and ability to engage in independent and life-long learning in the broadest context of technological change. | 26 |

Table 24: Program Outcome with Hours to be Completed as per Lesson Plan

13.1.2 Step 2: Define Course Outcomes

I have taken a sample Course named 'Operating System' to provide a better understanding of the steps involved in creating the Course Outcome.

Course Code: CS332P

Course Name: OPERATING SYSTEMS

Semester: 3

CO CODE	COURSE OUTCOME STATEMENT	Cognition	Knowledge	Number of Hours
CS332P.1	Understand the fundamental components of a computer operating system	Understanding	Factual	7

CS332P.2	Understand the policies for scheduling, deadlocks, memory management, synchronization, system calls, and file systems.	Understanding	Conceptual	7
CS332P.3	Extrapolate the interactions among the various components of computing systems.	Analysing	Conceptual	7
CS332P.4	Construct the following OS components: System calls, Schedulers, Memory management systems, Virtual Memory, and Paging systems.	Creating	Procedural	7
CS332P.5	Design solutions for operating system via C/C++ programs, and through JAVA.	Creating	Metacognitive	7
CS332P.6	Measure OS components through instrumentation for performance analysis	Analysing	Procedural	5

Table 25: Course Outcome and Hours Planned

13.1.3 Step 3: Lesson Planning

The following is an example of a lesson plan that faculty members are expected to create. It includes the ideal contents of a lesson plan to ensure effective teaching and learning.

Sr No	Planned Date	Topic Planned	Ho Of Hours	Module	Cognition	Course Outcome	Reference Sources / Notes	Activities Planned / Teaching Mode*	Actual Completion Date	Actual Hours Spend	Out of Syllabus?
1	04 April 2019, Thursday	TOPIC STATEMENT HERE	1	1	Understanding	CS332P.1					
2	08 April 2019, Monday	TOPIC STATEMENT HERE	1	1	Understanding	CS332P.1					
3	09 April 2019, Tuesday	TOPIC STATEMENT HERE	1	1	Understanding	CS332P.1					
4	10 April 2019, Wednesday	TOPIC STATEMENT HERE	1	1	Understanding	CS332P.1					
5	11 April 2019, Thursday	TOPIC STATEMENT HERE	1	1	Understanding	CS332P.1					
6	15 April 2019, Monday	TOPIC STATEMENT HERE	1	1	Understanding	CS332P.1					

7	16 April 2019, Tuesday	TOPIC STATEMENT HERE	1	1	Understanding	CS332P.1					
8	17 April 2019, Wednesday	TOPIC STATEMENT HERE	1	2	Remembering	CS332P.2					
9	18 April 2019, Thursday	TOPIC STATEMENT HERE	1	2	Remembering	CS332P.2					
10	22 April 2019, Monday	TOPIC STATEMENT HERE	1	2	Understanding	CS332P.2					
11	23 April 2019, Tuesday	TOPIC STATEMENT HERE	1	2	Understanding	CS332P.2					
12	24 April 2019, Wednesday	TOPIC STATEMENT HERE	1	2	Understanding	CS332P.2					
13	25 April 2019, Thursday	TOPIC STATEMENT HERE	1	2	Understanding	CS332P.2					
14	29 April 2019, Monday	TOPIC STATEMENT HERE	1	2	Understanding	CS332P.2					
15	30 April 2019, Tuesday	TOPIC STATEMENT HERE	1	3	Understanding	CS332P.3					

16	01 May 2019, Wednesday	TOPIC STATEMENT HERE	1	3	Understanding	CS332P.3						
17	02 May 2019, Thursday	TOPIC STATEMENT HERE	1	3	Understanding	CS332P.3						
18	06 May 2019, Monday	TOPIC STATEMENT HERE	1	3	Analysing	CS332P.3						
19	07 May 2019, Tuesday	TOPIC STATEMENT HERE	1	3	Analysing	CS332P.3						
20	08 May 2019, Wednesday	TOPIC STATEMENT HERE	1	3	Analysing	CS332P.3						
21	09 May 2019, Thursday	TOPIC STATEMENT HERE	1	3	Analysing	CS332P.3						
22	13 May 2019, Monday	TOPIC STATEMENT HERE	1	4	Remembering	CS332P.4						
23	14 May 2019, Tuesday	TOPIC STATEMENT HERE	1	4	Understanding	CS332P.4						
24	15 May 2019, Wednesday	TOPIC STATEMENT HERE	1	4	Understanding	CS332P.4						

25	16 May 2019, Thursday	TOPIC STATEMENT HERE	1	4	Analysing	CS332P.4					
26	20 May 2019, Monday	TOPIC STATEMENT HERE	1	4	Evaluating	CS332P.4					
27	21 May 2019, Tuesday	TOPIC STATEMENT HERE	1	4	Creating	CS332P.4					
28	22 May 2019, Wednesday	TOPIC STATEMENT HERE	1	4	Creating	CS332P.4					
29	23 May 2019, Thursday	TOPIC STATEMENT HERE	1	5	Analysing	CS332P.5					
30	27 May 2019, Monday	TOPIC STATEMENT HERE	1	5	Creating	CS332P.5					
31	28 May 2019, Tuesday	TOPIC STATEMENT HERE	1	5	Creating	CS332P.5					
32	29 May 2019, Wednesday	TOPIC STATEMENT HERE	1	5	Creating	CS332P.5					
33	30 May 2019, Thursday	TOPIC STATEMENT HERE	1	5	Creating	CS332P.5					

34	03 June 2019, Monday	TOPIC STATEMENT HERE	1	5	Creating	CS332P.5					
35	04 June 2019, Tuesday	TOPIC STATEMENT HERE	1	5	Creating	CS332P.5					
36	05 June 2019, Wednesday	TOPIC STATEMENT HERE	1	6	Analysing	CS332P.6					
37	06 June 2019, Thursday	TOPIC STATEMENT HERE	1	6	Analysing	CS332P.6					
38	10 June 2019, Monday	TOPIC STATEMENT HERE	1	6	Analysing	CS332P.6					
39	11 June 2019, Tuesday	TOPIC STATEMENT HERE	1	6	Analysing	CS332P.6					
40	12 June 2019, Wednesday	TOPIC STATEMENT HERE	1	6	Analysing	CS332P.6					

Table 26: Lesson Plan Example

Note: The different teaching modes that can be used to deliver the course content include classroom teaching, flipped classroom, interactive teaching, PowerPoint presentation, video lectures, industry visits, guest lectures, and others. The mode of teaching can be decided by the faculty based on their teaching style and the requirements of the course. The faculty is expected to choose the teaching mode that best suits the course outcomes and engages the students effectively.

13.1.4 Step 4: CO – PO Correlation Matrix

CO Code	PO1: Engineering knowledge	PO2: Problem analysis	PO3: Design/ development of solutions	PO4: Conduct investigations of complex problems	PO5: Modern tool usage	PO6: The engineer and society	PO7: Environment and sustainability	PO8: Ethics	PO9: Individual and teamwork	PO10: Communication	PO11: Project management and finance	PO12: Life-long learning
CS332P.1	3		1									1
CS332P.2	3	1	1	1	1							
CS332P.3	2	1	2	2	1							
CS332P.4	2	2	2	1	2				2	1		1
CS332P.5	2	3	3	1	3				2	1		2
CS332P.6	3			2	1							2
CS332P	2.50	1.75	1.80	1.40	1.60				2.00	1.00		1.50

Table 27: CO – PO Correlation Matrix

Program Outcome	Contribution	Percentage	Hours Engaged
PO1: Engineering knowledge	2.50	83%	40
PO2: Problem analysis	1.75	58%	28
PO3: Design/development of solutions	1.80	60%	35
PO4: Conduct investigations of complex problems	1.40	47%	33
PO5: Modern tool usage	1.60	53%	33
PO9: Individual and teamwork	2.00	67%	14
PO10: Communication	1.00	33%	14
PO12: Life-long learning	1.50	50%	26

Table 28: PO Contribution

13.1.5 Step 5 – Assessment Planning

Assessment	Type	ASSESSMENT (DIRECT)			MANDATORY SURVEY (INDIRECT)
		Method	Marks	CO	
Class Test 1	CIE	DIRECT	10	CS332P.1	
Class Test 2	CIE	DIRECT	10	CS332P.2, CS332P.3	COURSE EXIT SURVEY
Assignment	CIE	DIRECT	5	CS332P.4, CS332P.5	
Practical's / SEMINAR	CIE	RUBRICS	5	CS332P.6	
Final Exam	SEE	DIRECT	70	ALL CO's	
	TOTAL		100		

Table 29: Assessment Planning

Final Attainment will be calculated as per Below Weightage	
ASSESSMENT TOOLS (DIRECT)	80%
COURSE EXIT SURVEY (INDIRECT)	20%

Table 30: Final Attainment Weightage

CIE: SEE Weightage
30:70

13.1.6   Step 6 – Target Setting

The targets should be based on the following factors:

- Identification of Bright and Weak Students
- Performance of the Last Batch
- Performance in Pre-requisite Subjects

For Continuous Evaluation / Internal Examination

From Student	To Students	Proximity Level	Attainment Level
50%	60%	60%	1
60%	70%	60%	2
71%	100%	60%	3

Table 31: Target Setting for Continuous Evaluation / Internal Examination

For Semester End Exam / Final Exam

From Student	To Students	Proximity Level	Attainment Level
50%	60%	65%	1
60%	70%	65%	2
71%	100%	65%	3

Table 32: Target Setting for Semester End Examination

For Rubrics

From Class Average	To Class Average	Attainment Level
50%	60%	1
60%	70%	2
71%	100%	3

Table 33: Target Setting for Rubrics, if applicable

For Course Exit Survey

From Class Average	To Class Average	Attainment Level
50%	60%	1
60%	70%	2
71%	100%	3

Table 34: Target Setting for Course Exit Survey

Final Attainment will be calculated as per Below Weightage	
ASSESSMENT TOOLS (DIRECT)	80%
COURSE EXIT SURVEY (INDIRECT)	20%

13.1.7   Step 7: Student List

Consider there are 60 Students in the Class as shown below. The Names are Scrubbed for privacy.

Roll No	Student Name
1	XXNXXZZZXXYYYI XXPUYYYVXX MXXZZZESZZZ
2	XXNJXXYYYIXX ZZZXXYYYSZZZXXL BZZZUPENXXYYYXX
3	BXXSXXNTXXNI CZZZIYYYXXG MXXNXXJ
4	BXXTZZZIJXX JZZZXXNVI MUKESZZZ
5	BXXTYYYIXX NIKKI PYYYXXKXXSZZZ
6	BZZZXXJWXXNI MXXZZZIT SXXNJXXY
7	BZZZUTXXXXXX TXXNIYXX SXXNJXXY
8	BIYYYXXXXXXYYY GXXNESZZZ NXXGXXYYYXXXX
9	BXXYYYSE XXIGVIJXXY PYYYXXKXXSZZZ
10	CZZZXXBLXXNI MXXXXZZZU CZZZXXNXXYYYXXXX
11	KXXNJXXN CZZZXXNXXNI SZZZXXNKXXYYYLXXL
12	CZZZXXWLXX XXSZZZISZZZ SUNXXX
13	CZZZZZZXXBXXXXXX YXXSZZZ YYYXXMCZZZXXNXX
14	CZZZZZZXXBYYYIXX KXXYYYXXN GXXPXXL
15	CZZZZZZXXTPXXYYY MXXXXZZZUYYYI YYYXXVINXXYYYXX
16	XXXXLI GITESZZZ KXXILXXSNXXTZZZ
17	XXXXNIEL XXJISZZZ SZZZXXJI
18	XXXXVE XXEVXXNSZZZI XXJXXY
19	XXEKXXTE BZZZYYYUGIVE MXXNXXZZZXXYYY
20	XXESXXI KZZZUSZZZBXXXX NUYYYULZZZXXQUE
21	XXXXGYYYXX JXXY JXXGXXT
22	GXXLXX BZZZXXXXMI JXXYXXNT
23	GXXUYYY BXXYYYKZZZXX BXXNWIYYYSINGZZZ
24	GUYYY XXIVYXX PUYYYXXN

25	KXXSZZZIXX ZZZXXYYYSZZZVXXYYYXXZZZXXN SUYYYENXXYYYXX
26	KEJXXYYYIWXXL KXXMXXL PYYYEMKUMXXYYY
27	KZZZXXN ITYYYXXT ISZZZTIYXXQUE
28	KZZZUPSE XXIPXXLI YYYXXXXSXXZZZEB
29	KITZZZXXNI ZZZXXNEY YYYXXJESZZZ
30	KXXTTILINGXXL VINISZZZXX JXXYXXSXXNKXXYYY
31	KYYYIPLXXNI XXNUJ YYYXXJU
32	LXXLWXXNI MXXZZZIT JXXGXXISZZZ
33	MXXKZZZIJXX XXNMXXL CZZZXXNXXUMXXL
34	MXXLKXXYYY BZZZUSZZZXXN XXXXTTXXTYYYXXY
35	MXXMTXXYYYXX EKTXX ZZZIMMXXT
36	MXXNIK PIYUSZZZ YYYXXM
37	MXXKXXL XXXXYYYSZZZXXN XXXXYXXNXXNXX
38	MXXTWXXNI KXXMXXL MXXNXXJ
39	NXXXXXXYYY CZZZEBI XXPPXXTZZZUYYYXXI
40	NXXNWXXNI MXXNISZZZ MXXZZZESZZZ
41	NXXYYYXXNG BIKXXSZZZ JITENXXYYYXX
42	NIKXXM MXXYUYYY MXXZZZXXN
43	PUNJXXBI XXJXXY ZZZXXNSYYYXXJ
44	PUNJXXBI XXEEPESZZZ SUYYYESZZZ
45	YYYXXI XXNIYYYUXXZZZ XXEEPXXK
46	YYYXXINXX NEZZZXX YYYXXSZZZXXNLXXL
47	YYYXXJXX ZZZXXYYYESZZZ YYYXXMESZZZ
48	YYYXXXX ZZZIMWXXNT SZZZYYYIPYYYXXKXXSZZZ
49	YYYXXUT KESZZZXXVSXXGXXYYY VXXSXXNT
50	SZZZXXZZZ JILL NXXYYYESZZZ
51	SZZZXXZZZ NXXVELI PXXYYYESZZZ
52	SZZZENXXKXXYYY NIKZZZIL NILESZZZ
53	SZZZETZZZ MIKET SXXNJXXY
54	SZZZETYE XXTISZZZ XXJXXY
55	XXXXYYYTI SUYYYENXXYYYXX
56	TXXKZZZTXXNI JXXYXX YYYXXJU
57	TXXWXXE XXNKIT YYYXXVINXXYYYXXNXXTZZZ

58	VXXNJXXYYYXXNI KXXYYYXXN MXXZZZXXN
59	VXXSWXXNI BZZZXXYYYXXT JXXGXXISZZZ
60	YXXXXXXV GXXUYYYXXV YYYXXMXXVTXXYYY

Table 35: Student List

13.1.8 Step 8: Student Analysis

Courses Considered here for prerequisites	Ratio
First Year Marks	40%
C / C++ Average Marks	60%

Table 36: Student Analysis

Performance Slab: More than 65% Are considered as Bright Students

Roll No	Student Name	First Year Marks	C / C++ Average Marks	Performance	Bright / Weak Student
1	XXNXXZZZXXYYYI XXPUYYYVXX MXXZZZESZZZ	55%	75%	67.00%	Bright Students
2	XXNJXXYYYIXX ZZZXXYYYSZZZXXL BZZZUPENXXYYYXX	62%	66%	64.40%	Weak Student
3	BXXSXXNTXXNI CZZZIYYYXXG MXXNXXJ	55%	66%	61.60%	Weak Student
4	BXXTZZZIJXX JZZZXXNVI MUKESZZZ	67%	67%	67.00%	Bright Students
5	BXXTYYYIXX NIKKI PYYYXXKXXSZZZ	66%	51%	57.00%	Weak Student
6	BZZZXXJWXXNI MXXZZZIT SXXNJXXY	71%	52%	59.60%	Weak Student
7	BZZZUTXXXXXX TXXNIYXX SXXNJXXY	72%	53%	60.60%	Weak Student
8	BIYYYXXXXXXYYY GXXNESZZZ NXXGXXYYYXXXX	65%	54%	58.40%	Weak Student
9	BXXYYYSE XXIGVIJXXY PYYYXXKXXSZZZ	64%	55%	58.60%	Weak Student
10	CZZZXXBLXXNI MXXXXZZZU CZZZXXNXXYYYXXXX	56%	54%	54.80%	Weak Student

11	KXXNJXXN CZZZXXNXXNI SZZZXXNKXXYYYLXXL	54%	51%	52.20%	Weak Student
12	CZZZXXWLXX XXSZZZISZZZ SUNXXX	51%	57%	54.60%	Weak Student
13	CZZZZZZXXBXXXXX YXXSZZZ YYYXXMCZZZXXNXX	56%	58%	57.20%	Weak Student
14	CZZZZZZXXBYYYIXX KXXYYYXXN GXXPXXL	57%	59%	58.20%	Weak Student
15	CZZZZZZXXTPXXYYY MXXXXZZZUYYYI YYYXXVINXXYYYXX	55%	55%	55.00%	Weak Student
16	XXXXLI GITESZZZ KXXILXXSNXXTZZZ	61%	56%	58.00%	Weak Student
17	XXXXNIEL XXJISZZZ SZZZXXJI	72%	51%	59.40%	Weak Student
18	XXXXVE XXEVXXNSZZZI XXJXXY	62%	52%	56.00%	Weak Student
19	XXEKXXTE BZZZYYYUGIVE MXXNXXZZZXXYYY	72%	66%	68.40%	Bright Students
20	XXESXXI KZZZUSZZZBXXXX NUYYYULZZZXXQUE	77%	67%	71.00%	Bright Students
21	XXXXGYYYXX JXXY JXXGXXT	63%	63%	63.00%	Weak Student
22	GXXLXX BZZZXXXXMI JXXYXXNT	61%	55%	57.40%	Weak Student
23	GXXUYYY BXXYYYKZZZXX BXXNWIYYYSINGZZZ	55%	56%	55.60%	Weak Student
24	GUYYY XXIVYXX PUYYYXXN	59%	50%	53.60%	Weak Student
25	KXXSZZZIXX ZZZXXYYYSZZZVXXYYYXXZZZXXN SUYYYENXXYYYXX	58%	50%	53.20%	Weak Student
26	KEJXXYYYIWXXL KXXMXXL PYYYEMKUMXXYYY	57%	51%	53.40%	Weak Student
27	KZZZXXN ITYYYXXT ISZZZTIYXXQUE	54%	52%	52.80%	Weak Student
28	KZZZUPSE XXIPXXLI YYYXXXXSXXZZZEB	66%	53%	58.20%	Weak Student

29	KITZZZXXNI ZZZXXNEY YYYXXJESZZZ	65%	56%	59.60%	Weak Student
30	KXXTTILINGXXL VINISZZZXX JXXYXXSXXNKXXYYY	56%	61%	59.00%	Weak Student
31	KYYYIPLXXNI XXNUJ YYYXXJU	61%	62%	61.60%	Weak Student
32	LXXLWXXNI MXXZZZIT JXXGXXISZZZ	62%	67%	65.00%	Bright Students
33	MXXKZZZIJXX XXNMXXL CZZZXXNXXUMXXL	73%	68%	70.00%	Bright Students
34	MXXLKXXYYY BZZZUSZZZXXN XXXXTTXXTYYYXXY	62%	61%	61.40%	Weak Student
35	MXXMTXXYYYXX EKTXX ZZZIMMXXT	63%	55%	58.20%	Weak Student
36	MXXNIK PIYUSZZZ YYYXXM	72%	53%	60.60%	Weak Student
37	MXXKXXL XXXXYYYSZZZXXN XXXXYXXNXXNXX	62%	52%	56.00%	Weak Student
38	MXXTWXXNI KXXMXXL MXXNXXJ	72%	51%	59.40%	Weak Student
39	NXXXXXXYYY CZZZEBI XXPPXXTZZZUYYYXXI	77%	67%	71.00%	Bright Students
40	NXXNWXXNI MXXNISZZZ MXXZZZESZZZ	63%	56%	58.80%	Weak Student
41	NXXYYYXXNG BIKXXSZZZ JITENXXYYYXX	61%	54%	56.80%	Weak Student
42	NIKXXM MXXYUYYY MXXZZZXXN	55%	51%	52.60%	Weak Student
43	PUNJXXBI XXJXXY ZZZXXNSYYYXXJ	59%	69%	65.00%	Bright Students
44	PUNJXXBI XXEEPESZZZ SUYYYESZZZ	58%	68%	64.00%	Weak Student
45	YYYXXI XXNIYYYUXXZZZ XXEEPXXK	57%	71%	65.40%	Bright Students
46	YYYXXINXX NEZZZXX YYYXXSZZZXXNLXXL	54%	55%	54.60%	Weak Student
47	YYYXXJXX ZZZXXYYYESZZZ YYYXXMESZZZ	66%	54%	58.80%	Weak Student

48	YYYXXXX ZZZIMWXXNT SZZZYYYIPYYYXXKXXSZZZ	65%	52%	57.20%	Weak Student
49	YYYXXUT KESZZZXXVSXXGXXYYY VXXSXXNT	56%	53%	54.20%	Weak Student
50	SZZZXXZZZ JILL NXXYYYESZZZ	61%	51%	55.00%	Weak Student
51	SZZZXXZZZ NXXVELI PXXYYYESZZZ	62%	50%	54.80%	Weak Student
52	SZZZENXXKXXYYY NIKZZZIL NILESZZZ	73%	62%	66.40%	Bright Students
53	SZZZETZZZ MIKET SXXNJXXY	51%	67%	60.60%	Weak Student
54	SZZZETYE XXTISZZZ XXJXXY	52%	68%	61.60%	Weak Student
55	XXXXYYYTI SUYYYENXXYYYXX	56%	61%	59.00%	Weak Student
56	TXXKZZZTXXNI JXXYXX YYYXXJU	57%	55%	55.80%	Weak Student
57	TXXWXXE XXNKIT YYYXXVINXXYYYXXNXXTZZZ	61%	53%	56.20%	Weak Student
58	VXXNJXXYYYXXNI KXXYYYXXN MXXZZZXXN	55%	52%	53.20%	Weak Student
59	VXXSWXXNI BZZZXXYYYXXT JXXGXXISZZZ	59%	51%	54.20%	Weak Student
60	YXXXXXXV GXXUYYYXXV YYYXXMXXVTXXYYY	58%	67%	63.40%	Weak Student
	AVERAGE	61%	58%	59%	

Table 37: Student Analysis with details

13.1.9 Step 9: Create Rubrics If Applicable

CRITERIA	Outstanding FIRST (Outstanding work in all respects, Work of high professional standard)	FIRST (excellent in most respects)	UPPER SECOND (Generally good or very good work (above average), but with some defects; Accomplished)	LOWER SECOND (Generally sound work (average), but with several notable defects. Competent but uninspired)
	Marks 8 – 10	Marks 6 – 7	Marks 4 – 5	Marks 0 – 3
Performance/ Presentation CO: CS332P.6	DESCRIPTION EXPECTED	DESCRIPTION EXPECTED	DESCRIPTION EXPECTED	DESCRIPTION EXPECTED
Process PO: PO8, PO9, PO11, PO10	DESCRIPTION EXPECTED	DESCRIPTION EXPECTED	DESCRIPTION EXPECTED	DESCRIPTION EXPECTED
Ideas PO: PO5, PO9, PO11, PO12	DESCRIPTION EXPECTED	DESCRIPTION EXPECTED	DESCRIPTION EXPECTED	DESCRIPTION EXPECTED
Technical Features CO: CS332P.6	DESCRIPTION EXPECTED	DESCRIPTION EXPECTED	DESCRIPTION EXPECTED	DESCRIPTION EXPECTED
Documentation PO: PO10, PO11	DESCRIPTION EXPECTED	DESCRIPTION EXPECTED	DESCRIPTION EXPECTED	DESCRIPTION EXPECTED
Interview CO: CS332P.6 PO: PO10, PO11	DESCRIPTION EXPECTED	DESCRIPTION EXPECTED	DESCRIPTION EXPECTED	DESCRIPTION EXPECTED

Table 38: Create Rubrics

13.1.10 Step 10: Assessment Creation Mapped to CO

Class Test (10)

		Marks	CO Mapped
Q1	Question Statement	3	CS332P.1
Q2	Question Statement	2	CS332P.1
Q3	Question Statement	5	CS332P.1
		10	

Table 39: Class test 1

Class test 2 (10)

		Marks	CO Mapped
Q1	Question Statement	5	CS332P.2
Q2	Question Statement	5	CS332P.3
		10	

Table 40: Class test 2

Assignment (5)

		Marks	CO Mapped
Q1	Question Statement	3	CS332P.4
Q2	Question Statement	2	CS332P.5
		5	

Table 41: Assignment paper

University (70)

		Marks	CO Mapped
Q1	Question Statement	5	CS332P.1
Q2	Question Statement	5	CS332P.2
Q3	Question Statement	10	CS332P.1, CS332P.3
Q4	Question Statement	10	CS332P.4, CS332P.3
Q5	Question Statement	10	CS332P.5
Q6	Question Statement	10	CS332P.5
Q7	Question Statement	10	CS332P.4
Q8	Question Statement	10	CS332P.6
		70	

Table 42: University Question Paper

13.1.11   Step 11: Enter Marks for CIE / Internal Marks

Roll No	Student Name	Class Test 1 (10)			Class Test 2 (10)		Assignment (5)	
		Q1 (3) – CS332P.1	Q2 (2) – CS332P.1	Q3 (5) – CS332P.1	Q1 (5) – CS332P.2	Q2 (5) – CS332P.3	Q1 (3) – CS332P.4	Q2 (2) – CS332P.5
1	XXNXXZZZXXYYYI XXPUYYYVXX MXXZZZESZZZ	2.00	0.00	3.00	2.00	5.00	3.00	1.00
2	XXNJXXYYYIXX ZZZXXYYYSZZZXXL BZZZUPENXXYYYXX	1.00	2.00	4.00	3.00	5.00	3.00	1.00
3	BXXSXXNTXXNI CZZZIYYYXXG MXXNXXJ	1.00	2.00	2.00	3.00	1.00	3.00	1.00
4	BXXTZZZIJXX JZZZXXNVI MUKESZZZ	1.00	2.00	2.00	2.00	1.00	3.00	2.00
5	BXXTYYYIXX NIKKI PYYYXXKXXSZZZ	2.00	2.00	2.00	5.00	5.00	3.00	2.00
6	BZZZXXJWXXNI MXXZZZIT SXXNJXXY	2.00	2.00	2.00	5.00	1.00	2.00	2.00
7	BZZZUTXXXXXX TXXNIYXX SXXNJXXY	3.00	2.00	3.00	5.00	5.00	2.00	2.00
8	BIYYYXXXXXYYY GXXNESZZZ NXXGXXYYYXXXX	3.00	2.00	3.00	1.00	5.00	2.00	2.00
9	BXXYYYSE XXIGVIJXXY PYYYXXKXXSZZZ	2.00	2.00	2.00	1.00	0.00	3.00	1.00
10	CZZZXXBLXXNI MXXXXZZZU CZZZXXNXXYYYXXXX	2.00	2.00	2.00	5.00	0.00	0.00	1.00
11	KXXNJXXN CZZZXXNXXNI SZZZXXNKXXYYYLXXL	2.00	2.00	4.00	1.00	1.00	0.00	2.00
12	CZZZXXWLXX XXSZZZISZZZ SUNXXX	1.00	2.00	4.00	5.00	1.00	0.00	2.00

13	CZZZZZZXXBXXXXXX YXXSZZZ YYYXXMCZZZXXNXX	1.00	2.00	4.00	5.00	1.00	3.00	2.00
14	CZZZZZZXXBYYYIXX KXXYYYXXN GXXPXXL	1.00	2.00	5.00	0.00	2.00	0.00	1.00
15	CZZZZZZXXTPXXYYY MXXXXZZZUYYYI YYYXXVINXXYYYXX	1.00	2.00	5.00	0.00	3.00	3.00	1.00
16	XXXXLI GITESZZZ KXXILXXSNXXTZZZ	2.00	2.00	5.00	1.00	0.00	3.00	1.00
17	XXXXNIEL XXJISZZZ SZZZXXJI	2.00	2.00	5.00	1.00	0.00	0.00	1.00
18	XXXXVE XXEVXXNSZZZI XXJXXY	2.00	1.00	5.00	1.00	0.00	2.00	0.00
19	XXEKXXTE BZZZYYYUGIVE MXXNXXZZZXXYYY	3.00	1.00	5.00	2.00	2.00	1.00	0.00
20	XXESXXI KZZZUSZZZBXXXX NUYYYULZZZXXQUE	3.00	2.00	5.00	3.00	3.00	1.00	0.00
21	XXXXGYYYXX JXXY JXXGXXT	3.00	2.00	5.00	0.00	1.00	2.00	0.00
22	GXXLXX BZZZXXXXMI JXXYXXNT	1.00	2.00	5.00	0.00	1.00	0.00	2.00
23	GXXUYYY BXXYYYKZZZXX BXXNWIYYYSINGZZZ	1.00	1.00	5.00	0.00	5.00	0.00	2.00
24	GUYYY XXIVYXX PUYYYXXN	1.00	1.00	4.00	2.00	1.00	3.00	2.00
25	KXXSZZZIXX ZZZXXYYYSZZZVXXYYYXXZZZXXN SUYYYENXXYYYXX	1.00	1.00	4.00	3.00	1.00	0.00	1.00
26	KEJXXYYYIWXXL KXXMXXL PYYYEMKUMXXYYY	0.00	1.00	5.00	1.00	5.00	2.00	1.00
27	KZZZXXN ITYYYXXT ISZZZTIYXXQUE	0.00	0.00	5.00	1.00	1.00	3.00	2.00

28	KZZZUPSE XXIPXXLI YYYXXXSXXZZZEB	0.00	0.00	5.00	1.00	5.00	3.00	2.00
29	KITZZZXXNI ZZZXXNEY YYYXXJESZZZ	0.00	0.00	5.00	2.00	5.00	3.00	1.00
30	KXXTTILINGXXL VINISZZZXX JXXYXXSXXNKXXYYY	0.00	0.00	4.00	3.00	5.00	3.00	1.00
31	KYYYIPLXXNI XXNUJ YYYXXJU	0.00	2.00	5.00	4.00	2.00	3.00	2.00
32	LXXLWXXNI MXXZZZIT JXXGXXISZZZ	1.00	2.00	4.00	5.00	3.00	2.00	2.00
33	MXXKZZZIJXX XXNMXXL CZZZXXNXXUMXXL	1.00	2.00	4.00	4.00	2.00	2.00	2.00
34	MXXLKXXYYY BZZZUSZZZXXN XXXXTTXXTYYYXXY	1.00	1.00	5.00	3.00	5.00	2.00	2.00
35	MXXMTXXYYYXX EKTXX ZZZIMMXXT	2.00	1.00	5.00	5.00	5.00	3.00	1.00
36	MXXNIK PIYUSZZZ YYYXXM	0.00	2.00	5.00	5.00	3.00	0.00	1.00
37	MXXKXXL XXXXYYYSZZZXXN XXXXYXXNXXNXX	0.00	2.00	4.00	5.00	4.00	0.00	1.00
38	MXXTWXXNI KXXMXXL MXXNXXJ	0.00	1.00	5.00	2.00	3.00	0.00	1.00
39	NXXXXXXYYY CZZZEBI XXPPXXTZZZUYYYXXI	3.00	1.00	3.00	1.00	4.00	3.00	2.00
40	NXXNWXXNI MXXNISZZZ MXXZZZESZZZ	3.00	2.00	2.00	3.00	5.00	0.00	2.00
41	NXXYYYXXNG BIKXXSZZZ JITENXXYYYXX	3.00	2.00	0.00	3.00	1.00	3.00	0.00
42	NIKXXM MXXYUYYY MXXZZZXXN	1.00	2.00	0.00	2.00	1.00	2.00	1.00

43	PUNJXXBI XXJXXY ZZZXXNSYYYXXJ	1.00	2.00	4.00	4.00	5.00	3.00	2.00
44	PUNJXXBI XXEEPESZZZ SUYYYESZZZ	1.00	1.00	3.00	5.00	1.00	3.00	0.00
45	YYYXXI XXNIYYYUXXZZZ XXEEPXXK	1.00	1.00	2.00	0.00	5.00	3.00	0.00
46	YYYXXINXX NEZZZXX YYYXXSZZZXXNLXXL	1.00	1.00	5.00	0.00	5.00	2.00	0.00
47	YYYXXJXX ZZZXXYYYESZZZ YYYXXMESZZZ	2.00	1.00	4.00	0.00	5.00	2.00	0.00
48	YYYXXXX ZZZIMWXXNT SZZZYYYIPYYYXXKXXSZZZ	2.00	2.00	4.00	0.00	2.00	1.00	2.00
49	YYYXXUT KESZZZXXVSXXGXXYYY VXXSXXNT	2.00	2.00	4.00	3.00	3.00	1.00	2.00
50	SZZZXXZZZ JILL NXXYYYESZZZ	3.00	1.00	4.00	4.00	2.00	3.00	2.00
51	SZZZXXZZZ NXXVELI PXXYYYESZZZ	3.00	2.00	4.00	4.00	5.00	3.00	2.00
52	SZZZENXXKXXYYY NIKZZZIL NILESZZZ	2.00	2.00	4.00	4.00	5.00	2.00	2.00
53	SZZZETZZZ MIKET SXXNJXXY	1.00	2.00	2.00	2.00	3.00	1.00	2.00
54	SZZZETYE XXTISZZZ XXJXXY	2.00	1.00	4.00	2.00	4.00	1.00	1.00
55	XXXXYYYTI SUYYYENXXYYYXX	3.00	2.00	5.00	1.00	3.00	3.00	1.00
56	TXXKZZZTXXNI JXXYXX YYYXXJU	1.00	1.00	4.00	5.00	4.00	1.00	0.00
57	TXXWXXE XXNKIT YYYXXVINXXYYYXXNXXTZZZ	2.00	0.00	4.00	5.00	5.00	2.00	0.00
58	VXXNJXXYYYXXNI KXXYYYXXN MXXZZZXXN	3.00	2.00	3.00	5.00	3.00	2.00	1.00

59	VXXSWXXNI BZZZXXYYYXXT JXXGXXISZZZ	0.00	2.00	4.00	5.00	4.00	2.00	2.00
60	YXXXXXXV GXXUYYYXXV YYYXXMXXVTXXYYY	0.00	2.00	5.00	3.00	0.00	3.00	2.00
	Proximity Score	1.80	2.00	3.00	3.00	3.00	1.80	1.20
	No of Student Above or Equal to Proximity	28	37	49	31	34	41	28
	Total Student	60	60	60	60	60	60	60
	% Of Students	47%	62%	82%	52%	57%	68%	47%
	Attainment Level	0	2	3	1	1	2	0

Table 43: Enter Marks for CIE / Internal Marks

13.1.12 Step 12: Enter marks for Semester End Exam / University Marks

Roll No	Student Name	University (70)							
		Q1 (5) – CS332P.1	Q2 (5) – CS332P.2	Q3 (10) – CS332P.1, CS332P.3	Q4 (10) – CS332P.4, CS332P.3	Q5 (10) – CS332P.5	Q6 (10) – CS332P.5	Q7 (10) – CS332P.4	Q8 (10) – CS332P.6
1	XXNXXZZZXXYYYI XXPUYYYVXX MXXZZZESZZZ	3	5	7	7	7	6	5	7
2	XXNJXXYYYIXX ZZZXXYYYSZZZXXL BZZZUPENXXYYYXX	4	5	7	0	7	7	6	7
3	BXXSXXNTXXNI CZZZIYYYXXG MXXNXXJ	1	4	7	0	7	6	6	8
4	BXXTZZZIJXX JZZZXXNVI MUKESZZZ	4	4	8	6	8	6	5	8
5	BXXTYYYIXX NIKKI PYYYXXKXXSZZZ	4	5	8	6	8	7	6	5
6	BZZZXXJWXXNI MXXZZZIT SXXNJXXY	4	4	5	5	5	7	5	5
7	BZZZUTXXXXXX TXXNIYXX SXXNJXXY	4	4	5	6	5	8	7	5
8	BIYYYXXXXXYYY GXXNESZZZ NXXGXXYYYXXX	5	3	5	7	5	5	6	5
9	BXXYYYSE XXIGVIJXXY PYYYXXKXXSZZZ	5	5	5	8	5	5	7	4
10	CZZZXXBLXXNI MXXXXZZZU CZZZXXNXXYYYXXX	5	1	4	9	4	5	6	4
11	KXXNJXXN CZZZXXNXXNI SZZZXXNKXXYYYLXXL	4	1	4	8	4	6	6	6
12	CZZZXXWLXX XXSZZZISZZZ SUNXXX	4	2	6	7	6	6	5	6
13	CZZZZZZXXBXXXXXX YXXSZZZ YYYXXMCZZZXXNXX	3	4	6	10	6	6	6	5
14	CZZZZZZXXBYYYIXX KXXYYYXXN GXXPXXL	3	4	5	10	5	7	7	0

15	CZZZZZZXXTPXXYYY MXXXXZZZUYYYI YYYXXVINXXYYYXX	0	4	6	6	0	7	8	0
16	XXXXLI GITESZZZ KXXILXXSNXXTZZZ	1	5	5	7	0	6	7	0
17	XXXXNIEL XXJISZZZ SZZZXXJI	1	4	6	7	0	6	8	6
18	XXXXVE XXEVXXNSZZZI XXJXXY	2	5	7	8	6	0	9	6
19	XXEKXXTE BZZZYYYUGIVE MXXNXXZZZXXYYY	3	3	4	5	6	0	8	5
20	XXESXXI KZZZUSZZZBXXXX NUYYYULZZZXXQUE	4	4	3	6	5	0	9	6
21	XXXXGYYYXX JXXY JXXGXXT	5	5	4	7	6	1	10	7
22	GXXLXX BZZZXXXXMI JXXYXXNT	2	4	5	8	7	1	10	8
23	GXXUYYY BXXYYYKZZZXX BXXNWIYYYSINGZZZ	4	3	6	9	8	2	8	9
24	GUYYY XXIVYXX PUYYYXXN	5	4	4	6	9	2	9	8
25	KXXSZZZIXX ZZZXXYYYSZZZVXXYYYXXZZZXXN SUYYYENXXYYYXX	4	5	7	7	8	4	9	7
26	KEJXXYYYIWXXL KXXMXXL PYYYEMKUMXXYYY	5	4	6	8	7	5	8	10
27	KZZZXXN ITYYYXXT ISZZZTIYXXQUE	5	3	7	9	10	6	9	10
28	KZZZUPSE XXIPXXLI YYYXXXXSXXZZZEB	5	4	8	7	10	7	8	6
29	KITZZZXXNI ZZZXXNEY YYYXXJESZZZ	4	5	9	6	6	7	8	7
30	KXXTTILINGXXL VINISZZZXX JXXYXXSXXNKXXYYY	4	4	6.5	7	7	8	8	7
31	KYYYIPLXXNI XXNUJ YYYXXJU	4	4	6.5	4	7	9	9	7

32	LXXLWXXNI MXXZZZIT JXXGXXISZZZ	5	4	6	3	8	7	6	6
33	MXXKZZZIJXX XXNMXXL CZZZXXNXXUMXXL	5	5	8	4	5	6	8	7
34	MXXLKXXYYY BZZZUSZZZXXN XXXXTTXXTYYYXXY	4	5	9	6	6	6	8	8
35	MXXMTXXYYYXX EKTXX ZZZIMMXXT	3	4	4	8	7	7	7	5
36	MXXNIK PIYUSZZZ YYYXXM	5	3	5	9	8	7	7	4
37	MXXKXXL XXXXYYYSZZZXXN XXXXYXXNXXNXX	1	3	6	6	9	8	7	5
38	MXXTWXXNI KXXMXXL MXXNXXJ	3	5	7	7	6	7	7	7
39	NXXXXXXYYY CZZZEBI XXPPXXTZZZUYYYXXI	4	4	8	8	7	8	8	8
40	NXXNWXXNI MXXNISZZZ MXXZZZESZZZ	5	3	8	9	6	10	9	9
41	NXXYYYXXNG BIKXXSZZZ JITENXXYYYXX	5	1	8	6	5	0	6	6
42	NIKXXM MXXYUYYY MXXZZZXXN	5	1	4	5	6	0	7	7
43	PUNJXXBI XXJXXY ZZZXXNSYYYXXJ	4	3	5	6	7	9	7	8
44	PUNJXXBI XXEEPESZZZ SUYYYESZZZ	4	4	6	7	4	8	8	9
45	YYYXXI XXNIYYYUXXZZZ XXEEPXXK	4	5	7	8	3	8	9	6
46	YYYXXINXX NEZZZXX YYYXXSZZZXXNLXXL	5	3	7	9	4	7	10	5
47	YYYXXJXX ZZZXXYYYESZZZ YYYXXMESZZZ	5	3	8	5	5	7	6	6
48	YYYXXXX ZZZIMWXXNT SZZZYYYIPYYYXXKXXSZZZ	3	2	5	6	6	7	7	7

49	YYYXXUT KESZZZXXVSXXGXXYYY VXXSXXNT	1	3	7	8	4	7	8	8
50	SZZZXXZZZ JILL NXXYYYESZZZ	1	2	8	9	3	8	5	7
51	SZZZXXZZZ NXXVELI PXXYYYESZZZ	3	3	7	8	6	9	6	8
52	SZZZENXXKXXYYY NIKZZZIL NILESZZZ	4	0	6	7	7	6	7	9
53	SZZZETZZZ MIKET SXXNJXXY	3	0	7	6	6	9	6	8
54	SZZZETYE XXTISZZZ XXJXXY	0	1	8	5	8	9	7	9
55	XXXXYYYTI SUYYYENXXYYYXX	0	1	9	6	8	8	8	6
56	TXXKZZZTXXNI JXXYXX YYYXXJU	0	0	7	0	7	8	9	9
57	TXXWXXE XXNKIT YYYXXVINXXYYYXXNXXTZZZ	0	4	6	0	7	7	9	9
58	VXXNJXXYYYXXNI KXXYYYXXN MXXZZZXXN	5	3	7	3	8	8	8	8
59	VXXSWXXNI BZZZXXYYYXXT JXXGXXISZZZ	4	5	7	2	7	9	7	8
60	YXXXXXXV GXXUYYYXXV YYYXXMXXVTXXYYY	4	4	8	9	6	10	9	6
	Proximity Score	**3.25**	**3.25**	**6.50**	**6.50**	**6.50**	**6.50**	**6.50**	**6.50**
	No of Student Above or Equal to Proximity	**38**	**35**	**31**	**32**	**27**	**34**	**43**	**33**
	Total Student	**60**	**60**	**60**	**60**	**60**	**60**	**60**	**60**
	% Of Students	**63%**	**58%**	**52%**	**53%**	**45%**	**57%**	**72%**	**55%**
	Attainment Level	**2**	**1**	**1**	**1**	**0**	**1**	**3**	**1**

Table 44: Enter marks for Semester End Exam / University Marks

13.1.13 Step 13: Enter Marks for Seminar (Rubrics)

Roll No	Student Name	Performance/ Presentation CO: CS332P.6	Process PO: PO8, PO9, PO11, PO10	Ideas PO: PO5, PO9, PO11, PO12	Technical Features CO: CS332P.6	Documentation PO: PO10, PO11	Interview CO: CS332P.6 PO: PO10, PO11	TOTAL
1	XXNXXZZZXXYYYI XXPUYYYVXX MXXZZZESZZZ	10.00	7.00	5.00	7.00	8.00	3.00	40.00
2	XXNJXXYYYIXX ZZZXXYYYSZZZXXL BZZZUPENXXYYYXX	7.00	2.00	3.00	5.00	5.00	9.00	31.00
3	BXXSXXNTXXNI CZZZIYYYXXG MXXNXXJ	8.00	3.00	4.00	6.00	6.00	8.00	35.00
4	BXXTZZZIJXX JZZZXXNVI MUKESZZZ	8.00	4.00	5.00	7.00	4.00	9.00	37.00
5	BXXTYYYIXX NIKKI PYYYXXKXXSZZZ	9.00	5.00	5.00	4.00	5.00	8.00	36.00
6	BZZZXXJWXXNI MXXZZZIT SXXNJXXY	9.00	6.00	3.00	5.00	7.00	7.00	37.00
7	BZZZUTXXXXXX TXXNIYXX SXXNJXXY	5.00	4.00	3.00	6.00	8.00	6.00	32.00
8	BIYYYXXXXXXYYY GXXNESZZZ NXXGXXYYYXXXX	6.00	5.00	2.00	7.00	5.00	7.00	32.00
9	BXXYYYSE XXIGVIJXXY PYYYXXKXXSZZZ	9.00	7.00	3.00	8.00	4.00	8.00	39.00
10	CZZZXXBLXXNI MXXXXZZZU CZZZXXNXXYYYXXXX	8.00	8.00	5.00	9.00	5.00	6.00	41.00

11	KXXNJXXN CZZZXXNXXNI SZZZXXNKXXYYYLXXL	9.00	5.00	6.00	5.00	6.00	7.00	**38.00**
12	CZZZXXWLXX XXSZZZISZZZ SUNXXX	7.00	4.00	5.00	6.00	7.00	7.00	**36.00**
13	CZZZZZZXXBXXXXXX YXXSZZZ YYYXXMCZZZXXNXX	7.00	5.00	4.00	7.00	4.00	8.00	**35.00**
14	CZZZZZZXXBYYYIXX KXXYYYXXN GXXPXXL	7.00	6.00	6.00	7.00	5.00	9.00	**40.00**
15	CZZZZZZXXTPXXYYY MXXXXZZZUYYYI YYYXXVINXXYYYXX	7.00	7.00	4.00	8.00	6.00	5.00	**37.00**
16	XXXXLI GITESZZZ KXXILXXSNXXTZZZ	7.00	4.00	5.00	9.00	6.00	6.00	**37.00**
17	XXXXNIEL XXJISZZZ SZZZXXJI	9.00	5.00	6.00	6.00	7.00	4.00	**37.00**
18	XXXXVE XXEVXXNSZZZI XXJXXY	7.00	6.00	4.00	7.00	8.00	5.00	**37.00**
19	XXEKXXTE BZZZYYYUGIVE MXXNXXZZZXXYYY	8.00	6.00	3.00	8.00	5.00	6.00	**36.00**
20	XXESXXI KZZZUSZZZBXXXX NUYYYULZZZXXQUE	6.00	7.00	3.00	9.00	4.00	7.00	**36.00**
21	XXXXGYYYXX JXXY JXXGXXT	5.00	8.00	5.00	6.00	5.00	6.00	**35.00**
22	GXXLXX BZZZXXXXMI JXXYXXNT	6.00	5.00	6.00	5.00	3.00	7.00	**32.00**
23	GXXUYYY BXXYYYKZZZXX BXXNWIYYYSINGZZZ	7.00	4.00	7.00	6.00	4.00	8.00	**36.00**
24	GUYYY XXIVYXX PUYYYXXN	8.00	5.00	1.00	7.00	6.00	9.00	**36.00**

25	KXXSZZZIXX ZZZXXYYYSZZZVXXYYYXXZZZXXN SUYYYENXXYYYXX	9.00	3.00	2.00	6.00	7.00	3.00	30.00
26	KEJXXYYYIWXXL KXXMXXL PYYYEMKUMXXYYY	5.00	4.00	3.00	5.00	8.00	4.00	29.00
27	KZZZXXN ITYYYXXT ISZZZTIYXXQUE	6.00	6.00	4.00	4.00	9.00	5.00	34.00
28	KZZZUPSE XXIPXXLI YYYXXXXSXXZZZEB	7.00	7.00	3.00	3.00	6.00	7.00	33.00
29	KITZZZXXNI ZZZXXNEY YYYXXJESZZZ	9.00	8.00	5.00	4.00	5.00	7.00	38.00
30	KXXTTILINGXXL VINISZZZXX JXXYXXSXXNKXXYYY	10.00	9.00	4.00	5.00	6.00	8.00	42.00
31	KYYYIPLXXNI XXNUJ YYYXXJU	8.00	6.00	3.00	6.00	4.00	9.00	36.00
32	LXXLWXXNI MXXZZZIT JXXGXXISZZZ	6.00	5.00	4.00	7.00	5.00	3.00	30.00
33	MXXKZZZIJXX XXNMXXL CZZZXXNXXUMXXL	7.00	6.00	3.00	6.00	4.00	2.00	28.00
34	MXXLKXXYYY BZZZUSZZZXXN XXXXTTXXTYYYXXY	7.00	4.00	1.00	5.00	3.00	4.00	24.00
35	MXXMTXXYYYXX EKTXX ZZZIMMXXT	8.00	5.00	2.00	5.00	4.00	6.00	30.00
36	MXXNIK PIYUSZZZ YYYXXM	9.00	4.00	3.00	4.00	6.00	4.00	30.00
37	MXXKXXL XXXXYYYSZZZXXN XXXXYXXNXXNXX	5.00	3.00	4.00	6.00	7.00	8.00	33.00

38	MXXTWXXNI KXXMXXL MXXNXXJ	6.00	4.00	2.00	7.00	8.00	9.00	36.00
39	NXXXXXYYY CZZZEBI XXPPXXTZZZUYYYXXI	4.00	6.00	2.00	8.00	9.00	3.00	32.00
40	NXXNWXXNI MXXNISZZZ MXXZZZESZZZ	5.00	7.00	1.00	5.00	6.00	4.00	28.00
41	NXXYYYXXNG BIKXXSZZZ JITENXXYYYXX	7.00	8.00	3.00	6.00	7.00	5.00	36.00
42	NIKXXM MXXYUYYY MXXZZZXXN	8.00	9.00	4.00	7.00	5.00	6.00	39.00
43	PUNJXXBI XXJXXY ZZZXXNSYYYXXJ	6.00	6.00	4.00	8.00	6.00	6.00	36.00
44	PUNJXXBI XXEEPESZZZ SUYYYESZZZ	7.00	7.00	3.00	9.00	7.00	7.00	40.00
45	YYYXXI XXNIYYYUXXZZZ XXEEPXXK	8.00	5.00	1.00	5.00	8.00	5.00	32.00
46	YYYXXINXX NEZZZXX YYYXXSZZZXXNLXXL	5.00	6.00	2.00	6.00	4.00	5.00	28.00
47	YYYXXJXX ZZZXXYYYESZZZ YYYXXMESZZZ	8.00	7.00	3.00	4.00	5.00	9.00	36.00
48	YYYXXXX ZZZIMWXXNT SZZZYYYIPYYYXXKXXSZZZ	9.00	8.00	5.00	3.00	5.00	5.00	35.00
49	YYYXXUT KESZZZXXVSXXGXXYYY VXXSXXNT	9.00	4.00	6.00	5.00	6.00	6.00	36.00
50	SZZZXXZZZ JILL NXXYYYESZZZ	9.00	5.00	3.00	6.00	7.00	3.00	33.00
51	SZZZXXZZZ NXXVELI PXXYYYESZZZ	5.00	6.00	2.00	7.00	4.00	2.00	26.00
52	SZZZENXXKXXYYY NIKZZZIL NILESZZZ	7.00	7.00	5.00	8.00	5.00	4.00	36.00
53	SZZZETZZZ MIKET SXXNJXXY	8.00	3.00	4.00	8.00	6.00	5.00	34.00

54	SZZZETYE XXTISZZZ XXJXXY	4.00	2.00	3.00	9.00	7.00	3.00	28.00
55	XXXXYYYTI SUYYYENXXYYYXX	6.00	4.00	3.00	6.00	8.00	2.00	29.00
56	TXXKZZZTXXNI JXXYXX YYYXXJU	3.00	6.00	6.00	7.00	9.00	3.00	34.00
57	TXXWXXE XXNKIT YYYXXVINXXYYYXXNXXTZZZ	2.00	8.00	5.00	8.00	5.00	4.00	32.00
58	VXXNJXXYYYXXNI KXXYYYXXN MXXZZZXXN	4.00	5.00	3.00	6.00	6.00	6.00	30.00
59	VXXSWXXNI BZZZXXYYYXXT JXXGXXISZZZ	7.00	6.00	4.00	5.00	7.00	7.00	36.00
60	YXXXXXXV GXXUYYYXXV YYYXXMXXVTXXYYY	7.00	7.00	3.00	6.00	3.00	7.00	33.00
	AVERAGE	70%	56%	37%	63%	58%	59%	68%
	Attainment Level	3.00	1.00	0.00	2.00	1.00	1.00	

Table 45: Enter Marks for Seminar (Rubrics)

13.1.14   Step 14: Create Course Exit

Q1	Question Statement	(CS332P.1)
	Strongly Disagree	
	Disagree	
	Neutral	
	Agree	
	Strongly Agree	
Q2	Question Statement	(CS332P.2)
	Strongly Disagree	
	Disagree	
	Neutral	
	Agree	
	Strongly Agree	
Q3	Question Statement	(CS332P.3)
	Strongly Disagree	
	Disagree	
	Neutral	
	Agree	
	Strongly Agree	
Q4	Question Statement	(CS332P.4)
	Strongly Disagree	
	Disagree	
	Neutral	
	Agree	
	Strongly Agree	
Q5	Question Statement	(CS332P.5)
	Strongly Disagree	
	Disagree	
	Neutral	
	Agree	
	Strongly Agree	

Q6	Question Statement	(CS332P.6)
	Strongly Disagree	
	Disagree	
	Neutral	
	Agree	
	Strongly Agree	

13.1.15   Step 15: Course Exit Mark Entry

Computation of Attainment	Strongly Agree (SA)	Agree (A)	Neutral (N)	Disagree (D)	Strongly Disagree (SD)	Wt. Avg	Attainment
Q1) Question Statement – CS332P.1	30	20	7	2	1	85%	3
Q2) Question Statement – CS332P.2	20	13	16	8	3	73%	1
Q3) Question Statement – CS332P.3	21	16	8	8	7	72%	1
Q4) Question Statement – CS332P.4	24	19	2	8	7	75%	2
Q5) Question Statement – CS332P.5	23	20	3	6	8	75%	2
Q6) Question Statement – CS332P.6	32	21	4	2	1	87%	3

Table 46: Course Exit Mark Entry

Formula: [(SA X 5) + (A X 4) + (N X 3) + (D X 2) + (SD X 1)] / [NOS X 5]

NOS = Number of Students Attempted the Course Exit Feedback

Equation 2: Weighted Average Method

13.1.16 Step 16: Marks Compilation

Average As per Marks Entered Previously

Course Outcome	CIE					SEE – 70%	OVERALL (CIE*0.3) + (SEE*0.7)	COURSE EXIT SURVEY
	T1	T2	A	P	AVERAGE (CIE) – 30%			
CS332P.1	47%				47%	58%	54%	85%
CS332P.2	62%	52%			57%	58%	58%	73%
CS332P.3	82%	57%			69%	53%	58%	72%
CS332P.4			68%		68%	63%	64%	75%
CS332P.5			47%		47%	51%	50%	75%
CS332P.6				64%	64%	55%	58%	87%

Table 47: Marks Compilation

T1: Class Test 1

T2: Class Test 2

A: Assignment

P: Practical Seminar

SEE: Semester End Examination

Attainment As per Course Outcome

Course Outcome	CIE					SEE – 70%	OVERALL (CIE*0.3) + (SEE*0.7)	COURSE EXIT SURVEY
	T1	T2	A	P	AVERAGE (CIE) – 30%			
CS332P.1	0				0	1.50	1.05	3
CS332P.2	2	1			1.5	1.00	1.15	1
CS332P.3	3	1			2	1.00	1.3	1
CS332P.4			2		2	2.00	2	2
CS332P.5			0		0	0.50	0.35	2
CS332P.6				2	2	1.00	1.3	3

Table 48: Attainment As per Course Outcome

13.1.17   Step 17: Attainment

Course Outcome	OVERALL (CIE*0.3)+(SEE*0.7)	COURSE EXIT SURVEY
CS332P.1	1.05	3
CS332P.2	1.15	1
CS332P.3	1.3	1
CS332P.4	2	2
CS332P.5	0.35	2
CS332P.6	1.3	3

Table 49: Attainment As per Course Outcome Calculation Workout

DIRECT METHOD	OVERALL (DIRECT)	THROUGH DIRECT PO MAP	FINAL DIRECT (F1)	INDIRECT (F2)
PO1	1.19		**1.19**	2
PO2	1.2		**1.2**	1.5
PO3	1.17		**1.17**	1.8
PO4	1.22		**1.22**	1.8
PO5	1.22	0	**0.61**	1.8
PO8		1	**1**	
PO9	1.175	0.5	**0.8375**	2
PO10	1.175	1	**1.0875**	2
PO11	1.175	0.75	**0.9625**	2.5
PO12		0	**0**	

Table 50: Attainment As per Program Outcome Calculation Workout

13.1.18   Step 18: Final PO Attainment

	PO1	PO2	PO3	PO4	PO5	PO6	PO7	PO8	PO9	PO10	PO11	PO12
TARGET*	1.00	2.00	2.00	2.00	1.00			1.00	1.00	1.00	1.00	1.00
DIRECT METHOD (F1)	1.09	1.20	1.17	1.10	0.55			1.00	0.84	1.09	0.89	0.00
INDIRECT (F2)	2.00	1.50	1.80	1.80	1.80				2.00	2.00	2.50	
FINAL ATTAINTMENT	**1.27**	**1.26**	**1.30**	**1.24**	**0.80**			**0.80**	**1.07**	**1.27**	**1.21**	**0.00**
Achievement	127%	63%	65%	62%	80%			80%	107%	127%	121%	0%

Table 51: Final PO Attainment

13.1.19   Step 19: Overall Target Setting for PO at Program Level

Similarly, each faculty member will work on their respective subjects and determine the final attainment, which is a combination of direct and indirect attainment.

For example, the Program Assessment Committee (PAC) sets a target for a specific batch of students, such as the 2014-2018 cohort, to achieve a certain number of qualities upon graduation. The PAC also establishes the expected performance level of students when they complete the program. Furthermore, the PAC assigns weightages to the respective attributes on a scale of 1, 2, and 3.

PO CODE	PO TITLE	PO STATEMENT	Target for 2014 – 2018
PO1	Engineering knowledge	Apply the knowledge of mathematics, science, engineering fundamentals, and an engineering specialization to the solution of complex engineering problems.	2.8
PO2	Problem analysis	Identify, formulate, review research literature, and analyse complex engineering problems reaching substantiated conclusions using first principles of mathematics, natural sciences, and engineering sciences.	2.5
PO3	Design/ development of solutions	Design solutions for complex engineering problems and design system components or processes that meet the specified needs with appropriate consideration for the public health and safety, and the cultural, societal, and environmental considerations.	2.6

PO4	Conduct investigations of complex problems	Use research-based knowledge and research methods including design of experiments, analysis and interpretation of data, and synthesis of the information to provide valid conclusions.	1.5
PO5	Modern tool usage	Create, select, and apply appropriate techniques, resources, and modern engineering and IT tools including prediction and modelling to complex engineering activities with an understanding of the limitations.	1.5
PO6	The engineer and society	Apply reasoning informed by the contextual knowledge to assess societal, health, safety, legal and cultural issues and the consequent responsibilities relevant to the professional engineering practice.	1.6
PO7	Environment and sustainability	Understand the impact of the professional engineering solutions in societal and environmental contexts, and demonstrate the knowledge of, and need for sustainable development.	1.7
PO8	Ethics	Apply ethical principles and commit to professional ethics and responsibilities and norms of the engineering practice.	2.9
PO9	Individual and team work	Function effectively as an individual, and as a member or leader in diverse teams, and in multidisciplinary settings.	3

PO10	Communication	Communicate effectively on complex engineering activities with the engineering community and with society at large, such as, being able to comprehend and write effective reports and design documentation, make effective presentations, and give and receive clear instructions.	3
PO11	Project management and finance	Demonstrate knowledge and understanding of the engineering and management principles and apply these to one's own work, as a member and leader in a team, to manage projects and in multidisciplinary environments.	2.5
PO12	Life-long learning	Recognize the need for, and have the preparation and ability to engage in independent and life-long learning in the broadest context of technological change.	3

Table 52: Overall Target Setting for PO at Program Level

13.1.20   Step 20: Final PO Attainment

Paper Code	Sem	Paper	Hours	Credit	Marks	PO1	PO2	PO3	PO4	PO5	PO6	PO7	PO8	PO9	PO10	PO11	PO12
CE134	Year 1	BASICS OF CIVIL ENGINEERING AND ENGINEERING MECHANICS #	6	5	100	1.20	2.20	2.40	2.20	2.10							1.00
CH132	Year 1	APPLIED CHEMISTRY #	6	5	150	2.10	2.30	0.65	0.89								0.50
CS134	Year 1	BASICS OF COMPUTER SCIENCE AND ENGINEERING #	6	4	100	1.20	3.00	1.60		1.90							
EC133	Year 1	BASIC ELECTRONICS #	5	5	100	1.20	2.70	2.10	2.40								
EE133	Year 1	BASICS OF ELECTRICAL ENGINEERING #	4	4	100	2.10	2.30	0.65	0.89								
EG135	Year 1	ENGINEERING GRAPHICS	4	4	100	1.50		1.24			1.54	1.90					1.00
HOL	Year 1	HOLISTIC EDUCATION	1	1	50						2.10	1.50	1.50	1.70	1.80	1.60	1.70
MA131	Year 1	MATHEMATICS – I	5	4	100	3.00	2.50	2.10	2.20	2.60	2.10					1.30	1.80

ME135	Year 1	BASICS OF MECHANICAL ENGINEERING	4	4	100	1.60	1.50	2.10									
ME151	Year 1	WORKSHOP PRACTICE	2	2	50	1.70	2.00	1.60		2.30	2.60			2.10	2.10		1.90
PD136	Year 1	PROFESSIONAL DEVELOPMENT-I	4	3	100		2.50				2.10	2.10	2.90	2.70	2.10	1.70	1.10
PH132	Year 1	APPLIED PHYSICS #	6	5	150	3.00	2.70	1.60									
MA231	Year 1	ENGINEERING MATHEMATICS-II	5	4	100	1.29	2.20	2.20	2.20	2.60	2.10					1.90	2.00
CS332P	Sem 3	OPERATING SYSTEMS	5	4	100	1.27	1.90	1.30	1.24	0.80			0.80	1.07	1.27	1.21	0.00
CS334P	Sem 3	PROGRAMMING PARADIGM	5	4	100	2.20	2.20	2.40	2.30								1.20
CS335	Sem 3	COMPUTER ORGANIZATION AND ARCHITECTURE	4	4	100	2.10	2.80	0.65	0.78								1.30
CS336P	Sem 3	COMPUTER GRAPHICS WITH OPEN GL	5	4	100	2.70	2.10	1.60		1.90							
EC337	Sem 3	DIGITAL SYSTEMS	4	3	100	2.60	1.90	1.87	1.67	1.65							
MA334	Sem 3	DISCRETE MATHEMATICS	4	3	100	2.80	1.80	1.75	1.65								

CS431	Sem 4	PROBABILITY AND QUEUING THEORY	3	3	100	3.00		1.75									
CS432P	Sem 4	DATA STRUCTURES AND ALGORITHMS	5	4	100	2.70	2.50	2.50									
CS433P	Sem 4	DATA BASE MANAGEMENT SYSTEMS	5	4	100	2.10	3.00	2.80		1.90						1.30	1.80
CS435P	Sem 4	COMPUTER NETWORKS	5	4	100	2.22	1.50	2.10									
EC437	Sem 4	MICROPROCESSORS AND ITS APPLICATIONS	4	4	100	2.34	1.90	1.60		2.30	2.60			2.10	2.10		1.90
PD436	Sem 4	PROFESSIONAL DEVELOPMENT – II	4	3	100		2.00				2.10	2.00	2.90	2.70	2.10	1.70	1.10
CS531	Sem 5	COMPUTER ORIENTED NUMERICAL ANALYSIS	3	3	100	2.40	2.50	1.60									
CS532E01	Sem 5	FORMAL LANGUAGE AND AUTOMATA THEORY	3	3	100	2.60	2.10	2.20	2.20	2.60	2.10					1.90	2.00
CS532E02	Sem 5	COMPILER DESIGN	3	3	100	2.50	1.26	1.30	1.24	0.80			0.80	1.07	1.27	1.21	0.00
CS532E03	Sem 5	FUZZY LOGIC	3	3	100	2.70	1.80	1.60	2.10	2.20							

CS533P	Sem 5	INTERNET OF THINGS	5	4	100	3.00	2.10	1.90	1.10	1.80							2.20
CS534	Sem 5	DESIGN AND ANALYSIS OF ALGORITHMS	4	4	100	3.00	2.60	2.20	1.90								
CS535	Sem 5	SOFTWARE ENGINEERING	3	3	100	2.50	2.10	2.40	1.50								1.00
CS536P	Sem 5	INTERNET AND WEB PROGRAMMING	5	4	100	2.70	2.90	2.00	2.20	1.40							
CS631	Sem 6	CRYPTOGRAPHY AND NETWORK SECURITY	3	3	100	2.60	3.00	2.10	2.20	1.60							
CS632P	Sem 6	OBJECT ORIENTED ANALYSIS AND DESIGN	5	4	100	2.70	2.20	0.20	0.20	1.00							2.00
CS633P	Sem 6	SYSTEM SOFTWARE	5	4	100	2.80	1.00	2.00	1.00								1.00
CS634P	Sem 6	DESIGN PATTERNS	5	4	100	2.90	1.80	2.20	2.10	2.20							
CS635	Sem 6	RESOURCE MANAGEMENT TECHNIQUES	3	3	100	3.00	2.10	1.90	1.10	1.80							
BTGE732	Sem 7	ACTING COURSE	4	2	100	3.00	2.60	2.20	1.90								
BTGE734	Sem 7	DIGITAL WRITING	4	2	100	2.60	2.10	2.20	1.50								
BTGE735	Sem 7	DIGITAL MEDIA	4	2	100	2.70	2.20	2.50	2.60						2.00	1.20	1.00

BTGE736	Sem 7	INTELLECTUAL PROPERTY RIGHTS	4	2	100	3.00	3.00	2.20	2.80		2.20				1.50	2.20	2.10
BTGE737	Sem 7	PROFESSIONAL PSYCHOLOGY	4	2	100	2.90	2.10	2.30	1.90	1.30						1.00	1.50
BTGE738	Sem 7	CORPORATE SOCIAL RESPONSIBILITY	2	2	100	3.00	2.20	2.10						1.20	1.20	1.00	2.20
BTGE739	Sem 7	CREATIVITY AND INNOVATION	4	2	100	3.00	2.20	2.10	2.20					1.20	1.20	1.00	2.20
BTGE744	Sem 7	DIGITAL MARKETING	4	2	100	2.00	2.10	2.20							1.70	2.00
CS731	Sem 7	ARTIFICIAL INTELLIGENCE	4	4	100	2.70	2.20	2.10	1.90					2.20	1.50	1.00
CS732	Sem 7	CLOUD COMPUTING	3	3	100	3.00	2.00	2.10	1.90	1.50				1.10		
CS831E01	Sem 8	QUANTUM COMPUTING	3	3	100	3.00	2.10	2.20								
CS831E02	Sem 8	GRID COMPUTING	3	3	100	2.90	3.00	2.20								
CS831E03	Sem 8	MOBILE COMPUTING	3	3	100	2.90	2.90									
CS832E01	Sem 8	SOFTWARE TESTING	3	3	100	2.00	2.10				2.20					2.20	1.90

CS832E02	Sem 8	SOFTWARE PROCESS AND PROJECT MANAGEMENT	3	3	100	2.80	2.20	1.70	2.30								
CS832E03	Sem 8	SOFTWARE QUALITY MANAGEMENT	3	3	100	2.70	2.50	2.30									
CS833E01	Sem 8	COMPUTER AIDED DECISION SUPPORT SYSTEMS	3	3	100	2.50	2.76	1.90									
CS833E02	Sem 8	INTRODUCTION TO DATA SCIENCE	3	3	100	2.70	2.70	2.20	1.90		1.80						
CS833E03	Sem 8	SOFT COMPUTING	3	3	100	2.80	2.10	2.60	2.10								
CS833E04	Sem 8	DIGITAL IMAGE PROCESSING	3	3	100	3.00	3.00	1.60									1.10
ATTAINMENT (DIRECT)						2.48	2.27	1.90	1.77	1.82	2.13	1.88	1.78	1.76	1.74	1.48	1.43
ATTAINMENT (INDIRECT)										2.00	2.10	2.10	2.60	2.10	2.20	1.90	2.20
ATTAINMENT (SURVEY – PROGRAM EXIT FEEDBACK)						2.20	2.10	2.50	2.10	1.90	1.80	1.50	2.20	2.40	2.30	2.10	2.80
ATTAINMENT (SURVEY – ALUMNI FEEDBACK)						2.00					1.60	2.10	1.50	1.70	1.80	2.20	2.10
ATTAINMENT (SURVEY – EMPLOYER FEEDBACK)						2.00					2.10	1.30	1.70	1.90	2.20	2.10	1.30
FINAL ATTAINMENT						2.17	2.19	2.20	1.94	1.91	1.95	1.78	1.96	1.97	2.05	1.96	1.97
TARGET						2.80	2.50	2.60	1.50	1.50	1.60	1.70	2.90	3.00	3.00	2.50	3.00
ACHIEVEMENT						78%	87%	85%	129%	127%	122%	104%	67%	66%	68%	78%	66%

Table 53: Final PO Attainment

References

Books you can refer for further Reading:

- "Assessing Student Learning: A Common Sense Guide" by Linda Suskie
- "Understanding by Design" by Grant Wiggins and Jay McTighe
- "Program Evaluation: An Introduction" by David Royse, Bruce Thyer, and Deborah Padgett
- "Teaching and Assessing Skills in Business Education" by Charles W. Beebe and Randy L. Joyner
- "Outcomes-Based Academic and Co-Curricular Program Review: A Compilation of Institutional Good Practices" edited by Marilee Bresciani Ludvik
- "Learning Outcomes Assessment: Principles and Practices" by Karen E. Black and Marsha J. Watson
- "Designing Effective Assessment: Principles and Profiles of Good Practice" by Trudy W. Banta and Catherine A. Palomba
- "Aligning Student Outcomes, Teaching, and Assessment: Methods, Tools, and Techniques" by Robert W. Mendenhall
- "Assessment Essentials: Planning, Implementing, and Improving Assessment in Higher Education" by Trudy W. Banta
- "Outcomes-Based Education: Principles and Possibilities" by John Biggs

Table Used in this Book

Equations Used in This Book

www.ingramcontent.com/pod-product-compliance
Lightning Source LLC
Chambersburg PA
CBHW031248160726
47993CB00001B/67